Fourth Edition

ASSIGNING, RESPONDING, EVALUATING

A WRITING TEACHER'S GUIDE

Edward M. White

UNIVERSITY OF ARIZONA

BEDFORD/ST. MARTIN'S

Boston/New York

For Bedford/St. Martin's

Developmental Editor: Nathan Odell
Production Editor: Bernard Onken
Production Supervisor: Matthew Hayes
Art Director: Lucy Krikorian
Copy Editor: Eric Raetz
Cover Design: Kim Cevoli
Composition: Laserwords
Printing and Binding: Haddon Craftsmen, Inc., an R.R. Donnelley & Sons Company

President: Joan E. Feinberg
Editorial Director: Denise B. Wydra
Editor in Chief: Nancy Perry
Director of Marketing: Karen Melton Soeltz
Director of Editing, Design, and Production: Marcia Cohen
Managing Editor: Erica T. Appel

Library of Congress Control Number: 2006926056

Manufactured in the United States of America.

2 1 0 9 8
f e d c

For information, write: Bedford/St. Martin's, 75 Arlington Street, Boston,
MA 02116   (617-399-4000)

ISBN-10: 0-312-43930-X
ISBN-13: 978-0-312-43930-9

Acknowledgments

Lynn Z. Bloom, Edward M. White, Shane Borrowman. "Avoiding Plagiarism." From pp. 485–488 in *Inquiry: Questioning, Reading, Writing,* 2nd Edition. Reprinted by permission of Pearson Educa-tion, Inc., Upper Saddle River, NJ.

Erika Lindemann. "A Heuristic for Designing Writing Assignments." From *A Rhetoric for Writing Teachers* by Erika Lindemann. Copyright © 1995 by Erika Lindemann. Used by permission of Oxford University Press, Inc.

Edward M. White. "The Scoring of Writing Portfolios: Phase 2." Adaption of the original selec-tion published in *CCC,* 56.4, June 2005, pp. 581–99. Copyright © 2005 by The National Council of Teachers of English. Reprinted with permission.

PREFACE

Some educators feel that evaluation in general and testing in particular have little to do with teaching and learning. Composition instructors have good grounds for feeling that way in light of the many abuses and misuses of testing in American schools, especially in writing programs. Many writing tests are imposed from outside the classroom by administrators or commercial testing firms unfamiliar with the teaching situation and are scored in more or less mysterious and reductive ways; in recent years the scoring of writing by computers instead of people adds to the mystery and suspicion, since the algorithms for scoring are closely guarded trade secrets. The widespread use of multiple-choice mechanics and usage tests as if they were writing assessments distorts the teaching of writing from earliest schooling through many university programs. And test results are routinely used to support or suggest incompetence on the part of the students, the teachers, or both. It is no wonder that so many of those teaching in American schools — from first-grade teachers wondering about the mechanisms that might prevent some children from getting into second grade to college professors seeing their best undergraduate students attempting to pass graduate record, medical school, or law school entrance examinations — consider evaluation the enemy of learning. Teachers of writing in particular, charged in part with the responsibility for supporting the creativity and individuality of their students, normally resist evaluation and the effects of grading on their students.

At the same time, everyone knows that some sort of evaluation is crucial for learning ("How'm I doing?") and most teachers of writing spend many hours a week responding to and grading papers in an attempt to help students write better. Clearly, despite their usual dislike of grading, writing instructors need and use evaluation to do their jobs. Some kinds of evaluation are obviously more valuable — and less offensive — than others.

Let's distinguish, in the first place, two general purposes for evaluation: (1) evaluation as an administrative sorting device, to make institutions more efficient, more accountable, and more clear about their standards; and (2) evaluation as a personalized teaching device, to help students learn more effectively. Not all evaluation devices fall neatly into these categories, of course, and some of the most useful are able to work at both the institutional and the personal level. For instance, a good placement system (somewhat of a rarity) is institutionally efficient because it arranges students in convenient teaching groups and is also valuable for instructors because it gives them relatively homogeneous groups to work with. But most of the testing devices that rightly bother postsecondary writing teachers have both strict institutional purposes and negative effects on students: admission tests to screen out those less prepared, "value-added" tests to convince legislators that students have accumulated information, proficiency tests designed to identify failures, and the like. Such tests have little to do with the teaching of writing. When teachers are forced to choose between tailoring their teaching to an inappropriate institutional test and helping their students learn how to write, they are bound to consider evaluation an intrusion into the classroom. One reason for the much-increased use of portfolio assessment in recent years is that it seems to enhance student learning while minimizing negative institutional use.

My concern in this book is largely with the second purpose, evaluation as a way of helping students learn more effectively. Because part of such evaluation includes giving reliable, fair, and valid tests, I will suggest some ways in which these evaluation devices can support institutional goals, such as placement or outcomes assessment. But our primary concern is personal: how can evaluation help the teacher help the student? Further, this book is designed to accomplish that task while saving the instructor time and labor. Readers of earlier editions will notice, however, the increased space given to institutional assessment in this edition, a reflection of the increasing external pressures on writing classes and, indeed, all education.

Although this book is addressed generally to all who teach writing or use writing in their courses, it often speaks directly to those teaching first-year students in American colleges and universities, responsible for instructing over a million students a year in rhetoric and composition. I do not intend to exclude either high school teachers (whose honors and advanced placement courses are often at a higher level than many college composition courses), teachers of advanced composition courses, or those involved in writing across the curriculum programs. In fact, all of us face the same problems of developing worthwhile writing assignments, responding sensitively to what students write, and evaluating that work intelligently and fairly. In addition, I will from time to time speak to writing program administrators (WPAs), a role many writing teachers will assume in the course of their careers and an increasingly important leadership position in American universities. When I say "we," I will usually mean those of us in the community of writing teachers, but (as in life) "we" are sometimes charged with assessment and mentoring activities beyond our classrooms.

The first chapter opens with a series of concrete and practical suggestions about constructing and giving writing assignments — a topic not usually attended to in the training of teachers of college writing courses despite its being the crucial first stage in working with student writers. The focus is on the development of clear topics for a wide variety of purposes and student populations. The sample assignments present a variety of successful topics that call for specific skills in the context of the writing course. Each assignment is followed by a brief discussion ("Teaching and Scoring Tips") that is designed to help with prewriting instruction, class use of the topic, and evaluation.

The second chapter focuses on the immediate practical problems of giving and responding to essay assignments, including essay tests; it also addresses ways to help students avoid plagiarism. Teachers who take the time to work through this material with their students will earn enduring gratitude, for nowhere else will students encounter systematic help with these problems; at best, some students will pick up versions of these ideas from their friends or from a writing center tutor. An additional advantage to instructors is that by seeing essay assignments from the students' point of view (how quickly we forget!), we can avoid the most common problems and construct better assignments than those we struggled with as students — and thereby elicit better and more satisfying writing from our students.

Chapters 3 and 4 turn to a sorely neglected matter — responding to student writing. Responding means much more than grading, just as grading means much more than marking errors. In recent years, studies of responding patterns have taught us much about what is useful — and not useful — to say to students about their written work. Chapter 3 attends to new options for responding — such as peer reading — and to new reading theories, which suggest that the reading of texts (including student texts) is more complicated than we used to think it was. It contains suggestions for handling the paper load, always a problem for those who assign student writing, and presents a student paper in two drafts: a good first draft and an even better revision, along with a description of how teacher and peer response led to this improvement. Chapter 4 focuses on how teachers can use an artifact common to large-scale grading sessions, the scoring guide (or "rubric"), as a labor-saving and clarifying device in their classrooms.

Chapter 5 opens with an overview of the many issues related to writing assessment: grading, placement testing, the new so-called "writing" portion of the SAT and ACT, various kinds of proficiency assessments, writing assessment and special needs students, and computer scoring of writing. Chapter 6 narrows the focus to the use of personal experience impromptu writing, giving several examples of such assignments, with scoring guides, sample student papers, and discussion of the use (and possible misuse) of such assignments. Chapter 7 continues that focus, turning to impromptu writing based on texts rather than experience and includes a discussion of the uses of literature in writing courses. Most teachers will find that the assignments in Chapters 6 and 7 (all of which have been developed and used successfully both on tests and in college freshman composition classrooms) are good ways to help their students do college-level writing. The topics are appropriate, with clear demands, and are interesting to most first-year students; they allow students to examine their own writing processes and to make entries in their writing logs; they are relatively easy to grade (using the scoring guides), will allow for direct diagnosis of writing problems, and can lead to useful conferences with students.

Finally, Chapter 8 examines the most valuable form of writing evaluation we now have: portfolio assessment. These collections of materials offer additional instructional and assessment options to instructors and have a greater scope than any other method for valid institutional assessments that support classroom teaching. While offering practical suggestions on the use of portfolios, this chapter summarizes the accumulated experiences that writing instructors and writing programs have had with portfolios and offers a method of scoring them that is reliable, economical, and theoretically sound. This chapter gives useful information on classroom uses of portfolios and moves to the uses of portfolios for outcomes assessments for writing and other kinds of college programs.

Assigning, Responding, Evaluating offers teaching faculty a new kind of support for the writing class. It is not a mere collection of tests and assignments, though it includes both, but is rather an evaluation guide based on writing and reading theory and integrally related to the teaching of writing. It is designed to help the teacher create writing assignments, evaluate student writing, and respond to that writing in a consistent and explainable way.

ACKNOWLEDGMENTS

Without the encouragement and advice of Andrea Lunsford and Robert Connors this book would never have been begun, and without the firm editorial support of Nancy Perry and Nathan Odell at Bedford/St. Martin's it would not have endured and developed. I must also thank the many colleagues who have worked with me on various testing projects, including the California State University Freshman English Equivalency Examination and the pilot essay project of the Medical College Admissions Test, for ideas that have worked their way in some form into this book.

Finally, I would like to offer thanks to Pat Belanoff of the State University of New York at Stony Brook, Bill Condon of Washington State University, and Kim Flachmann of California State University, Bakersfield. Their thoughtful reviews and comments guided this revision in many matters, large and small.

Edward M. White

CONTENTS

CHAPTER 4

Issues in Grading Writing and Using Scoring Guides   73

CHAPTER 5

Using Writing for Placement and Assessment   87

CHAPTER 1

WRITING ASSIGNMENTS AND ESSAY TOPICS

Devising writing assignments for students in writing courses is one of the most taxing and least understood parts of any teacher's job. There is no escaping this task, not even if we believe that students should select their own topics. That just shifts the difficult job of selecting assignments to the students, who themselves need much help in figuring out what to write about and how. Besides, there must be some kind of curriculum in any course, which in turn suggests that certain things are to be learned at different points in the course. Some kinds of writing and some kinds of topics will suit the curriculum better than others. Which? The teacher must decide.

We need to keep in mind that the writing of topics is, after all, writing. All the problems and all the stages of writing are part of the process of devising topics, and no one should imagine it to be easy. Many rhetorical problems add to the unique difficulty of crafting writing topics: the extraordinary compression of the form, the need for clarity and exactness of communication, the requirement that topics elicit a response from a range of students with disparate interests and varying levels of creativity, and the pressures of grading and the curriculum. It is no wonder that most attempts fall short. Yet we must offer the best assignments we can devise in order to stimulate our students' creativity and convince them to learn what we teach. This chapter suggests some concepts to guide the development of writing assignments, followed by a series of examples.

CONSTRUCTING WRITING ASSIGNMENTS

Planning Assignments for Discovery and Revision

Writing courses should undermine the night-before, all-night typing frenzy and its product — the McPaper — a fast-food version of writing that offers little nutritional value to students and is frequently indigestible for readers. Although the pattern is more prevalent outside of composition courses, it is a strong enough pattern that students are likely to use it unless the assignment makes it impossible. Few students really expect, as they begin college, to produce more than one draft of an essay; many students tend to feel that the first draft is a fully formed text, to be changed as little as possible. Even good students will, at most, proofread an initial draft for neatness, spelling, and footnote format — the primary criteria for good grades according to folklore (and experience). This expectation that school writing is essentially first-draft writing does not diminish as students move through college and into their major fields of study, unless their teachers continue to reinforce the need for revision as an essential part of the writing process. (See the "Outcomes Statement" of the Council of Writing Program Administrators, on the first pages of *The Outcomes Book* [Harrington et al.], for suggested principles for teachers outside of the first-year program to apply to help students continue to grow as writers.) Certainly one of the most important tasks we can accomplish in a first-year college writing course is to insist that the first draft is the beginning of the writing process, not the end of it.

Because virtually all professional writers spend substantial amounts of time revising their work, the designers of useful writing courses — and of writing assignments in all courses — should follow that model and recognize the importance of revision by seeking to establish new patterns for both students and teachers that emphasize revision. The most effective writing assignments set up a continuum of drafting and revising that begins when the assignment is distributed and concludes at the end of the term — if then.

Sequencing Writing Assignments

Most students experience writing assignments as a series of discrete tasks with little overlap. Many writing courses are actually designed so that the assignments are unrelated — a narrative followed by a comparison/contrast paper, analysis of a poem followed by analysis of a short story. Even teacher comments on papers, which are intended to lead to improvement on later work, may only affect revisions of the same paper as the student turns to new and apparently unrelated tasks.

If writing assignments can be sequenced so that each one builds directly on the one before it, students are more likely to incorporate revision into their writing process and produce better work. If revisions on the present paper can be included as part of the next paper, they will seem a natural part of the writing process; the instructor's comments will appear as helpful suggestions for the task to come, rather than as judgments to be filed away or disregarded. If entries in a writing journal can lead to class papers, both the journal and the papers will become parts of the overall writing process. Similarly, if readings can be sequenced and connected, the information will compound, have context, and will resemble the academic reading in other courses.

One way to sequence assignments is to divide a complex task so that it can be approached as a series of smaller jobs. Some customary writing assignments include a sequence of accomplishing tasks, and understanding the different nature of these tasks can help the instructor and the student understand what is involved in the larger assignment. For example, a comparison/contrast paper might call for a series of tasks, each of which could be the focus of a separate assignment: (1) summarize text A; (2) summarize text B; (3) list similarities and differences between texts A and B; (4) write an essay in which you develop an idea about the similarities and differences between texts A and B.

The complexity of the comparison/contrast paper makes many teachers unwilling to assign it, for such writing is rare outside the classroom and students require substantial help in understanding its demands. Yet its very complexity is attractive to some teachers of advanced students, who are ready to rise to its challenge when it is part of a coherent sequence. If a class is working with summaries and book reviews, a good assignment might ask students to compare and contrast two reviews from different kinds of publications (say, a newspaper and Web site) of the same book. As students work through the sequence of tasks, they learn about differences in media, audience, and conventions as they construct their own essays. The next assignment might call for the writing of a book review to be submitted to a particular publication.

Similarly, an assignment to write about an important event from childhood could be approached as a series of steps, each building on the one before: (1) describe the setting of the event, using clear and vivid detail; (2) narrate the event chronologically, combining the story with its setting; (3) speculate about why the event stays in your mind, why it remains significant to you, and why it might be interesting to the reader; (4) narrate the event, rearranging it so that significance, rather than chronology, becomes the organizing feature; (5) revise the writing so that the meaning of the event is shown (embedded in the narration), rather than told.

A sequenced assignment could also be organized according to a progression of skills. For example, before a student can complete a research paper successfully, many separate skills are required, and a series of assignments could focus on each of them. A single-source assignment (such as the one given on pages 19–21) will help students understand the most difficult problem when writing a research paper: how to use someone else's idea as support for an idea, rather than in lieu of an idea. Most students simply insert quotations without comment or connection into their texts, and students need to learn ways to use this kind of evidence before they can handle research; the concept can be learned by writing and revising a single-source paper. Research requires library and online search skills, which can be taught separately as students begin their research. Even advanced college students have problems with summarizing and evaluating sources; short assignments on choosing sources are appropriate after research has gotten under way. Most students are entirely unaware of scholarly journals and their important role in developing knowledge, so assignments that lead the more capable and advanced students into these journals will help them understand and join in academic discourse. An underlying problem for many students is to find ideas of their own to pursue and develop in the face of all the authoritative source materials they have discovered. An assignment asking them to write about differing interpretations of the same material will help them find their own topics and their own voices. Such an assignment will also sharply reduce problems with plagiarism (see the discussion on pages 43–47), since many instances of plagiarism are the result of the improper use of sources, rather than deliberate fraud.

Another opportunity for sequencing writing assignments will emerge from a designed sequence of reading assignments. Because so many writing instructors are graduates of literature programs, the usual writing curriculum centers on a series of reading assignments, with the writing assignments appended to the reading. Often these reading assignments are more or less random, designed to deepen understanding of each piece of literature. But a more effective writing course would be based on a sequenced series of writing assignments designed to help students attain a clear set of writing goals, with the readings serving as models and stimulation for those assignments. The reading in a course could present a series of fictions moving from simple narratives to postmodern stories with the narrator interwoven with the characters; writing assignments on narrative point of view could increase in complexity with each selection, perhaps moving toward postmodern personal essays themselves. But there is a serious temptation, if you are particularly interested in literature, to teach a course in literature instead of the writing course described in the course bulletin — with student writing serving only or principally the function of understanding the reading.

One way to keep a writing course from turning into a literature course is to organize the syllabus around a sequence of writing assignments designed to achieve certain writing goals before selecting the reading. For instance, if your students are reading Joseph Conrad's *Heart of Darkness*, you might select one of the editions with a series of critical essays from different perspectives in an appendix. Your goal might be to use student writing as a way to enforce the fact that a work of literature has no one "correct" reading, that students must come to terms with their own reading amid the complexity of interpretations. Thus an early assignment might focus on a formalistic reading, based on close reading of a passage. The students might investigate what assumptions about the meaning of a work of literature are embedded in such an approach. A subsequent assignment might ask the same questions of a contrasting viewpoint, such as a psychological reading asking about Conrad's voyage into his own subconscious. A historical essay could be the focus of the next assignment, looking at colonialism and perhaps the African novel *Things Fall Apart*, a book the Nigerian author Chinua Achebe deliberately set out as a reply to the Conrad novel. By this time, the students will have used their own writing as a way to understand a series of critical perspectives and be in the position to argue for a satisfying one of their own. While students will certainly learn a good bit about how to read fiction and how to make some sense of critical differences, the goal for the writing course is for them to learn to write analytic and argumentative essays using citations, interpretations they may not agree with, and a coherent expression of their own views.

Writing Assignments Presented in Written Form

After planning the assignment, the next step in eliciting good writing from students is to distribute a written assignment. Many teachers fail to hand out a written assignment, simply telling the class what they want, or jotting something on the chalkboard to be copied (or miscopied). Such casual treatment of the assignment suggests that a similarly casual response is called for. Even a written and discussed assignment can lead to misunderstanding by students; less careful assignments routinely lead to confusion. "Oh," the student will say, "I didn't remember what you wanted." Many experienced teachers have learned that they must write out, distribute, and discuss their assignments if they are to be taken seriously and if a particular goal is to be made clear.

Consider, for example, the simple assignment given on page 121 for an essay test:

> *Describe a person you knew well when you were a child. Your object is to use enough detail that your readers can picture the person clearly from the child's perspective and at the same time understand from the tone of your description and from the particular details you choose how you felt about the person you describe.*

That assignment is discussed in detail at the beginning of Chapter 6, but for our purposes here, notice just what the student is asked to accomplish: the student needs to use detail as evidence for some conclusions, without telling the reader how to interpret those details. The class discussion of the assignment, with students taking notes on the assignment sheet, can make clear the difference between this assignment and the more vague "Describe a person you knew well when you were a child" — which is all that students will take away from an oral assignment. The written assignment and subsequent discussion make clear that the description has a rhetorical purpose and that it has a connection to later assignments using evidence to support conclusions.

Some teachers prefer to let students choose their own subjects for writing, on the grounds that such openness will encourage creativity and a greater sense of ownership of the topic. With undefined topics, however, a large part of the student's energy available for writing must go into selecting, defining, and redefining a topic. If more than one or two such exercises are included in the writing course, students have less opportunity to learn other aspects of the writing process, such as development and demonstration of ideas, use of sources, and revision. Open topics, in my experience, are more likely to reflect an unclear and problematic course design than a commitment to independent and creative thought; such topics are also an open invitation to the insecure to purchase ready-made essays, which are widely available on the Internet.

Despite these problems, some superior writing instructors remain committed to open assignments; they are convinced that students will write better when they are free to choose what they will write about. If the assignment is, say, a brief open response to a reading or a personal narrative, the unstructured assignment should pose no problems. But more complex writing tasks call for planning to overcome the problems I have been describing. Before students begin work, they should receive a description of the purpose of the assignment, its format, and the criteria that will be used in evaluating it. Students need to internalize and own the underlying purpose of the assignment so that they can select topics that will fulfill that purpose. Much class time has to be spent discussing topics and helping students define, limit, and focus what they expect to say. Class time alone is insufficient for many students, who will need individual attention during (and after) office hours. During the writing process, students should be required to submit plans, outlines, drafts, bibliographies, and other components because an open assignment makes it easy for them to omit parts of the complex task. Students should ask themselves at every stage, "Is this work fulfilling the original purpose of the assignment?" Meanwhile, both teacher and student must develop a common set of standards, and the teacher needs to know — by their frequent submissions — that the student is actually doing the work.

There is no doubt that this system helps some students write more effectively; it represents a student-centered classroom and an ideal of teacher involvement with student writing that some institutions support for all assignments. But not often do we see this elaborate and labor-intensive pedagogy; few writing teachers have the time available. Open assignments more often reflect a lack of time than a commitment to intensive extra time with individual students. If you use open assignments, the job of developing individual topics is continuous. Nonetheless, many writing teachers are so committed to student-centered classrooms, with responsibility and authority shared between teachers and students — or even mainly in the hands of students — that they willingly take on the additional work.

Heuristic for the Writer of Writing Assignments

Erika Lindemann proposes a series of questions for faculty to ask themselves about their writing assignments; the following version of that heuristic (adapted from Lindemann 220–21) exemplifies the kind of thinking that ought to go into the making of assignments that can support constructive writing instruction.

A. Task Definition, Meaning, and Sequencing.   What do I want the students to do? Is it worth doing? Why? Is it interesting and appropriate? What will it teach the students specifically? How does it fit my objectives at this point in the course? What can students do before they undertake the assignment, and where do I expect them to be after completing it? What will the assignment tell me? What is being assessed? Does the task have meaning outside as well as inside the class setting? Have I given enough class time to discussion of these goals?

B. Writing Processes.   How do I want the students to do the assignment? Are the students working alone or together? In what ways will they practice prewriting, writing, and revising? Have I given enough information about what I want so that students can make effective choices about subject, purpose, form, mode, and tone? Have I given enough information about required length and about the use of sources? Have I prepared and distributed a written assignment with clear directions? Are good examples appropriate? Have I given enough class time to discussion of these procedures?

C. Audience.   For whom are the students writing? Who is the audience? If the audience is the teacher, do the students really know who the teacher is and what can be assumed? Are there ways and reasons to expand the audience beyond the teacher? Have I given enough class time to discussion of the audience?

D. Schedule.   When will students do the assignment? How does the assignment relate to what comes before and after it in the course? Is the assignment sequenced to give enough time for prewriting, writing, revision, and editing? How much time inside and outside of class will students need? To what extent will I guide and grade the students' work? What deadlines (and penalties) do I want to set for collecting papers or for various stages of the project? Have I given enough class time to discussion of the writing process?

E. Assessment.   What will I do with the assignment? How will I evaluate the work? What constitutes a successful response to the assignment? Will other students or the writer have a say in evaluating the paper? Does the grading system encourage revision? Have I attempted to write the paper myself? What problems did I encounter? How can the assignment be clarified or otherwise improved? Have I discussed evaluation criteria with the students before they began work, and will I discuss what I expect again as the due date approaches?

These guidelines for examining assignments must, of course, be adapted to fit the students, the curriculum, and the assignment. For instance, not every question would be applicable to a typical short writing assignment or an in-class writing assignment. But the heuristic is particularly valuable for longer assignments. For example, if the writing is to be developed over a significant period of time, the questions in point D relate directly to a deadline schedule for submitting stages of the work. Depending on the assignment, this schedule could call for notes, bibliographies, abstracts, plans, outlines, sections, drafts, or whatever is most appropriate. A simple deadline schedule for each assignment has two important benefits: (1) it enforces the need for the student to get going quickly and to work steadily at the task, instead of trying to handle the assignment the night before the due date, and (2) it largely ensures that the work is the student's own, as early stages of a bought or borrowed paper are unlikely to be available.

Class Discussion of the Assignment

The written assignment must be discussed carefully with students. To illustrate just what the task calls for and how it will be assessed, I often hand out scoring guides (or develop one with the class) and samples of successful papers. Because few students will have experience meeting deadlines for plans or drafts, students will probably ignore them unless they are explained in detail or given some kind of grade (like a simple check-off). If enough time is allowed for discussion of the assignment, students will leave the class session with an understanding of what is required, why, and how to approach the job. They may even have developed some enthusiasm for the task, and they will know that a last-minute first draft will not be adequate. A properly discussed assignment reinforces the need to draft and revise drafts and distinguishes the cognitive work of revision from the editorial work of correcting errors. This last point is best made by distributing a former student's first draft (a good early draft, showing the discovery of the topic by the end), followed by that student's revision (rearranged so that the topic begins at the beginning and develops). For an example, see pages 57–63.

The construction of appropriate writing assignments is one of the hardest jobs for the teacher of undergraduates and is exacerbated by the dearth of supportive material available. Every teacher should keep in mind that designing assignments is a particularly demanding form of writing, calling for the teacher to use the entire writing process. Careful consideration of the needs of the audience and class discussion of the assignment (over the entire period when students are working on it) will help the teacher find out where students are having problems; reflection about these problems will often lead to a revised assignment for future classes.

Prewriting

Students will write better if they are required to think systematically before they put pen to paper. Although scholars debate what kinds of prewriting are most effective, there is a clear consensus that active engagement with an assignment before writing begins is immensely valuable; prewriting not only improves the quality of the work to be done but also trains students in a crucial part of the writing process. Some composition faculty use formal methods derived from logic or problem solving (sometimes called heuristics); other teachers use various forms of brainstorming, cognitive mapping, or clustering of ideas. Still others ask students to do unstructured five-minute writes, freewriting, or aptly named discovery drafts as ways to uncover or develop ideas. These are all forms of what classical rhetoric called invention: the finding of topics for development. (The word *topic* comes from the Greek word for "place," suggesting that the thinking process is a kind of geographic quest, a hunt for a place where ideas lurk.)

Many students will have learned to do prewriting on the computer, a great convenience for all kinds of brainstorming. But working on a computer prompts students to edit constantly and preserve their texts, which are the least important issues when prewriting. For some students, the computer will restrict their inventiveness, particularly if they spend most of their time using a search engine to find out what others have had to say, or if they limit their thinking to the strict outline formats some business-oriented software displays. Other students will be so accustomed to using the computer creatively that it is liberating in the same way it is for professional writers. It is important to find out just where your students are along this spectrum. Many students are still liberated by the use of pencil and paper for prewriting. But others are amused by this ancient technology and resist using it.

Any assignment demanding substantial student effort is worth discussing in class as the work progresses. The most valuable discussion often emerges from presentations of what the other students in the class are working on. As students listen to their peers' plans, they begin to envision new possibilities. As they express their own thoughts on the subject, they begin to acquire ownership of their topic. Moreover, early notes and reading give them an unaccustomed start toward more satisfying writing than their previous training and habits may have led them to expect. Some teachers will break the class into small groups on the day that plans or outlines are due so that all students will be able to present their ideas to others in the class. The pressure of such a presentation is healthy; some students don't mind being unprepared for the teacher, but very few students are willing to look foolish before their peers.

SAMPLE ASSIGNMENTS FOR A WRITING COURSE

When we isolate writing assignments from the multitude of simultaneous tasks a teacher must accomplish, as this chapter does, we focus attention on a major aspect of the writing course. Because writing tasks are the focus of this sort of course, most student time should be spent writing to a planned sequence of topics, while most teacher time should be spent responding to student writing. Class time should largely be spent preparing for and responding to various stages in the writing process. Thus it is appropriate to consider carefully each writing assignment and how it fits into the instructional plan for the course.

No set of writing assignments automatically equates to effective writing instruction. Effective instruction requires a clear plan for what each assignment should teach and how the assignments should be sequenced. Thus the assignments that follow are not set out as a curriculum to follow in a single course, but rather as examples of assignments that might fit into an overall teaching plan. Every suggestion in this chapter will have to be modified according to your class goals and your particular student population. The following assignments offer many specific ways to plan successful and interesting assignments that have been proven to work in composition classrooms. They move from simpler assignments (typically used in the early part of a course) to more complicated topics (appropriate for later on). Some of the assignments are short classroom exercises; others are more elaborate. Some are designed as tests, others as papers to be revised and graded, and still others as material for small group discussion with or without evaluation. In every case, the topic is followed by a few tips for scoring and for teaching. No writing assignment should ever be given without discussion of its expected purpose, audience, level of finish, and criteria for evaluation. If you give extended attention to these matters in class, you will get the best writing your students can produce, and you and they are likely to experience the satisfaction of achievement.

Understanding the Writing Process

Topic.   Write a short paper in which you describe in detail your usual writing process. Then evaluate that process, giving its strengths and weaknesses.

Teaching and Scoring Tips.   Class presentation of plans or drafts will let students see that everyone follows a writing process and that this process relates to individual styles of learning. Don't forget to describe your own writing process, too. When you describe criteria for assessing the paper, point out that you will reward vivid detail in the description of the writing process and clear connections between that detail and the evaluation of the student's own process. Weak papers will contain general descriptions and stock phrases ("I know I shouldn't write at the last minute, but that's life"). Remember that an unconventional and inappropriate writing process (for example, drafting the night before without revising) could still yield a good essay on this topic and that a good writing process does not guarantee a good essay. An interesting class exercise on the day the assignment is due asks students to write a brief description of the process they used to write this particular assignment; did they follow what they said about their usual writing process?

Planning and Drafting

Understanding Writing Assignments

Analytic Topic.   Define the possible meanings of the word "discuss" on a test. (Often that word follows a quotation.) Do you consider "discuss" to include defining, describing, comparing, contrasting, or evaluating? What else? "Discuss" a test question that you have been given recently; state the question if you can remember it, and tell how you handled it.

Teaching and Scoring Tips.   This is a difficult and abstract topic. Students who can't come up with an example may be lost; you might suggest using a dictionary to start with, or you might give a "discuss" question of your own for reference. Prewriting exercises and some discussion in class are essential. For example, ask students how one would write an essay that "defines." Good students have usually learned the knack of redefining vague questions to fit what they know best while still responding to the question, a skill that other students need to learn. These latter students will learn it more effectively from listening to and discussing their peers' writing than from a lecture. The best essays will be able to draw clear distinctions among the options contained in the term "discuss" and will illustrate those distinctions in some detail.

Personal Experience Topic.   Choose a topic about which you have special knowledge. In your essay, tell your readers just how you gained that knowledge and how the way you gained it has affected what you know. How is your knowledge different from that of others who may have learned it differently?

Teaching and Scoring Tips.   This is also difficult and abstract, but an interesting challenge for students. Rather to my surprise, I've never found a student unable to come up with an interesting essay on this topic; everyone seems to have special knowledge of something. Examples I remember are the student who began working with his father repairing cars at the age of five, the students who associate cooking with a loving grandmother, a student expert in flamenco dancing, and so on. Students may need help seeing the three parts of the assignment, as they tend to get caught up in the narrative of their experience.

Thinking of Your Audience

Topic.   Think of the last really good cultural, social, or sports event you attended, and describe it in three different ways: first to your best friend, then to your parents, and then to a group of high school students attending an open house at your college. Finally, describe the variations in content, organization, and wording that writing for different audiences led you to make.

Teaching and Scoring Tips.   This is a four-part assignment (the last part of which calls for examination of the first three, according to three categories, which actually makes it a twelve-part assignment). Be sure to make clear just what you really want, because the assignment looks simpler than it is. If you want all twelve parts, give the students enough space and time to do them; if you want less, make clear what an acceptable response will include. This is a good topic for peer evaluation in small groups, where the audience is visible.

Exploring a Topic

Topic.   Describe how you would write a paper on the following topic: "White-collar crime poses a greater danger to the economy than more visible forms of street crime." Include (1) a list of actions you would take to gather information and define your terms and (2) an outline or other plan for presenting your ideas. In your presentation, make clear that you see the difference between asserting ideas and demonstrating ideas.

Teaching and Scoring Tips.   Help students see that this is a topic about planning a paper — a brand-new concept for many. The best papers will show awareness of the complexity of definition, familiarity with the use of sources, and some sense of the process of demonstrating ideas. Weak papers will slide into clichés about crime (instead of focusing on the topic) and may use an outline format without real reference to the problems at hand. If the plans look promising, you might ask students to go ahead and write the paper. They should keep notes in writing logs or journals (if you have your students keep them) about changes in the plan as they proceed.

Revising and Editing

Topic.   Select a paper of more than two pages in length that you have written for this (or another) course. In preparation for revision, number each paragraph and write a single complete sentence that states what each paragraph is saying. (If a paragraph is saying more than one thing, without a unifying connection, it probably needs to be divided into two or more paragraphs.) Examine your list of sentences, and write a response to each of the following questions:

1. How have you organized the main ideas of your paper? Spatially? Chronologically? Logically? Or do they occur at random? Is the organization effective?

2. Do all the ideas relate to a central idea and to one another?

3. Can you identify any confusing leaps from point to point?

4. Looking at the sentences and your paper, can you identify transitional words or phrases that connect ideas? Do any others need to be added?

5. Have any important points or connections been left out?

6. Are any included points irrelevant?

7. Where is the best, most original, most interesting, most important idea located? If it comes late in the paper, as it often does in early drafts, write a new outline putting that idea up front in a prominent place. Then rearrange the other paragraphs as needed.

8. What are the strengths and weaknesses of your original organization? How might the organization of the paper be improved?

Hand in (1) the original paper, (2) your numbered series of sentences outlining the paragraph structure, and (3) your responses to the eight questions (including the new outline, if needed).

Teaching and Scoring Tips. Most students are reluctant to go back to a paper they have "finished" and rework it, so class time will be necessary to help them understand the importance of revising and reading their own writing critically. Some students have acquired the romantic belief that writing is the result of inspiration and that revision is a betrayal of the muse. (It is a major irony that the most professional writers revise all the time, whereas the least skilled writers almost never do.) And many students have no experience reading their own writing critically. For many, this will be the first time they have ever seriously had to rethink, revise (which literally means "see anew"), or rewrite (as opposed to edit) a paper. A successful response to this assignment will show that the student has been able to see the original paper anew and to move beyond editing to reorganizing it; the exercise is designed to free the student from the limits of the early draft, which to inexperienced writers often seems so fixed that nothing can be dropped or added or shifted about.

Constructing and Analyzing Argument

Topic.   Create a complete argumentative thesis statement for two of the following general topics:

1. The Arab-Israeli conflict
2. Mandatory testing of prison inmates for HIV
3. Acquaintance rape
4. The increasing cost of college and its effect on realizing the American dream
5. A college ban on fraternities and sororities

Teaching and Scoring Tips.   Note that the thesis statement should specify the following components: purpose, audience, definite position, and reasons why the position is true. In essence, the thesis will state, "In this essay, I plan to [explain, argue, demonstrate, illustrate] for an audience of _____ that _____ because _____." This appears to be a dry formula, but students will give it life as they apply it to real arguments and relate it to their own experience; meanwhile, its very rigidity requires that they consider the crucial issues for a thesis statement. You will want to help students understand the difference between arguable and nonarguable statements and between asserting and demonstrating ideas. The thesis statements and opening paragraphs written on this topic are particularly useful for small group discussion; the groups could give one point for each of the components required and two points for an arguable assertion. Though you may not want to ask students to complete the essays for which they have written thesis statements, you might want to discuss with them ways of developing the planned arguments — in particular, how to narrow a wide-open topic, what sources might be used, what tone might be most effective, and what sequence of arguments might be most convincing. The creation of thesis statements also helps students make an informed choice of topic; the most complete, best-argued thesis statement will identify not only the topic on which they are likely to be most successful but also the most interesting one. (This procedure will help students perform well on the many essay tests that give a choice of topic.)

Constructing Paragraphs

Constructing Unified, Coherent, and Well-Developed Paragraphs

Topic.   Select a well-developed paragraph from an essay you have written recently. At the top of a sheet of paper, copy that paragraph. Below it, write another paragraph showing why the paragraph you selected is a good one: identify its central idea (usually embodied in a topic sentence), show how each sentence relates to the central idea, and describe the pattern of development (illustration, definition, comparison/contrast, and so on). If you see ways in which the paragraph might have been improved, go ahead and rewrite it.

Teaching and Scoring Tips.   Even weak students know more about paragraphing than they are consciously aware of. But conscious awareness of paragraphing often extends no further than the notion of indenting the first line. This exercise asks students to use what they are learning about paragraphs as part of their own revision process. Because many students have great difficulty reading what they have written (clouded by what they perhaps meant to say), small group discussion of this exercise should compare the paragraph analysis of the author to that of others in the group.

Developing Main Ideas

Topic.   Choose one of the topic sentences that follow, and write a unified paragraph that develops the main ideas.

1. I found out quickly that college life was not quite what I had expected.
2. Being popular used to be important to me.
3. My work experience has taught me several important lessons.
4. Until recently, I never appreciated my parents fully.
5. I expect my college education to do more than simply get me a job.

Teaching and Scoring Tips.   The best paragraphs will (1) supply details and evidence, (2) use a clear organizational plan, (3) be cohesive and employ transitional devices, and (4) be developed enough to present a convincing argument. Each of these four aspects of developed paragraphs is worth discussing when the assignment is given, and each of them should be attended to when you (or peer groups) respond to and evaluate the paragraphs produced. One prewriting exercise would be to select one of the topic sentences (or to come up with a similar one) for the class to develop on the chalkboard. Write out the proposed sentence, and act as scribe as students propose sentences to follow; revise steadily, with an eye to the four issues you expect to evaluate in a finished paragraph. How good is the paragraph you come up with? If you wanted to take more time and effort, how might it be improved further? Keep asking yourself how well you have modeled a revision process.

Constructing Grammatical Sentences

Topic.   The following sentences contain unnecessary words and phrases. Rewrite them so that they are clear and concise.

1. At the present time, many different forms of hazing occur, such as various forms of physical abuse and also mental abuse.

2. Many people have a tendency toward the expansion of their sentences by the superfluous addition of extra words that are not really needed for the meaning of the sentences.

3. One of the major problems that is faced at this point in time is that there is world hunger.

4. After I stopped the practice of exercising regularly, I put on ten pounds of weight in a relatively short amount of time.

5. There are numerous theories that have been proposed by scientists as to why dinosaurs reached the point of becoming extinct.

Teaching and Scoring Tips.   Improving the bad sentences that other people write is good fun and not very difficult, even for students who have a hard time producing good sentences of their own. Take enough class time with this set of sentences to discuss both the problems and the alternative improvements that the students will suggest. (Do not imply that there is only one correct answer for any sentence.) The challenge in teaching this kind of useful exercise is tranferring these skills from the exercise to the students' prose. Much research has shown that the ability to see or correct errors in other people's writing does not lead a person directly to being a better writer; one's own sentences are designed to carry meaning for a purpose and an audience, not merely to be correct. Nonetheless, knowledge about ways to improve writing can provide a context for improvement when student writing is carefully annotated for a particular trait. This exercise will not by itself lead to the production of improved sentences by your students, but exercises like this are worth doing if you make them meaningful by connecting them to actual sentences in the students' own writing.

Hence, you must make explicit connections between this set of sentences and student work. One way to do this would be to follow the exercise with small group readings of draft paragraphs from work in progress. Each student should seek sentences that need improvement in the paragraphs before the group. But in every case, the group will have to be sensitive to the purpose and audience of the work in question and not merely simplify for the sake of simplifying; it is easy to simplify sentences out of context but far more difficult to do so with attention to the complex meanings and emotions of real writing.

Another way to make connections is for you to relate one or two sentences in student work to sentences in the exercises: "This sentence," you might write in the margin, "has some characteristics of sentence 5 in our last exercise. Try to improve it along the lines of our revision of that sentence in class."

Some teachers will want to focus on the grammar of the sentence as a way to accustom students to a more systematic language for analyzing sentence structure. Since most writing teachers have had some work in linguistics, it is hard to resist the temptation to share that knowledge with students. But almost all of the research on the use of grammar to teach writing shows that formal grammatical instruction does not improve student writing; even when they learn grammatical concepts, they tend not to apply them when they compose, though they may use them for editing. Nonetheless, some teachers are committed to the concept that knowledge of grammar will at least help them talk about faulty sentences with their students.

Using Dictionaries

Topic.   Look up the word *sophistication* in several dictionaries, and write an essay in which you explain the meanings the word may have in various contexts. In your essay, consider the Greek root and the complex history of the word.

Teaching and Scoring Tips.   This topic is interesting because of its complexity; most students think it a compliment to be called a "sophisticated" person, but wine connoisseurs are appalled at "sophisticated" wine. Buried inside the word are the contradictory attitudes we tend to feel about wisdom and ignorance (or innocence). Intelligent use of the dictionary leads to awareness of this complexity — not, as some "unsophisticated" students believe, to simple answers. Students at a stage of development where they expect things to be either right or wrong or expect authorities (such as the dictionary) to settle problems will have a hard time with this essay. They will need some help coping with ambiguity and with approaching the dictionary as a start rather than an end to questions about words.

Varying Tone

Topic.   Write five sentences about one of the subjects listed here in which you use the familiar tone, as if you were writing or talking to a very close friend. Then work those sentences through the necessary changes to make them first informal and then formal. You should have produced fifteen sentences. Finally, write a short essay of three or four paragraphs on the problems you encountered as you tried to change tone for different audiences.

1. New friends versus old friends
2. The difficulty of getting homework done
3. Balancing schoolwork and a job
4. Gaining or losing weight

Teaching and Scoring Tips.   This is a surprisingly difficult task for inexperienced writers, so it should be treated as a learning exercise not to be graded. You may have to devote class time to explaining and defining tone (basically, the relation between reader and writer), or you may refer students to that section in their handbooks. (Some handbooks will call this by other terms, including *register*, *style*, or *voice*.) If appropriate, you could remind students of the parlor game that uses four synonyms for the same concept: "I am curvy. He is stocky. You are husky. She is fat." Many students, when they arrive at college, will have many tones for speech but only one for writing, a dead formal tone they have grown accustomed to using in school. Such a tone is often rewarded by high grades, praised as "objective," and even required in some disciplines. This exercise is intended to free students from these restraints, loosen them up, help them find new possibilities, and move toward a more genuine voice. One way to help students see the many options they have is to begin with the many oral tones they use with their families, friends, and social groups. You may wish to substitute topics more suited to your particular group of students, as long as the topics elicit genuine sentences for a variety of audiences.

Analyzing Experience

Topic.   Describe and analyze an institution or a group of some sort that you knew well as a child: a school, school group, scout troop, dancing class, summer camp, club, Sunday school — any group with an obvious and consistent set of values will do. You have two specific tasks to accomplish: to describe clearly what it was like to be a member of the group at the time and to assess from your mature perspective the meaning of the group's values.

Teaching and Scoring Tips.   This assignment draws on descriptive personal writing and then requires analysis. The first task here is to help students select an institution to describe and analyze. Because almost any group can meet the demands of the assignment, they have many possible choices. As part of the job will be to see the institution from two different time perspectives (past and present), it should be a group that they remember well enough to describe clearly but from which they have some distance.

The first essay test topic in Chapter 6 (p. 121) of this guide is excellent preparation for this assignment, and the sample student papers in that chapter can lead to useful class discussion. Note that the essay test topic, designed for forty-five minutes of writing time, is simpler in its demands than this essay. You might want to bring in some examples of professional writing on this topic such as Paul Fussell's "The Boy Scout Handbook" (1982) or George Orwell's "Such, Such Were the Joys" (1952; available at no cost online).

Suggestions from you and from students in the class will make the possibilities clear. Perhaps, you might suggest, a summer camp a student loved (or hated) as a child would be fun to revisit in writing, but it may be just as rosy (or bleak) in memory today as it was in the past; maybe there isn't much to say about it beyond description. But as students reflect on, say, the high school band, some questions arise that would be interesting to pursue: one of my students wrote that she loved music when she joined but learned to dislike music because of the intense competition inside the group; that is a topic rich with possibilities. Or perhaps a scout troop changed the way someone thinks and feels even today: how did the group do that? Perhaps as students think about the values of the groups they remember, they may find some conflict between what was said and what was done; such inconsistencies are always interesting to examine.

Early drafts are likely to be mostly description, for analyzing values is a difficult task that usually requires both distance and insight; good description, particularly if it handles the two locations in time clearly, surely deserves praise and reward. But a revision should move beyond description into analysis of meaning. Because the topic is inherently interesting to students, they will often be able to come up with creative insights into what was really going on in their pasts.

Expect a wide variety in students' ability to examine their pasts, a skill that depends on the development of metacognitive skills and maturity. For instance, some students will be able to look at a church school designed to keep them from asking questions about religion with amusement and insight; other students will be defensive and protective about their childhood religions. Again, some students will be able to analyze the competitive aspects of American education (such as spelling bees) as evidence of a competitive society more interested in failure than in success, while others may be so committed to competition as a value that they see in those phenomena only reason and good sense. Some students may even feel that to question the institutions they knew as children is subversive (which in fact it is) and un-American (which it is not). One good way to help unsophisticated students develop the needed analytic skills is to form small groups for discussion of possible topics after class discussion; students will learn well from each other and be less defensive than they will in the class as a whole.

A sample response to this assignment, in two drafts, along with commentary by the teacher on the drafts and in conference, appears in Chapter 3 of this book.

Becoming a Researcher

Topic. Write a short essay examining what the anthropologist Jules Henry means in the following passage and showing the extent to which the passage applies to your own schooling.

Another learning problem inherent in the human condition is the fact that we must conserve culture while changing it; that we must always be more sure of surviving than of adapting — as we see it. Whenever a new idea appears, our first concern as animals must be that it does not kill us; then and only then can we look at it from other points of view. In general, primitive people solved this problem simply by walling their children off from new possibilities by educational methods that, largely by fear (including ridicule, beating and mutilation), so narrowed the perceptual sphere that other than traditional ways of viewing the world became unthinkable. . . . The function of education has never been to free the mind and the spirit of man, but to bind them. . . . Schools have therefore never been places for the stimulation of young minds.

(Henry 286–88)

Teaching and Scoring Tips.   The basic problem in teaching the research paper is to reverse students' preconception that research means collecting other people's opinions and patching them together with a bit of rhetorical glue. Thus it is a good idea to begin with an analytical reading of a single source such as this one to demonstrate ways of using a source as part of one's own paper. This passage is particularly good for such a purpose because many conventional students have a hard time understanding that a respectable person would make such a radical statement about the schools they have been told to love; other students may find that Henry is saying what they have often felt but never quite dared to say. So students must begin by understanding the meaning of what the writer has to say (through class discussion of the passage and its context) and how that meaning relates to what they have to say about their own schooling. Then they must integrate what Henry says into their papers.

The students' abilities should determine how much class time to give to prewriting. If the class is very able, you might wait for submission of first drafts before discussing the passage, even though many of the students will misunderstand what Henry says and will write essays defending school spirit. Well-trained students enjoy the challenge of discovering a new idea on their own and will come to class primed for discussion. Numbers of good students may misread the passage as an attack on American schools instead of a statement about the function of all schools. Resist discussion of bad examples of student writing, which do not teach as well as good ones. Some of the drafts will be good enough to illustrate for the rest of the class the way to respond to a quotation that seems to attack values one treasures. The writers of these papers will understand and discuss the Henry passage, refer to it in proper form, and bring some experiences from their own schooling to demonstrate the degree to which the passage helps them understand those experiences.

A weaker class will need more help, though ironically it may be more ready to deal with what Henry says about schools. Put *Culture against Man* on reserve in the library, or find a legal way to photocopy the chapter and ask such a class to read the chapter from which the passage comes and to write a summary of its argument. Help students understand some of the ways in which anthropologists observe cultures; Henry is applying these techniques to our own culture rather than one in a far-off land. When the summaries are brought in, you might well analyze the chapter with the class and construct on the chalkboard an outline of the principal assertions in the chapter. A lively discussion of school experiences will surely follow, leading to many ideas about ways to handle the topic assigned. Several drafts may be necessary before the students have learned how to refer to a source in the course of developing their own essays. But until they have reached that point, it is of no value to assign a research paper.

Assigning a Research Paper

Why Require a Research Paper?

The research paper has been slipping out of fashion in recent years. Many educators see it as a product- and footnote-oriented exercise with little meaning. They will argue that research depends on a background of knowledge that first-year students do not have, so students wind up going through the motions of research without assimilating its substance. Besides, the argument goes, different disciplines have different ways of doing and writing about research, reflecting unique discourse communities; teaching research techniques must therefore be the job of faculty in a student's major. Some writing teachers enlist the aid of faculty in the various disciplines to support discussion of discourse communities; more advanced courses might even require students to choose a field or even a professional journal as their audience.

The advantages of requiring a research paper in beginning college writing courses remain clear, however, despite the power of these arguments for specialization. All first-year students need to learn how to incorporate source material into their own writing, and that task cannot wait for advanced courses in the major, which are likely to assume that students have already learned general research skills. Evidence from research is not much different from other kinds of evidence that students must learn to use in papers to demonstrate ideas, and hence first-year composition can, or even should, teach this aspect of exposition.

It is certainly possible to assign a research paper and to teach the use of research materials in the writing course without resorting to empty forms and formats. If you decide to use a research paper, you might want to restrict the number of sources and the extent of the paper, and you will probably want to emphasize the various stages of the paper at least as much as the final product. Above all, you will want to emphasize that research uses sources to answer interesting questions — not to impress with their quantity, length, or style. Any quotation inserted into a paper must be discussed and connected to the controlling idea; quotations can support ideas but may never substitute for them.

The research paper can remain in the writing class, if it loses its curse as a dead exercise in compiling quotations in correct form. It has an appropriate place as an important kind of writing, with its own process issues and its own problems with evidence. Indeed, some teachers will design the entire writing course as a sequence of assignments (including ones like those I suggest in this chapter) linked to the writing of the research paper, which might incorporate earlier assignments. This is one way to give coherence and continuity to the sequence of writing assignments — though not, of course, the only way. Those who see this as an appropriate curriculum will find a number of textbooks entirely devoted to writing research papers.

Selecting Topics

Many teachers are reluctant to prescribe topics for research because they believe that research depends on the writer's individual curiosity about a subject. (See the discussion of this issue earlier in this chapter.) Such a view makes sense as long as the development of a clear and manageable topic becomes the joint responsibility of the student and the teacher, with early decisions about a topic required. Inexperienced writers will confuse identification of an area of inquiry with selection of a writing topic, and they normally need help in seeing the difference. An area of inquiry is usually too large to manage: "What is the meaning of love in poetry?" A writing topic focuses and narrows that area of interest and poses a question that can be addressed in the time and space allowed: "Sexual love versus spiritual love in the poetry of John Donne." For students with sufficient ability and teachers with sufficient time, the selection of a topic might well be part of the writing task and the writing process. But other faculty, faced with this problem of clear topic definition but with insufficient time to spend with each student (or, perhaps, concerned about the ready availability of commercial research papers), will prefer to assign a particular area of inquiry for their students. The students' freedom of choice becomes restricted, but the advantages of precision, focus, and economy of time may well compensate.

Sample Topic

The following topic is an example of a research paper assignment that narrows focus for the student sharply but also allows considerable choice.

Topic.   The term *popular art* is loosely used to describe the kind of literature, music, painting, architecture, and other cultural matter that is produced for unsophisticated mass consumption. Some popular art sometimes turns out to be very sophisticated indeed (Dickens's novels, for instance), but most popular art is designed to reaffirm and comfort popular attitudes and tastes, not challenge or examine them.

Choose for this paper a relatively unsophisticated form of popular art for analysis. If you choose a type, or genre, be sure that it is a coherent genre; not "popular music" but, say, "sentimental love songs of the 1950s"; not "comic books" but "Disney comics" or "monster comics" or "superhero-type comics." Popular art exists in almost all areas, for all kinds of specialized interests. Be sure to select a form of popular art in a field you find interesting to begin with.

Your object will be to have something worth saying about the material you analyze and then to express what you have to say convincingly. That is, while you will need to use detail to describe the popular art you have chosen, mere description is not enough. You need to develop an argument, a thesis topic, a controlling idea that will be supported by your evidence. Evidence for your argument will probably come for the most part from analysis or descriptions of the popular art. But one requirement of the paper is that you consult relevant material about popular art and find a way to make use of at least three different sources on your subject in your paper. An incidental but required job is for you to use standard ways of referring to these sources as you make your argument.

Teaching and Scoring Tips.   This assignment has several strengths as a research paper topic. It combines considerable focus with openness of choice for the student. That is, students can write about a wide variety of material — from comic books to tract homes, from horror movies to bumper stickers, from Nancy Drew to Neil Simon — but they have already been given a substantial head start on ways to approach the material. Similarly, the range of sources has been limited, and attention is placed on the development of ideas rather than on the accumulation of note cards. Class time should be spent discussing topics (perhaps giving each student a few minutes to present ideas for consideration), sources (students should know about the *Journal of Popular Culture*, for instance), and ways of using sources to develop ideas. It is advisable to specify at least three deadlines: (1) an early one, requiring a thesis statement of the main idea and an annotated bibliography; (2) an intermediate one, requiring a completed draft for peer group evaluation of ideas, organization, and use of sources; and (3) a final deadline for the edited draft, with a high level of polish. Most students will need yet another chance to revise that final draft before the product is satisfactory.

SELECTED REFERENCES

Harrington, Susanmarie, et al., eds. *The Outcomes Book: Debate and Consensus after the WPA Outcomes Statement.* Logan: Utah State UP, 2005.

Henry, Jules. *Culture against Man.* New York: Random House, 1963.

Lindemann, Erika. "Developing Writing Assignments." *A Rhetoric for Writing Teachers.* 4th ed. New York: Oxford UP, 2001.

Roen, Duane, et al., eds. *Strategies for Teaching First-Year Composition.* Urbana: NCTE, 2002.

Ruth, Leo, and Sandra Murphy. *Designing Writing Tasks for the Assessment of Writing.* Norwood: Ablex, 1988.

Walvoord, Barbara E., and Virginia Johnson Anderson. "Managing Assignments Worth Grading." *Effective Grading: A Tool for Learning and Assessment.* San Francisco: Jossey-Bass, 1998.

White, Edward M. "Assessment and the Design of Effective Writing Assignments." *Teaching and Assessing Writing: Recent Advances in Understanding, Evaluating, and Improving Student Performance.* 2nd ed. San Francisco: Jossey-Bass, 1994. 21–51.

CHAPTER 2

HELPING STUDENTS DO WELL ON WRITING ASSIGNMENTS

ESSAY TESTS AND WRITING ASSESSMENT

Twenty years ago, the timed impromptu essay test was everywhere defended by English faculty as the most effective, responsible, and teacher-supportive assessment device available — a humanistic response to the machinery of multiple-choice tests. But essay testing has been under attack recently in the professional literature for requiring first-draft writing to a set topic under artificial, tension-producing circumstances; though essay testing remains standard practice in many college courses, educators emphasizing the writing process and the importance of revision are often suspicious of the results of an assessment device that now seems distant from their teaching. For such instructors, the assessment tool of choice is likely to be portfolios, which can include a wider range of writing and writing processes.

Writing assignments that lead to portfolios tend to be quite different from assignments that prepare students for essay tests, most obviously because they demand repeated revision. But students will need to produce the kind of impromptu writing called for by essay tests in much of their college coursework, which is preparation for the essay tests now common for admission to post-graduate study — and on the job. We must give students practice in writing on demand. At the same time, we cannot restrict ourselves to teaching to tests, to making writing less about critical thinking, self-awareness, and creativity and more about mere test preparation. The best writing courses will help students learn how to write under different circumstances, for different kinds of audiences, and under different kinds of restrictions.

The essay test has gained credibility as a direct measure of writing ability and has made important inroads against the prevailing tendency to use multiple-choice tests for that purpose. Even the SAT and ACT college admissions testing programs added essay test portions to their multiple-choice exams in 2005, though the usefulness of their "writing" scores have been much disputed. And although we know that writing is a process, we might agree that evaluation of an achieved writing product is appropriate under some circumstances; the only way to come up with the product is through some sort of process. Essay tests have important strengths as well as limitations, and we ought not exaggerate either.

The limitations of the timed impromptu essay test have become clear as portfolios have become prominent, since portfolios are a kind of expanded essay test — covering much time, allowing for revision, and including several topics. Here are the most important limitations of essay tests:

- Most essay tests define writing as first-draft writing, thereby contradicting the definition of writing as a process.

- Most essay tests yield a score on a one-question test, which may disadvantage a student who cannot do well with that particular question.

- If the essay test has only one question, its results have been shown to be unreliable, even when it is scored carefully.

- The essay test is an artificial exercise — under anxiety-producing test conditions and requiring writing to a set topic — and hence may not represent more natural writing circumstances.

- Essay test scores are often misused and treated as if they reflected students' true writing ability, rather than their responses to a particular question on a test under time constraints.

We must recognize the existence of these limitations, even if we note that the strengths of essay testing may compensate for them. Here are some of the strengths of essay tests:

- Essay tests are much preferable to multiple-choice tests because writing requires students to generate ideas, sentences, and conclusions rather than merely react passively to given choices.

- The intense concentration required by an essay test, particularly one with more than one question, can lead to representative writing that correlates well with the way students write under less pressured conditions.

- A well-designed essay test allows students to demonstrate their writing process.

- Essay test scores are no more likely to be misused than other assessment results, but if they are scored responsibly by the writing staff, they can support the teaching of writing.

- An essay written under test conditions is indisputably the product of the student being assessed. And test conditions are not necessarily improper, considering that all school writing is artificial and all writing induces a certain amount of anxiety in most students.

- Using focused holistic scoring, we can grade an essay test rapidly and reliably. (For a detailed description of the process, see White [*Teaching and Assessing Writing,* Chapter 10].)

In light of these arguments, many institutions will continue to ask writing teachers to develop, supervise, and score essay tests. And instructors in all disciplines will see such tests as a reasonable way to assess student writing for in-class as well as institutional purposes. Hence, writing teachers should continue to take seriously their opportunity to help students do well on essay tests, which will recur throughout the college years.

Some students do very well on essay tests. If they have learned how to read essay questions (which often means mentally revising the questions into clearer and more manageable ones), if they have experience at organizing their thoughts quickly, if they are very fluent in the school dialect (without oral dialect or foreign language interference), and if they have quick editing skills, they are much more likely to succeed. However, many students have never learned those skills and consequently do much worse than they should on essay tests. Many students from weak educational systems have done very little writing, and the little they have done has been more or less the mechanical repetition of information. For most students, writing means retelling something that they have read or that the teacher has said, and such impersonal and unorganized writing may have been rewarded with praise and high grades — particularly outside of English courses. Suddenly, in college, these students are confronted with essay tests that call for original thought, organization, and editing — all within a tight time limit. Moreover, for a significant number, the dialect required is very different from that spoken everywhere but at school. Little wonder that essay tests provoke fear and hostility in these students!

We will be doing our students a great service if we spend some time helping them learn these test-taking skills or, in the case of good test takers, helping them understand what they have been doing and how they might do it even better. Furthermore, students who have learned a writing process for essay tests will be able to use a similar process on other writing assignments. While poorly conceived essay tests will reinforce the notion that writing is essentially first-draft writing, better tests can reinforce the need for planning, revising, and editing, which leads to the best student work.

UNDERSTANDING THE ASSIGNMENT

Two problems cloud student understanding of essay questions: teachers often do not make clear what is called for, and even when they do, students do not attend carefully to the demands of the assignment.

Writing Clear Essay Questions

Well-constructed essay questions often use a series of code words that students must understand: describe, discuss, compare, contrast, explain, comment, and others with even less obvious meanings. Some handbooks and manuals define these terms, making clear distinctions among them. Unfortunately, teachers spend little time reading these handbooks, so students must expect considerable overlap and ambiguity — even when the words seem distinct. The problem is not that teachers or students do not understand what the terms mean; the fact is that the terms have no fixed meaning and can mean whatever the teacher expects them to mean.

For example, many teachers will use *compare* as a direction to show similarities between two objects or views and *contrast* as a direction to show differences; most handbooks define the terms in this way. Thus "compare and contrast" will often mean to do both: describe similarities and differences. But other teachers (and handbooks) will take *compare* to include *contrast*, on the logical grounds that comparing two things means placing them side by side and describing what matters. A diligent student who has learned the narrower definition of *compare* and cites only similarities in such a case will receive half credit; a protest that the teacher should have asked specifically for contrasts if differences were to be shown is likely to fall on deaf ears.

Because of the uncertainty of these terms, careful question design is likely to avoid them or explain them, for clarity's sake. The best way to explain them is probably to take class time to define and illustrate the meaning of such terms for a particular class, perhaps referring students to this section in the handbook you assign or keep in a writing lab. An awkward substitute would be to define the terms on the test itself. Another useful way to proceed is to create questions with explicit instructions. Thus instead of directing students to "compare and contrast" two quotations, a question could ask students to "show in what ways these two quotations are saying similar things and in what ways they are saying different things." The longer version is somewhat cumbersome, but it does not depend on students' knowing the ill-defined meanings of *compare* and *contrast*. But, of course, a student would have to know what *show* means (does it include "use specific detail"?) in order to proceed, so there is no way to avoid using some sort of code.

An even more common example of a confusing direction is the overused term *discuss*. Many teachers will use this directive when they mean something as vague as "say something about the subject." For many students, this turns out to be an activity analogous to what in computer talk is called a "file dump": an undifferentiated list of all information available, without organization, coherence, or context. A high grade can be earned for such a file dump — if that was the teacher's intent. But the teacher may well mean — indeed, ought to mean — something much more precise, such as an argument about the strengths and weaknesses of a particular position. In that case, the file dump will elicit a low grade and complaints about student inability to focus and organize. In fact, the teacher has received what was asked for but not what was really sought. The miscommunication that results from imprecise question design leads students into confusion and teachers into frustration.

Students will benefit from practice-reading essay questions with pen in hand. In the first place, they should recognize and circle the key directions and consider what the words mean. Many students interpret all directive words as "say something about" (which is in fact all that many teachers mean) and need to understand that different directions may actually call for different kinds of responses. They should be aware that *describe* usually requires specific detail, that *explain* is likely to call for definitions and analysis, that *analyze* suggests taking something apart to see what it is made of, and so on. Here are some other terms that teachers use in question design, along with what they often mean by them:

List Name one by one, explaining or commenting when appropriate

Enumerate List in a meaningful sequence

Outline Give an overall plan for proceeding in some kind of order

Design Present a more elaborate overall plan than an outline, using descriptions, sketches, drawings, or the like

Summarize State the main points in as concise a way as possible, without commentary

Review Give a quick survey of several positions, using summaries with commentary

Interpret Explain in detail what something means to you and how you came to that understanding

Define Present in detail the essential traits or characteristics of something and how it differs from similar things

Prove Provide evidence to establish that something is true

Demonstrate Add to your proof examples of applications of what you have shown to be true

This list is not by any means complete, but we can draw two conclusions from this brief look at examination terminology: teachers who have a clear sense of what they want their students to do on a writing assignment need to use directions beyond the confusing code words, and teachers who do not have a clear sense of the task they are requiring should understand (and perhaps attempt to complete) their own assignments before they ask their students to do so.

Furthermore, students should be taught to note and circle the different parts of the question. A common cause of low grades on essays is simply failing to answer all parts of the question. It is easy to get caught up in responding to the first directive and to forget everything else. If students circle and number the parts (which may be buried in a complex sentence), they are more likely to deal with them. Even advanced students will often miss key parts of complex questions. One question type asks for a single coherent essay in which several topics are addressed. Many students will answer the subquestions in a series of paragraphs, sometimes numbering them diligently, but then fail to connect these parts into the single coherent essay required.

Finally, students need to be aware of the mode of discourse that the question requires. This can be a serious problem for first-year students, who often have little experience with expository writing. We seem, as we enter the twenty-first century in America, to have reversed the findings of James Britton and his team of researchers in the London schools some decades ago. They found very little personal writing and a great deal of rote expository writing. Today many of our students have very little practice with expository writing; personal narratives are all they can produce. It is now common to find personal essays as responses on college placement tests, even when the question specifically asks for exposition or argument. One sure way for a student to fail an institutionally administered expository essay question is to answer it with a personal experience.

Some questions may intentionally mix modes: "Analyze the quotation and then illustrate it by some personal experience." Students need to see that such a question expects the narrative to be subordinate to the discussion of the quotation and connected to it. Sometimes the emphasis seems to be reversed: "Describe an occasion in which you _____, and tell what you learned from it." This question normally elicits a personal narrative with a perfunctory moral tag on the end. Perhaps such a narrative and tag are what the question actually seeks, but often what is really required is very much like the analysis in the preceding question. If there are good reasons to believe that the question is in fact basically looking for exposition, the student should decide on the concept first and use the description to illustrate the concept — writing an expository paper, with its evidence drawn from personal experience, not a personal narrative.

Sometimes, particularly on short placement tests, a narrative or a description is all that the question calls for. Though not all students find personal or descriptive writing easier than expository writing, most do; such writing poses few organizational or interpretive problems, for a simple chronology will usually serve quite well and the student is the final expert on the meaning of their own experiences. Such a test will examine a student's ability to marshal memories in reasonably error-free Standard English — useful information for some situations, but hardly information about a student's ability to turn out college-level writing.

The point is to train students to read questions carefully and to gain sufficient experience at writing in different modes so that they can make a rapid, accurate judgment of the kind of writing that may be required on an essay test. As more and more instructors are learning to ask precise questions, students are more and more likely to encounter clear directives. They may not know why the clear test strikes them as a good one or why they feel more capable and successful as they answer it, but they will be pleased with teaching and testing that clarifies rather than confuses.

Responding to Unclear Essay Assignments

Unfortunately, many essay assignments (of whatever scope) are not designed with sufficient care or precision, and students have come to expect vague directions for writing tasks. Even well-trained and experienced students may be surprised to receive low grades on a precise essay question because they have not responded to the question asked; some students are so used to unclear questions that they have become accustomed to ignoring them and writing whatever they choose on the general topic. Writing teachers should prepare students for the unclear questions they will be asked in various courses and should help students differentiate among types of unclear questions. Most of all, students need to know when a question makes precise demands that they must follow and when it requires them to construct their own question.

When a question is not clear, it becomes the student's responsibility to construct a clear question and then answer it. This way of handling the question is never evident, and many students will respond to unclear questions as they do to the ubiquitous *discuss* — by simply dumping everything they know about the topic on the page in the hope that they will somehow hit on whatever the teacher is looking for. Sometimes that works, for a vague question suggests that the teacher has no clear response in mind. But a much more productive tactic for students is to figure out what a reasonable question might be in relation to what is asked and to the context of the test.

For example, on the final exam in a course dealing with nineteenth-century European symphonies, the class might find the following question: "Beethoven and Brahms. Thirty minutes." Many possibilities open up. Some students in the class begin writing immediately, telling everything they know about Beethoven (mostly his biography, with dates of the symphonies), followed by whatever they can list about Brahms, with dates; at the end, when time is up, they stop in mid-sentence and scrawl, "Out of time."

More experienced test-taking students do not start writing without revising and clarifying the question. They take five of the thirty minutes to list on scratch paper a few connections between the two composers, recognizing that the question must represent some kind of comparison and contrast. They know that they can write only three or so paragraphs, so they decide that one paragraph will deal with similarities and a second with differences; a final paragraph will address the importance of the two composers in the history of music; an opening paragraph is uncertain, so they leave space for it to be added at the end of the test, stating the question that they have answered. These successful students might produce an opening paragraph stating that Beethoven and Brahms are both German romantic composers who displayed different forms of romanticism; two paragraphs might follow, comparing and contrasting a few aspects of their romanticism; and a closing paragraph could suggest that later composers such as Bruckner and Mahler drew on both forms of romanticism. These students plan their time so the writing ends with a few minutes to spare; they then reread their essays, fix up the spelling, insert a missing word or two, and move on to the next question.

The excellent students I have just described may or may not happen to know more about nineteenth-century music than the mediocre students, writing as fast as they can without a plan, but they will certainly get higher grades. They will also find essay tests more rewarding and less exasperating than the other students will.

Sometimes the questions are even less clear than "Beethoven and Brahms." A typical one will give a quotation with no directive at all, or the quotation may be followed by the direction "Discuss." But what is the student to discuss? Again, most students will proceed with a file dump, disgorging as much of what they know as possible on the page. But the careful, well-trained student will pause to construct a question before responding so that the essay can follow some kind of organization. What is the quotation saying, and how does it relate to the material of the course? (Most essays written in response to texts fail to examine the text in much detail.)

These students will mark up the quotation and sketch out meanings and connections as they decide on the central idea of their response. If time is short, they may begin by leaving space for an opening paragraph and proceed to write an analysis paragraph, expecting their own point to become clear as they write. Soon they realize that the quotation illustrates a particular point of view, perhaps a common mistake or a particular insight, in the field; the task then becomes to show how the quotation achieves its goal — an analysis question. Or perhaps the quotation needs to be proved, or disproved, by an ordered citation of evidence: the question calls for an argument. Whatever the students decide, it is impossible for them to write out an answer until they have a good sense of even a badly written question.

For example, consider the first question in Chapter 7 of this book, a question based on a Samuel Clemens quotation:

> The best swordsman in the world doesn't need to fear the second best swordsman in the world; no, the person for him to be afraid of is some ignorant antagonist who has never had a sword in his hand before; he doesn't do the thing he ought to do, and so the expert isn't prepared for him; he does the thing he ought not to do; and often it catches the expert out and ends him on the spot.

An early draft of this question used the quotation with only a vague directive, and many students had a great deal of trouble with it. Some were convinced that they should devote themselves to a discussion of dueling; others decided to call up whatever they knew about Clemens and so relate the quotation to Tom Sawyer and Huckleberry Finn. Many students began writing about dueling as an example of something, only gradually coming to realize the essence of the quotation; by then it was too late to revise and reorganize the essay. The most astute and test-wise students marked up the quotation carefully, usually by underlining the three characters whose actions are being described: the best swordsman, the second best swordsman, and the ignorant antagonist. These students listed descriptors and examples for the three character types. A typical example looked like this:

Best swordsman: expert, like the Redcoats in 1776

Second best swordsman: good, plays by the rules, the French

Ignorant antagonist: makes his own rules, like the Revolutionary Americans

As the experienced students marked up the quotation and reflected on it, they became aware that the best way to "discuss" it would be to explain the three character types and then relate them to some area they knew (here, the American Revolution). Those of us on the test development committee for a major nationwide test decided that we would even the field for the test takers and devise a precise directive that pointed out the most effective way to handle the question: "Write an essay that explains what Clemens means by his description of the 'best swordsman' and the 'ignorant antagonist.' Relate Clemens's concept to an area about which you are well informed." By giving these directions, we changed the examination from one testing students' experience with handling unclear essay questions to one testing their ability to write an essay handling complex concepts. The results still showed a great range of abilities, as the sample papers given in Chapter 7 demonstrate (beginning on page 144), but the more precise question allowed the examination to elicit the information about the students that we really wanted.

Teachers helping students do their best on essay assignments will use their knowledge about directives in two ways: to revise their own questions to make them more answerable, clearer, and more precise in their demands; and to give students advice on and practice in responding to essay questions that are none of these — and hence require that students construct a question before answering it.

It is often very difficult for teachers, who (as good test takers themselves) always understood the code terminology and readily constructed test questions to answer when necessary, to realize that many students simply do not understand what they are supposed to do in response to essay questions. The questions may seem obvious to initiates, but time spent in class on this issue will lead to much better essay test writing and greatly improved grades.

Finally, all the issues this section deals with apply not only to essay tests but, even more pointedly, to all essay assignments. Ask any director of a college writing center the problem most often posed by frustrated students to tutors and the response will be, "I don't understand what the teacher wants me to do." The tutor is in an awkward position, since most of the time she doesn't know either, even after reading the assignment carefully. Sometimes the tutor will call the professor with a delicately framed version of that question, only to discover that the teacher has only a vague notion of what the assignment really calls for. So the tutor and the student spend time trying to figure out what the task at hand is and how it will be assessed. If the assignment were clear to begin with, that time — and every student's time — could be spent doing the job instead of guessing what the job might be.

The Role of Memory

Most essay tests contain a hidden demand: to call up material from memory for the essay. Many students have a rich and full memory store, stocked with personal experiences, reading, history, arguments, and much more. Such students are never at a loss for a topic, though they often need help in organizing, focusing, and developing the material they have at the ready. Most essay questions simply assume that students have access to a rich store of material.

But many students do not have that access, nor do they have the background in remembered reading, intellectual conversation, and reflective introspection that the typical essay question draws on. This problem surfaces regularly in writing classes that focus on autobiography or other versions of personal experience, just as we see it in the uneven performance of students on personal experience essay tests or those that draw on history that everyone supposedly knows. Because writing not only depends on but also increases memory, writing teachers ought to pay more attention to that relationship than other instructors do.

One strong argument for assigning personal experience writing is that such writing enriches memory. As students learn to write about themselves, they gain new access to the material of their own lives; it is common for an adult to comment, after writing a paper about a childhood experience, that only now do they really *own* the experience. In a similar way, the advocates of writing across the curriculum argue that the act of writing about anything gives ownership and immediacy to material that may have been distant and unrelated to the self. In short, we normally teach in our writing classes deep forms of understanding and learning, about both the self and the subject. For many of our students, this use of writing to internalize and understand is novel and difficult; it also turns out to be profoundly instructive, sometimes even transformative.

Essay testing is particularly frustrating for some students until they have learned how to call up from memory the events, details, and examples that are needed for most essay questions. Further, they will be expected to take an analytical and evaluative stance toward these memories, a stance that may seem unnatural to some who are not used to the academic culture. We ought to help such students understand and practice the kinds of memory exercises that most essay questions take for granted. One effective way to do this is through group discussion of responses to typical essay questions. Another way is to help students draw up lists of personal memories, historical references, and other matters likely to be of use on a particular test.

Let's use the Clemens question as an example. What historical events besides the American Revolution would illustrate (or argue against) the quotation? What personal experiences might the student be called on to use for the essay? (One student used his knowledge of chess to show that the quotation was dead wrong under conditions where skill alone mattered.)

WORKING WITHIN TIME CONSTRAINTS

The essential time problem with essay tests comes from the fact that most first-draft writing is usually faulty, disorganized, unclear, and unfocused. The secret to helping students do well on timed essay tests is to suggest ways, even under severe time limits, to hand in second or third drafts without writing earlier drafts. (The single greatest waste of time during an essay test comes from re-copying drafts.) In other words, the good test taker will find a way to think through a first draft in scratch notes and then write a more finished draft in the time allowed. In addition, time must always be saved for rereading and editing during the last few minutes. Students should be encouraged to write on only one side of the page and write on every other line so that there will be plenty of room for neat revisions; they should also leave space at the start for a new open-ing to be written after the essay is finished.

This kind of time management ought not to be taken as only a test-taking skill. A pervasive problem with all kinds of writing is poor planning. Though different students will use different writing processes, a writing process that al-lows no time for revision usually produces weak work. As any writer with a deadline knows, planning is crucial for success. Most students will appreciate some help in planning for successful essay test writing, and experience with re-vision in the testing situation will carry over to more leisurely writing tasks.

How long should an essay test take? Sometimes the institution establishes an exam schedule and the instructor must simply fit into the schedule. But often the teacher or test committee can design a time span that is appropriate for the purpose of the test. A test is, in one sense, a means of gathering infor-mation, and the time required for the test should depend on the complexity of the information being sought. Essay tests usually follow one of four patterns, which we will discuss in turn.

The Twenty-Minute Essay

Twenty-minute essay tests are designed to elicit two or three paragraphs that show mechanical competence and fluency. If the question is well constructed, it will allow students to begin writing almost immediately by (1) drawing on per-sonal experience or simple description and (2) asking for a straightforward chronological structure. If the question is not clear, poses organizational prob-lems, asks for much reflection, or makes other unreasonable demands for the time allowed, students will have to rewrite the question so that it can be an-swered in two or three paragraphs of hasty writing. Some students are very di-rect at doing this in their opening paragraphs: "I can't possibly write about the three most impressive teachers I have had, so let me tell you about my high school advanced placement teacher, who is the main reason I am now in col-lege. . . . " It may seem risky to do this, but the people grading the test should recognize the good sense of accomplishing the possible, particularly if they are reading many essays that show the despair and confusion of attempting the impossible.

The Thirty-Minute Essay

In recent years, numbers of large-scale testing programs have begun to use the thirty-minute essay, often at the college graduation level; the best known are the California Basic Educational Skills Test (CBEST) for teacher candidates and the Medical College Admissions Test (MCAT). The time frame is administratively convenient, for two essays will fit neatly in one hour — the same reason essays of this length appear often on final examinations.

In contrast to the twenty-minute test, thirty minutes will allow for an organized and coherent essay of limited complexity. But successful students will need to manage their time with great care: five minutes or so for close reading of the question and brainstorming (on paper), another five minutes to arrange and focus the ideas (deciding on the one central idea the essay will demonstrate), fifteen minutes to write three or so focused paragraphs, and five minutes to edit and revise. Even with so little time, it is a good idea to write on every other line so that corrections and additions can be inserted neatly at the end of the time span.

The Forty-Five-Minute Essay

Forty-five minutes remains the standard essay time span, and it allows for thoughtful, organized, and somewhat creative responses. The first ten minutes or so can be spent analyzing the question and outlining a response, almost half an hour can be spent writing, and time still remains for careful editing before the end of the test. Students should resist the impulse to recopy their drafts, which becomes more of a temptation as the time span increases; they should use all of the time allowed for organizing, writing, and editing. There is time to do extensive editing or even revision in the space between lines, on blank left-hand pages, and in the blank on the opening page. An opening paragraph that relates to the closing paragraph and points to the best ideas of the essay might, with luck, start the writing; more often, it should be written last.

Some instructors give their students a formula for writing the forty-five-minute essay, such as the "five-paragraph theme" — a widely used strategy that can lead to limited success. This formula for writing essay tests requires that the student have three things to say about any topic, no more and no less; the first and last paragraphs list the three points, and the three middle paragraphs assert each idea and give a bit of evidence for each. The formula persists because it provides an easy, all-purpose organizational scheme; however forced or mechanical, it does help students who cannot come up with an organization that reflects what they have to say. Those who dislike the formula complain that it provides an organizational scheme as a substitute for having something to say and so discourages creative thinking. When students use the formula mechanically, they are likely to produce essays that stick out during essay readings like a mannequin on a cheerleading squad. Most students will have more or less than three things to say; some students will have nothing to say, and dividing nothing by five (paragraphs) still leaves nothing, despite the appearance of an essay. The strategy is particularly weak on development (it disallows more than one paragraph for each subtopic) and coherence (which it almost ignores), not to speak of its inappropriateness for some kinds of essay questions (such as comparison/ contrast). But many instructors continue to teach it, on the grounds that some organizational scheme is preferable to none.

Instead of providing such formulas, teachers would be more helpful to students by offering them a range of organizational possibilities and idea-generating devices, recognizing that different students will learn and write in different ways. Some students will do best using formal outlines; others will be most productive using clustering (jotting down ideas any which way on the page and later organizing them with lines and circles); still others will profit from structured problem-solving mechanisms (heuristics). Some may even need to learn some stress-reducing techniques before they can begin to write well under time pressure.

The essays presented in Chapters 6 and 7 of this book were all written in forty-five minutes. Those at the top end of the scoring scale show how much can be said in this time span, if the time is well used. While it still seems a short span of time for a considered essay, all too many student papers written at home or in the computer center are "finished" in less time.

One-, Two-, and Three-Hour Essays

As the time span increases, questions can become more complicated. A typical two-hour test, for example, may be an open-book question on essays read in advance, calling for detailed analysis of several of them, comparison/contrast, and connections to the student's experience. Curiously, writing quality does not seem to improve very much beyond that of the forty-five-minute exam; the essays will simply be longer. Much of the additional time seems to be spent on worrying, rereading, and recopying of drafts.

Students taking long essay tests should spend the extra time thinking the question through and organizing their responses so that the draft they write will seem to be a second rather than a first draft: it will be focused on a single controlling idea, organized around a sequence of connected assertions, and developed by use of examples and detail. In addition, students should save a substantial amount of time at the end for writing the first paragraph, revising the rest of the essay to develop and demonstrate the controlling idea, and editing it so that the essay they hand in is almost a third draft — despite the fact that it has been written and edited only once. The best preparation for such tests is extensive practice in organizing and revising complex papers.

ORGANIZING THE RESPONSE

Despite all the good advice given by teachers and books such as this one about organizing writing on essay tests and other writing assignments, very few students actually do it — so few, in fact, that it is worthwhile trying to figure out why. I think that there are both theoretical and practical reasons for this resistance to a practice that would surely improve students' writing and grades.

Some students have so little practice in reading and writing about ideas (as opposed to experiences) that a discussion of organization may be premature. They need experience in reading and discussion to gain an understanding of ways to pursue ideas and arguments; they are likely to need help with invention and development strategies before there is much to organize. In spite of the fact that most students have plenty to say, some experience with exposition and argument, and a reasonable background of information to draw on, many still resist the very idea of organizing their writing.

Numbers of students have picked up a half-baked theory of writing, based on the muse theory of poetry: either you will be inspired to write a terrific piece of first-draft writing, or you won't — and no amount of work will produce anything worth reading. In either case, there is no point in organizing or revising — in fact, such activities are an outrage to the muse, an attempt to impose reason on a mystical process.

Even without this dimly perceived romantic theory, most fluent college students see no point in organizing their work, for fluent first drafts (really discovery drafts) have often won them praise and high grades in the past. Too often, what has really mattered about writing has been correctness in mechanics and a certain amount of repetition of key ideas from the text or from lecture notes. When we speak of organizing thoughts and going through a series of drafts, we are changing the rules of a game that some students have learned to play successfully. "You can make me write," one student wrote on an essay test, "but you can't make me think!" We need to make clear that we are intentionally changing the rules. Avoiding thinking and revising may have been tolerated in the past, but writing and thinking now must go together; we must emphasize that organization and revision are an indispensable part of successful writing.

One good way to combat these destructive attitudes toward writing, I am convinced, is by way of assessment. Not until students have become able to distinguish good from weak responses will they realize that their work both needs improvement and can be improved with planning. They need to be exposed to scoring guides and other student papers, gradually internalizing critical standards that they can then begin to apply to their own work. And they need enough practice with revision to see that they are capable of recognizing their own best ideas, organizing them, providing evidence and connections for them, and rearranging them in improved order. In short, organization as a concept assumes that we are looking at writing as craftsmanship in critical thinking, not as inspiration or mechanics. Not until students have made that conceptual leap will advice on organization or practice in it have much effect.

Some teachers have found that regular practice in writing and writing assessment in class are the best means of helping students conceive of writing in this new way. If we value writing as a discovery process, which need not be organized or edited in preliminary form, we help students understand the difference between discovery drafts and finished drafts. A writing journal in which students both summarize and react to reading assignments, ungraded but collected and checked, is a powerful tool for reshaping attitudes about writing. Opening class with a "five-minute write," during which the pen must keep moving, can launch students directly into discussion. Such activities accustom students to writing as part of their regular thinking, talking, and reading activities and can help them understand the necessarily unshaped nature of draft writing. Materials such as journal entries and five-minute writes must be molded before they can become products submitted for grading. Peer grading and peer response sessions conducted in class when papers or drafts are due can open students' eyes to the possibilities of organized writing as critical thinking. Practice in writing timed tests and peer grading of those tests will reinforce the need for planning, organization, and revision.

The world seems filled with organizational schemes, and for a very good reason: people have a wide variety of ways of proceeding, depending to a great extent on their learning styles. Outlining works very well for those who proceed in a linear fashion, comfortable with categories and subcategories. But outlining feels like a straitjacket for other students, who need a more open and more holistic way of coming up with and arranging ideas.

We can help our students learn the most effective ways to organize their essays by giving them a series of options and by recognizing that our own way of organizing will not work for everyone. Besides outlining, we should be able to illustrate nonlinear procedures — clustering, cognitive mapping, listing of assertions, and other useful schemes for grouping and ordering ideas. We should demonstrate that only organization before writing will allow a student to write "second drafts" on essay tests, as there is never time to write two full drafts. And we need to make clear that writing on an essay test needs to use the same process that leads to good writing under more leisurely circumstances, that organizing a test essay is much easier than organizing a long research paper or an honors thesis but is nonetheless a similar activity. Students who learn that organized thinking is the essence of expository writing will visit you during their senior year to thank the teacher who helped them understand that most important lesson.

REVISING AND EDITING

It is important to distinguish editing from revising, a much more elaborate activity. During revision, we move paragraphs about, insert new pages, discard whole chunks of prose, reorganize, and come up with new ideas. Editing is a humble cousin of revision, though it may sometimes lead to revision. For example, work on sentence structure that is awry may reveal that the concept is poorly formed; work on paragraph coherence may lead to revision of the paragraph, breaking it into two or more new ones. But in general, editing is the last phase of writing, a matter of tidying up the mechanics so that readers will not be distracted by errors or inconsistencies.

Not until we get to the forty-five-minute essay can we reasonably talk about revision; shorter essay tests simply do not allow time for that activity. (As mentioned earlier, this limitation of essay tests, which makes it difficult for writers to use an extended writing process to produce good drafts, has led to the recent emphasis on portfolio assessment; we return to this matter in Chapter 8.) So the final few minutes of every essay test should be spent on rereading and editing what has been written. Good writers will be able to do some revision (usually additions and deletions) as they edit, but most students should probably use this time for polishing and cleaning: inserting the occasional missing words typical of a hasty draft, correcting the inevitable spelling errors, replacing commas with semicolons where necessary, checking subject-verb agreement, and so on. No matter how much the grader of the essay tries to allow for hasty errors on exams, a cleaned-up paper will almost always receive a higher grade; some teachers find it extremely hard to respect the views of writers of error-filled prose, regardless of how intelligent the writing may be.

Some students want to bring dictionaries or thesauri to tests so that they can look up troublesome words. Though we must respect the impulse to use reference materials, they usually do more harm than good on timed essay tests. The dictionary may help on spelling problems, but the time lost is usually not worth the improvement; in most cases, the presence of the dictionary suggests that the student should do editing while composing, instead of as a cleanup operation afterward, and the constant interruptions while writing destroy the essay. The thesaurus is even worse; it encourages the students to use longer and odder words rather than the clear ones they have in mind. There is so much to do during the usual timed essay test that reference books become distractions rather than supports. Some students feel so insecure without their references that it would be unsettling to forbid them, even on brief tests, but we might suggest that they are more helpful if left unopened during the limited time allowed for most essay tests. Not until we get into two-hour or longer tests will they be of much use. Of course, the kind of assignments that lend themselves to portfolio assessment are likely to assume or even depend on the use of reference works and other sources. Editing for portfolios will then include consistent citation format as well as organizational clues to readers.

COMPUTER ASSISTED WRITING
AND RESPONDING

The various uses of computers for all stages of writing and research have so increased over the past few years that we can only deal with general tendencies and principles here. We will focus on the computer scoring of writing and the now-common problem of distinguishing proper from fraudulent uses of sources. Our concern here is the use of computers as part of the development of writing assignments, since we can expect most of our students to write on computers as they meet those assignments.

We need to consider ways to integrate computer possibilities into a new generation of writing assignments. A microcosm of this issue is clear in any essay testing room. If computers are not permitted, some students will be so unaccustomed to handwriting that they will be at a disadvantage. If the test is given in a computer center, every student will be using the same software, but again that will give an unfair advantage to those who happen to be familiar with that software. If students bring their own laptops, they might bring preprepared text on their computers ready to import into their essay responses. One trend in computer centers, and in more and more classrooms, is to offer wireless technology for students to use on their own computers. This solution to the need for constantly updating hardware and software in computer labs is so economical for colleges that we may see it becoming the standard arrangement. Whatever the technological solution, and whatever the time length of the examination, an essay question can now employ resources unimaginable a generation ago. But with the teaching of writing, every solution brings with it new problems. For instance, the division between students from well-to-do homes and those without much privilege is now exacerbated by their differing knowledge of and access to computers. (Some computers-in-composition specialists call this "the digital divide.") And despite the many advantages computers have brought to the writing process, recent experience with student writing — which is now almost universally composed on and printed by computer — shows that it is no panacea. Many students mistake the neat appearance of printed texts for good writing, and the mechanical correctness suggested by the spelling and grammar checkers is no substitute for organized, original, or creative thinking.

Computers have the potential for changing writing and the teaching of writing in many additional ways. Like the typewriter, whose advocates predicted conceptual revolutions from writing by machine, the computer does ask writers to compose in a different way than the pen does; every experienced writer knows that word processing aids revision and increases production. But unlike the typewriter, computers can also alter the way we read and respond to writing. Some writing classes in well-equipped schools are using course management software, Internet research resources, and networked computer labs that facilitate constant and wide-ranging responses from readers. Indeed, many computer enthusiasts in the rhetoric and composition professional community are convinced that the use of computers for writers and writing teachers is a genuine revolution in thought as well as in technology. I am somewhat skeptical about such claims, but I notice that my own practice as a writer and as a teacher is dramatically different now from what it was ten years ago. I communicate with my students using class listservs; I no longer carry stacks of papers around, since all work is submitted by computer, as e-mail attachments; I respond to their work by adding comments to their electronic texts and e-mailing them back; I "track changes" on their revisions. I wish I could say that all of these conveniences had led to a vast improvement in student writing, but I haven't experienced that change, nor have I seen evidence from composition research that has persuaded me. Of one thing I am sure: computers have increased the workload of teachers even as they have given us new tools for responding conveniently to student writing.

It is inevitable that new assessment devices will emerge from such practices, and commercial firms are now busily promoting computer scoring as a great economy in time and money for teachers and institutions. I have not seen much evidence yet for the usefulness of these innovations for assessment, though they do have their enthusiastic supporters. The teaching of writing is so tied to teacher involvement in student writing processes and to teacher response and evaluation of writing products that it is hard to imagine how handing such matters over to a machine will improve either teaching or learning.

AVOIDING PLAGIARISM

I tend to avoid the term "plagiarism," since it is a scare term that has many and varied meanings. Certainly, students need to learn how to use sources properly, and they need to learn that they are subject to penalties if they present the work of others as if it were their own. And they need to understand that the ready availability of, and ease of copying from, the Internet does not relieve them of that responsibility. Yet there are degrees of copying, some of which are more acceptable than others (Rebecca Howard sees "patchwriting" — the incorporation of scraps of quotable material into one's own — as common in professional writing), and the issue is not at all simple. Outright fraud does exist, but most of what teachers call plagiarism is a result of students' genuine confusion about what is proper and what is not — that is, how to use sources responsibly.

The following description of the issue derives from a class handout, initially prepared by my former colleague Peter Schroeder and much adapted by me. It is addressed to students and you are welcome to adapt and distribute it to your classes for discussion. This version appeared in the writing textbook *Inquiry: Questioning, Reading, Writing*, edited by Lynn Z. Bloom and me (485–88).

Suppose you are writing a paper on American civil disobedience. You are particularly interested in the relation between idealism and lawbreaking. You decide that the following passage from Henry David Thoreau's essay in the previous chapter is relevant to your topic, and you want to use it as a source:

> Unjust laws exist: shall we be content to obey them, or shall we endeavor to amend them, and obey them until we have succeeded, or shall we transgress them at once? Men generally, under such a government as this, think that they ought to wait until they have persuaded the majority to alter them. They think that, if they should resist, the remedy would be worse than the evil. But it is the fault of the government itself that the remedy is worse than the evil. It makes it worse. Why is it not more apt to anticipate and provide for reform? Why does it not cherish its wise minority? Why does it cry and resist before it is hurt?

What Thoreau has to say is clearly useful for your topic. But how are you to use it? And how are you to avoid using it improperly?

Let's take a moment to look at the wrong ways to handle sources, for many students are nervous about falling into plagiarism — using sources as if they were your own idea — by mistake. Very few students will be deliberately dishonest and foolish enough to plan plagiarism — that is, to copy what Thoreau said word for word and hand it in as if it were original. But honest and sensible people still have trouble using sources properly and sometimes stumble unaware into plagiarism, unless they understand clearly how to incorporate other people's ideas into their own work.

For instance, one way to misuse Thoreau's material would be to copy what he says word for word and put a note at the end referring to the source of the quotation. Sometimes plagiarism happens if you take careless notes that fail to distinguish quotations from your summaries of what you have read. There is no intention to deceive in this case, but plagiarism is still going on since (without quotation marks) Thoreau's words and ideas are put forward as your own.

It is more responsible to put the quoted material in quotation marks, of course, but even that does not complete the job of using the source responsibly. Why is the quotation in your text? How does it relate to what you have to say?

The whole point of writing a paper using sources is not just to include relevant quotations and to cite sources, but rather to demonstrate that you have thought about your quotations and your sources in relation to your topic. If you just string together sources, quoted or paraphrased, with a bit of connection to hold them together, you are not accomplishing the inquiry that lies behind writing itself. Sources will help you demonstrate your ideas, but they cannot substitute for your ideas.

One way many students would use this source would be to figure out what Thoreau is saying and to put it into their own words:

> People suffering under unjust laws have to decide if they should obey the laws or not. Most people decide to obey them while they work for change, since breaking the law might be worse than the unjust law itself. But it is better to break the law, since the law itself should allow the best citizens to make changes.

But inserting this rewording of Thoreau's idea into your paper (while it shows that you understand his idea) is still not by itself a responsible use of the source, particularly if you fail to cite Thoreau at the end of the paraphrase. The idea is still his, even if the words are yours, and just placing someone else's ideas into your paper represents a failure to use the source properly. And even if you do cite Thoreau after the paraphrase, your reader will not know what the citation means. How much of what you say is yours, how much is Thoreau's, or is there any difference?

The problem you must handle as a writer using sources is not only to understand Thoreau but also to come to some personal understanding of the material at hand (here, the moral and legal problem of either obeying or disobeying unjust laws). You must regard Thoreau critically; if you end up agreeing with him, you should say so explicitly. If not, point out where and why you differ.

So we return once more to the topic. Is Thoreau's argument (those in a "wise minority" should break laws they feel to be unjust) an idea you wish to support, in whole or in part? What does your own experience say? What do other sources (for instance, Martin Luther King, Jr.) say about the same subject? Does Thoreau's location in nineteenth-century New England in any way determine what he will see? How does Thoreau's view relate to your own?

To think this way is to come to terms with the problems of writing a paper using sources. If you decide to put the whole quotation into your paper, you will need to introduce it, analyze it, comment on it, and relate it to your own ideas. You might begin, after the quotation, something like this:

> When we look closely at what Thoreau has to say, we can argue that he over-simplifies the issue; as the last 150 years have made plain, it is hard to decide exactly what is an unjust law. Few of us today can be so certain that any law is wrong. But Thoreau's arrogant certainty has undeniable power. . . .

But perhaps you do not want to focus so heavily on Thoreau's views; in that case you may want to quote a small portion of what he says, as part of another argument:

> Disobedience to law in our time has proven to be a powerful force for change. The idea that we should always obey laws while seeking to change them has repeatedly been shown to be the way governments perpetuate evil; they argue that breaking laws is worse than any evil the law may bring about. But I would argue, as does Thoreau, that "it is the fault of the government itself that the remedy is worse than the evil." A truly democratic government will provide ways for those who object to its laws to protest legally and effectively.

Or you may just want to allude to what Thoreau says as part of a survey of various ideas on your subject:

> Among the most well-known proponents of disobeying laws they felt to be un-just are Thoreau (who briefly went to jail for opposing a government support-ing slavery) and Dr. Martin Luther King, Jr., who . . . .

There are many ways to use sources responsibly, but the important principle to keep in mind is that you must understand what the source is saying and how it relates to your own ideas. In using sources you must not simply be a sponge, soaking up uncritically everything you read. You must distinguish between the opinions of another and the opinion that you yourself, after careful considera-tion, come to hold. The quotation then becomes a fact, the fact that a particular writer has said something, which you as author of your own work must inter-pret as you would any other fact; you need to show how the evidence provided by the quotation relates to what you yourself have to say. Every writer has their own intellectual identity, though most ideas inevitably come from outside sources. A responsible use of sources recognizes that identity and distinguishes clearly between what you think and what the sources think. It is no sin to accept another person's idea: "But I would argue, as does Thoreau, that . . ." But you must interpose yourself between the sources and your writing, thus making other people's ideas your own through a process of critical scrutiny.

SELECTED REFERENCES

Bloom, Lynn Z., and Edward M. White. *Inquiry: Questioning, Reading, Writing.* Upper Saddle River: Prentice-Hall, 2004.

Kirch, Ann. "A Basic Writer's Topoi for Timed Essay Tests." *Journal of Basic Writing* 15.2 (1996): 112–24.

Roy, Alice M., and Lisa Buranen, eds. *Perspectives on Plagiarism and Intellectual Property in a Postmodern World.* Albany: State University of New York Press, 1999.

Shafer, Gregory. "Using Letters for Process and Change in the Basic Writing Classroom." *Teaching Developmental Writing: Background Readings.* Ed. Susan Naomi Bernstein. Boston: Bedford, 2001. 354–64.

White, Edward M. "An Apologia for the Timed, Impromptu Essay Test." *College Composition and Communication* 46.1 (1995): 28–43.

——— . "Selecting Appropriate Writing Measures" and "Organizing and Managing Holistic Essay or Portfolio Readings." *Teaching and Assessing Writing.* 2nd ed. San Francisco: Jossey-Bass, 1994. 171–96.

CHAPTER 3

RESPONDING TO STUDENT WRITING

Though there is much debate these days about the most effective methods of responding to student writing, there is a clear consensus about the least effective ways to handle student papers. Far too much of what teachers do with student writing is picky, arbitrary, unclear, or generally unhelpful. Most of us model our teaching behavior on the instructors we have had in school, and more than likely they used negative responses rather than effective patterns. To help us avoid merely repeating what our instructors did, we need to make conscious decisions about how we will handle student papers if we are to use the most appropriate methods for our own classes.

We shouldn't press the analogy too far, but teaching writing has a lot in common with parenting. It combines discipline and nurturing, encouragement and warning, even perhaps love and hostility. There is a curious intimacy to the whole business, as we read student response journals, hold one-on-one conferences, and write notes to one another. This parallel to parenting becomes particularly apparent as we consider how we have absorbed patterns of behavior without conscious awareness. Unless we make a serious effort, we simply adopt the parenting or responding styles of our early experience. And some of those styles may have been destructive or even abusive. We have to become conscious of and dissatisfied with these ways of responding before we will consider replacing them.

This chapter will focus on the wide range of options teachers have for responding effectively to student papers.

PURPOSES AND EFFECTS OF RESPONDING

The educational purpose of responding to and evaluating student writing ought to be the same as the purpose of the writing class: to improve student writing. (We also must serve one other administrative purpose, to screen out students who do not write well enough, but I will discuss that gatekeeper function later.) We seek to improve student writing in many ways, but in responding to writing we have one overriding goal: the student needs to see what works and what does not work in the draft so that revision can take place. Hence, it does little good for the instructor to judge or grade writing without providing responses that allow the writer to understand the reasons for that judgment. If the student can simply dismiss the teacher's views as mere personal opinion, the writing will not improve. Writers (like all learners) improve when they can internalize evaluation — when they can themselves see what needs to be changed and how to make those changes. Conversely, if the draft is truly finished (and very few are), the writer needs to see just where its excellences lie so that they can be repeated.

As an analogy, a batter in a batting cage hits the ball and gains an immediate response; if the ball isn't hit well, the player will make immediate corrections, steadily practicing until the player's hitting improves. The coach closely observes the performance and offers suggestions, sometimes modeling the most productive behavior, but the player is the only one who can make the changes needed. It is patently absurd for batters to blame coaches for their strikeouts, and no coach (however kind and supportive) can pretend that bad play will win games; nor can an irascible and competitive coach gain improvement by continuous harassment if the player will not practice. Writing is, of course, more complex than batting (though perhaps not more difficult), but writing teachers can learn a good bit about teaching from watching a good coach.

Clearly a grade on a paper, with no comment or only a cryptic phrase or two, will not add much to student learning. Sarcastic or harsh comments will allow the student to displace dissatisfaction with the paper (the teacher's intention) with dislike of the teacher and thereby short-circuit learning. Steady red-marking of all possible errors will bewilder and frustrate students, who cannot profit from an overload of correction; such papers tend to receive a cursory glance from the student before being thrown away. Puzzling abbreviations (k, d, fs) are abstruse to the student; they may mean "awkward," "diction," and "fused sentence" to the teacher, but for whom are they intended? Even vague positive comments ("Nice work," "I enjoyed reading this") frustrate students, who want to know what the teacher found "nice" and what made reading enjoyable. With so many teachers responding to student writing in such negative or uninformative ways, those of us who respond more professionally to student work can anticipate warm student appreciation and a genuine attempt to improve as we surprise them by taking their writing seriously and respecting it and them.

For many of us in our student days, the writing and submitting of papers was just one battle in the war between student and teacher. We did our best to figure out what the teacher really wanted, often puzzling for hours over obscure directions (or no directions). Then we would hand in the paper and hold our collective breath while we waited for the more or less mysterious judgment that would be handed down when the papers were returned. If we made mechanical errors, we could expect snarls — but we often received those snarls anyway for unpredictable reasons. However, we didn't complain much because in our heart of hearts we knew we were guilty of unknown sins. We didn't pretend to know "grammar," which was an impenetrable puzzle of arbitrary rules of linguistic conduct, and we thought that the teacher did and would punish us for our unintentional and inevitable violations. It was all part of the war, and — like Marine recruits — we expected random humiliation. The grade was all that really counted — revision was rarely required or rewarded — so we developed various ways of ignoring the comments a few teachers sometimes provided.

Since so many of these patterns remain, it is interesting to consider what purposes they served and continue to serve. At the outset, it seems clear that the pattern I just described *is* a pattern: unclear assignment, harsh commentary, lack of expected revision, emphasis on grades — all add up to an exclusionary design, with concern only for product. In other words, this pattern rewards the academically canny and privileged, who can be depended on to know already what is being taught. The purpose of the grade and comment was to reward virtue and punish vice, and the moral overtones of the conflict led naturally to harshness. Students who did not show evidence of good writing were socially and morally offensive, wasting the time of the university and the professor. The teacher's red pen symbolized the scarlet letter, which on English papers was rarely an "A." It demonstrated the moral offense of the "errors" it excoriated and the pain of the teacher who was forced to mark them. Some instructors maintain this metaphor still in their conversation, unaware; they will talk of taking a batch of papers home for the weekend and "bleeding all over them."

What this pattern most obviously lacked was a concern for writing as learning, for the teaching of writing as supportive of learning. What it unconsciously enforced was the gatekeeper function of schooling — rewarding the privileged and excluding almost all whose parents were of the wrong class, income, or national origin. Instructors who unrepentantly continue this pattern today claim that they are upholding "standards," as if it were somehow wrong to help students learn.

The concern for standards is real and important but should not serve as an excuse to indulge in negative responding patterns. An essential part of the writing teacher's job is to teach and enforce standards of performance that will allow students to succeed in college. This is the gatekeeper function of writing courses, an institutional (rather than educational) function that makes many instructors uncomfortable. Some large state universities make freshman composition virtually a wing of the admissions office — expecting the staff to winnow out the unqualified rather than "waste" university resources teaching them. The moral dilemma posed by such a situation is difficult indeed, and every instructor will resolve the conflict between teaching and selecting in an individual way; but this conflict should not lead to the use of evaluation and responding only as an administrative selecting tool. Nor should it lead to a narrow definition of writing as a mere test of certain skills that the institution may define as necessary.

The uses of writing are so large — as a tool for learning new material, as a means of power in a verbal world, as a way to understand complex ideas, as a route to understanding the self, and so on — that we do not want to narrow our purpose as writing instructors to merely judging and enforcing group standards. We must accept some responsibility for standards, for the sake of both the institution and the students who will be required to fulfill its demands. But if we accept the profound value of writing and its many uses, responding to writing becomes extraordinarily complex, calling for some special thoughtfulness on the instructor's part.

The pressures of time and the force of tradition often keep us from thinking through the purposes and effects of responding to a particular set of student papers. Most teachers proceed to "mark" a set of papers without much consideration of options. They read each paper through, red pen in hand, marking mechanical errors as they go, writing comments of one sort or another in the margins, and concluding with a grade and a comment justifying the grade at the end. Such a procedure can give sensitive and supportive help to students, for it demonstrates a careful reader's responses, but it does not make sense to respond to every assignment in the same way.

Must every assignment be graded — or be graded on the same scale? Must the teacher read and mark every word of every piece of writing done in a writing class? What is the point of marking careless mechanical errors on drafts that will be revised or that are not designed for a demanding audience? Are we taking ownership of the paper away from the student by our markings and asking the student to say what we want instead of what he or she wants? Are we sufficiently aware of what recent literary theory has taught us about the problematics of reading texts, including student texts? What are some useful ways of involving students themselves in the evaluation and response that every writer needs? How can we structure our comments, and student peer comments, so that students will want to revise their texts for their own sake rather than for ours? Questions such as these ought to arise before the red ink begins to flow. The answers to such questions should make the immense amount of time spent with student papers more productive, more interesting, and (perhaps) less time-consuming.

RESPONDING TO DRAFTS

Responding to writing does not begin when you start to read student essays; it starts much earlier, at the point when the assignment is made. Earlier chapters in this book have spoken at some length about the problem of devising appropriate writing assignments; we need only note here that a careful assignment makes the task of responding to the papers it elicits easier for the instructor and more useful for the student.

Perhaps the most useful responses of all occur very early in the writing process. The teacher may discuss the assignment and ask students to go through some prewriting exercises; some examples of previous class work may be distributed and analyzed. Surely this is valuable. But more valuable still is the presentation by the student (to the class or to a small peer group) of early ideas for writing. The advantages of making such presentations are obvious: the student will gain ownership of the ideas presented, will get to work early on the task, and will come up with ways of demonstrating the major concept of the essay and making it interesting to others. The response to these presentations must be a delicate combination of support, encouragement, and rigor. If the topic is unworkable for some reason, this is the moment to help the student see the problem — when there is sufficient time for a change. If the evidence is unconvincing or weak, the student needs to hear that from the teacher or from the peer group. But responses at this early stage need not be harsh, for their only function is to help the student do good work. No grades or editing issues (the nightmares of so many students) need enter here. Good responding practice will begin with class discussion of the assignment, continue with class or group discussion of individual plans for the assignment, and then move into a consideration of steps for development and revision of discovery drafts.

We may talk about writing as discovery and revision and even schedule due dates for work in progress, but unless we build respect for revision into our evaluation of writing, our students will not believe us. If we continue to give a single grade for the finished (or unfinished) writing product, we are in fact saying that the product is all that we value. Therefore, the logic for rewarding the work in progress is compelling, and not only for the reasons I have been stating. Term papers, and student essays in general, are among the least valuable products in a world of wastepaper; only a tiny percentage of them are saved, and only a minuscule percentage are published. True, they serve as products to be graded, but the only real reason for their production is as testimony to student learning. In many cases, that learning is better measured through the steps of production than through the final formal product alone.

This is a delicate balance, for too much grading oversimplifies responding. Some instructors manage this balance by giving grades on one kind of scale for drafts, bibliographies, and the like — say, a numerical scale similar to that used in many holistic scoring sessions (typically, 6 [high] to 1 [low]). The final draft can then be graded on the usual "A" to "F" scale. Others, concerned about the imposition of authority and ownership implied by constant grading, use peer group responses and a simple check-off system to note the completion of parts of the task. It all depends on the goals of the course and the assignment. But the central point remains: any composition instruction that attempts to inculcate good writing habits should both require and respond to stages of the discovery and revision process.

We need to be careful about our real messages in this regard; if we intend to value revision as part of the writing process for everyone, we cannot treat revision as punishment for bad work. Unfortunately, numbers of well-meaning writing instructors include revision in their course plans either as an unpleasant option or as required only for bad work. Sometimes papers graded below "B" may or must be revised; sometimes revision is a possibility only if the students wish to raise their grades. In a great many classes, revision means merely editing for mechanics or making only the teacher's proposed changes. But every real writer and writing teacher know that revision means a "new vision" of what is being said, responding to internal as well as external demands; most writing in a writing class should be revised as a matter of normal routine, a natural part of the thinking process that writing expresses.

Whatever the grading or responding system, the comments on drafts should focus primarily on the conception and organization of the paper. There is no point in spending time on editing issues — aside, perhaps, from a note reminding the student that the final copy needs to be edited. Premature editing is the enemy of revision; some writers pay so much attention to spelling and punctuation that they neglect to attend to what they are saying.

To demonstrate that the ideas of the paper are what matter in early drafts, some teachers will require an outline of some sort to be submitted along with the draft, to make it easier for both student and teacher to see the ways in which ideas are developed. The basic job of draft writing is to discover and develop the subject, not to worry about mechanics. Hence, it is always helpful for the teacher to mark and respond to the clearest and most inventive statements about the subject; this is another place for encouragement and stimulation of the student. If you are really bothered by errors in the draft, you might want to write something like "Be sure to clean up the copy after you revise so that readers will be able to understand and respect what you have to say." But red-marking the errors would be destructive at this point.

Experienced teachers have developed various schemes for reading early drafts and concentrating on their ideas, development, and structure. Some make a point of skimming the work before commenting, attending particularly to the opening and closing paragraphs; sometimes the first sentence of each paragraph will give a clear clue to the structure, or lack of structure, of the paper. It is always useful to identify the central or controlling idea, circle it, and comment on its interest and possibilities. Questions are more useful to students than assertions at this stage. Instead of writing "coherence" or "coh" in the margin, we might say, "I've underlined the two separate ideas you are pursuing in this paragraph; can you connect them? If not, focus on one or the other," or, "Your point in this paragraph makes good sense, but it seems to conflict with what you said in your opening. How do the two ideas relate?"

Finally, if we want students to profit from our reading, we should apply two commonsense rules: do not overburden students with more commentary than they can handle, and find positive and encouraging ways to suggest improvements.

AUTHORITY, RESPONSIBILITY, AND CONTROL

One major difference between the teaching of writing and the teaching of other subject matter has to do with the role of the teacher. In most college courses, the teacher demonstrates authority (through expertness in the field), is responsible for the substance of what students are to learn, and maintains control over the course. However, each of these concepts operates differently in the writing course.

The teacher continues to exercise the authority that derives from knowledge and experience. The teacher knows more about writing than the students and has, of course, done more of it. The teacher is certainly a more practiced and skillful reader and is able to apply that skill to the reading of student texts. Therefore, the teacher has the authority to structure the syllabus, make assignments, and evaluate student writing. But students will not learn much about writing if they are merely passive recipients of the teacher's knowledge. Many studies support the need for active participation by students in the writing class if effective learning is to take place. Because the students must think their own thoughts, invent, discover, write, and revise, they must themselves develop some kind of authority; no one can write very well without having something to say, which implies a certain kind of authority over the material.

Thus the teacher must be willing to share some of the authority that comes inevitably with the instructor's role. If students are to write with a real voice, they must believe that they have, or can gain, authority over their subjects. When they write about personal experiences, that authority usually comes naturally enough: they are the only ones who really know what happened, and they have the right to speculate on what it means. But that tenuous sense of authority tends to disappear in the face of analytical assignments or printed sources. Frequently, students will merely describe what the assignment asks them to evaluate (or summarize or quote someone's argument), even though the assignment asks them to relate it to their own or someone else's ideas. Adolescent assertiveness about everything turns, in college, to a trained unwillingness to take a stand or to claim authority before the "expert" professor or the printed source. Therefore, the writing instructor must find ways to help students understand the kind of authority all writers can claim (or earn). Some students simply cannot write for professors who assert, or seem to claim, too much authority over too many aspects of the material. I remember well a diligent student's hesitant question after I gave the class an assignment to write about a Renaissance poet: "Are we supposed to like Skelton?" Like many passive students, she had given all authorial authority (note the relation of the two words) to the teacher — or, more likely, I had unwittingly laid claim to so much authority that she saw no space to assert any of her own. Until I was able to convince her that her response to the poem was important and could not come from outside, she was voiceless.

Many conscientious writing instructors not only deprive their students of the authority all writers need but also unintentionally assume responsibility for the papers their students produce. The most obvious sign of this shifting of responsibility from the student to the teacher occurs when the student tries to revise an early draft in light of the teacher's comments. Almost invariably, the student will not change anything that the teacher left alone; all revisions focus on the corrections suggested by the teacher. The result is often very odd, sometimes considerably worse than the original. The revised portions of the paper are often much better, particularly if the instructor's comments led the student to rethink and reorganize their best ideas (as comments should). But the paper as a whole is now out of balance, with the original untouched portions — which seemed all right in the draft — now in need of work. When we say this, the student is often outraged: "You saw nothing wrong with it before!" In the student's eyes, and perhaps in our own, we have become responsible for some (or all) of the paper. "Is this what you wanted?" we may hear, as if it were now our paper.

The attitude we take in our comments is crucial here. We must convey to student writers that responsibility and control remain with them and that they need to do more than merely respond to our comments. We ought not assume the role of editor for the student (marking every error is a common mistake, leading to student frustration or apathy in the face of too much red ink), nor ought we tell the student what the paper should do. We should rather express any problems we perceive in the paper, point out the questions that the paper raises in our minds, and ask the writer to attempt to resolve these problems. We should always be friendly, even when we are feeling overburdened and crabby, and we should always find something to praise and encourage. At most, we might suggest some options or alternatives, but we must refrain from taking over the paper — even if we are convinced that we know just what it ought to be doing. As I suggested earlier, pointed questions are often more effective than assertions: "This seems to be your central idea; why does it first appear here, in the next-to-last paragraph?"; "The second half of this paper seems to be on a different topic than the first half; which topic do you want to focus on?"; "This original idea opens up exciting possibilities; can you find a way to examine them?"

A sensible posture to take toward drafts is to comment only on a few central matters: the ideas, the structure, the author's perspective or voice, for example. Certainly, sound pedagogy suggests that all comments contain something positive. Perhaps a comment about mechanics at the end ("The paper has sentence errors that ought not to appear in the final draft") might be useful in some cases. But good teaching is clear about goals; therefore, if we assume that substantial rewriting of the current draft will take place, we ought not to fuss about the spelling of words that may later be edited. We need to encourage risk taking in drafts, the trying on of ideas and arguments that may not work out or may turn out to be very exciting.

Finally, we have to have a healthy portion of humility in the face of student texts, even texts we have trouble respecting. After three decades of post-structural theory, we can no longer imagine that the text is a simple object or that our reading of it is somehow objective or neutral. We must be aware that the value of a text is negotiated, culture-bound, and grounded in social structures. We come to student texts as we come to any texts, out of our own positions as people of a particular class, color, gender, age, and background. We respond as sensitively as we can, and we must finally record our evaluations on grade sheets, but the arrogance and arbitrariness of some teachers of the past might well be left behind along with their lessons in elocution and penmanship.

SAMPLE STUDENT PAPER IN TWO DRAFTS

Here are two drafts of a student paper written in response to the Analyzing Experience assignment given in Chapter 1. This is the assignment the students received:

> Describe and analyze an institution or a group of some sort that you knew well as a child: a school, school group, scout troop, dancing class, summer camp, club, Sunday school — any group with an obvious and consistent set of values will do. You have two specific tasks to accomplish: to describe clearly what it was like to be a member of the group at the time and to assess from your mature perspective the meaning of the group's values.

Here is the first draft brought to class by Robert, a first-year student, whose writing developed from discovery drafts about his Boy Scout Explorer post. Robert felt that the paper was "finished" but not really satisfactory, and he read it to his writing group with mixed feelings. I just happened to be sitting in with the group.

Explorer Post 14: Not Intellectually Prepared

I was a member of Explorer Post 14 for two years. We were a rather unorthodox Explorer post in that we wore no uniforms, had a constitution, elected officers, and had a nuclear physicist for a scoutmaster. Also, we did not go on camping trips, hikes, and other things of this type that one would normally associate with scouting. On the contrary, we studied, heard lectures and saw films on math and science, and worked on science projects, or at least that's what we were supposed to do.

We actually did hear lectures and see films, but having a serious discussion about any subject or working on a project, that was out of the question. I believe that this will become clear as I describe one of our typical meetings.

We would meet at Aerospace about 7:30 p.m. every other Wednesday night. Before the meeting began there was always a period of utter havoc. Loud talk and laughter, writing on the blackboard, making paper airplanes and other juvenile actions were common until the scoutmaster arrived. We then began the meeting with the flag salute, which was led by the president of the post. We quickly passed over the subjects of new and old business, project discussions, future plans, and other things of relative unimportance. We would then have a film or a lecture followed by a short, abortive discussion. This was not always the case. At times we did have lengthy intelligent discussions, but these were rare. Then we would adjourn the meeting and all go home. This is hardly the sort of meeting that would be expected of this type of group.

Another good example is projects. Each member of the group was expected to work on a project, individually or with another member. The only thing was, nobody ever worked on projects. With a group of this type, one would expect the members to be eager to work on projects and present them to other members for discussion, but this was just too much work.

I don't believe that the failure of our group to function as it was originally planned can be blamed on our scoutmaster as might at first be believed. On the contrary, I believe it was a direct result of the attitudes of the majority of the members toward doing anything that appeared to be work. Part of the members were the playboy type. They received good grades in school but preferred to chase around and go on dates three or four times a week rather than spend a little extra time working on a project or preparing a topic for a general discussion. Others were just plain lazy. All of the members had above average intelligence and the ability to think and reason, but thinking was just too much like work. Thus it appears to me that the members of this group were not intellectually prepared for an Explorer program of this type as it was originally designed.

Responding to "Explorer Post 14: Not Intellectually Prepared"

The writing group began by praising the paper, which fulfills the assignment quite well. Though it is weak on description, it does give a sense of what it was like to be a member of the group at the time, and the writer does analyze and point out the significance of the description. Since the first task for the group was to point out what was done well, they praised Robert for using enough detail to give them a sense of the scout troop. But along with the writer, the group was not really satisfied with the paper, though they struggled to figure out why.

I suggested that they look closely at its tone, the relationship of the writer to both the reader and the topic. First-year writing groups tend to be particularly sensitive to tone, for many young students are at an age when nuances of feelings have become particularly important. They noticed a conflict between the Robert they knew and liked as a person and the harsh, judgmental tone of the essay he had written. They pointed out some of the terms and phrases that establish his relationship to the troop: "that's what we were supposed to do" (paragraph 1); "that was out of the question" (paragraph 2). They also pointed out some problems with the writer's attitude toward the reader, asking the reader to condemn the other boys in the troop without much real evidence. An acute listener in the group had noted that the fourth paragraph begins "Another good example is projects" ("good example of what?"), which sounds whiny — as if there were a list of petty grievances. "You seem so stuffy and hostile to the other guys," another student in the group said, "didn't you like them at all?" Robert protested that he liked the other boys at the time and was still friends with many of them. Others in the group pointed out that Robert was a warm and accepting person, not at all like the tone he took in the essay, and wondered why he took the attitude he did; after all, the group was a Boy Scout troop, not a seminar of rocket scientists. Robert thought for a while and then smiled.

"I was trying to find something important to say, a controlling idea like Professor White here says we need. I guess I really forced things." He agreed with the group that the tone rang false; he had taken an attitude toward the boys in the troop that he really didn't feel, and that led to a false attitude toward the reader as well. He didn't much like the voice in the paper either.

Yet he felt sure that he had a good topic in the paper, even though he hadn't yet found a good controlling idea. The group went on to talk about scout troops and how they help kids find out who they really are. Robert joined in, saying that every scout troop is a kind of "explorer" troop in that they help their members explore themselves as well as their world. "Now that's an interesting idea," one of his friends said, "why don't you go with that?" I concurred that the idea of exploration sounded promising as a concept for the next draft.

"I think I'll try it," Robert replied. A week later he had completely revised the essay, as follows.

Explorer Post 14: The New World

Explorer Post 14 customarily met in a room at Aerospace usually used by scientists to discuss such vital subjects as defense projects and space exploration. The walls of the spacious, well-lighted room were blank, except for the west wall, which was decorated by a map of the world showing all of the routes taken by the early explorers to the New World. But this map was covered by a large motion picture screen whose pale blankness gave the room an air of sterility.

The twelve sixteen-year-old boys supposedly gathered together for the purpose of exploring the world of math and science. But actually this was just a guise for their real purpose — the exploration of the novel, quick-paced world of the teenager.

The meeting began, supposedly, with the flag salute. Actually the meeting began fifteen minutes earlier as the group gathered in the room that was to be their uncharted world for the next hour and a half. In these first fifteen minutes, the initial exploration began with the boys testing each other with silly comments about the day's activities at school and home. W. T. Jones III, the leader of the particular expedition, pulled the blackboard out to the middle of the room and began to map out their course. As it turned out, the map resembled the figure of Britney Spears and therefore was appropriately named The Temptation. About this time, Dr. Nevin, the nuclear physicist/scoutmaster, entered the room, and the expedition reached a temporary impasse.

After the flag salute, the lights went out and the motion picture screen flashed with brilliant colors and the blank walls reverberated with the sounds of a film titled The Exploration of the Planets and Beyond. It was the story of the astronauts and spacecraft that were venturing into the black reaches of space to explore the Earth's nearest neighbors, Mars and Venus. As the film ended, the bright lights again flicked on, and Dr. Nevin engaged the boys in a discussion of space exploration that lasted about twenty minutes.

But then the inevitable happened. The screen came down, revealing the world map. The temporary impasse overcome, the boys returned to their exploration with more vigor than before. Their path led them to cars, the date W. T. had had the night before, and girls in general. But soon they were forced to end their journey, for the meeting was at an end.

During the last part of the meeting, Dr. Nevin had just sat with the boys, laughing with them and only occasionally entering a comment of his own. Why had he done this? Why didn't he try to make the boys continue their discussion along more intellectually oriented lines? The reason is simple. He understood that in the strange, exciting world of the sixteen-year-old, self-exploration is much more intriguing than a journey into the world of science. For it is at this age when a person must find himself so that someday he will be a mature individual both mentally and physically. So each week Dr. Nevin took up the role of a silent guide so that a group of sixteen-year-old boys could engage in the exploration of life.

Responding to "Explorer Post 14: The New World"

The major changes from the first version to the second occur in the writer's attitude toward the boys in the scout troop and, consequently, in the controlling idea for the essay. The almost ritualistic condemnation of the boys, sometimes inappropriately bitter in the earlier draft, changes to sympathetic understanding as a result of more careful analysis and more original thought. As the writer examines his attitude toward the boys, he plays with the nicely ambiguous value of the "space exploration" of his topic: adolescents are inevitably involved in exploring their own worlds, even when they are supposedly finding out about planetary space. Perhaps the scoutmaster knew what he was doing after all.

In my written response to this draft, I praised the revision for its new depth of thought. I made some notes in the margins, showing that I noticed the more understanding attitude the writer takes to the boys in the scout troop in the revised draft. I also noted the changes in the writer's relationship to the reader: "Instead of asking us to condemn, you ask us to understand," I wrote. I also noted in the margins that the details are now richer and focus on reactions to his controlling idea, whereas the previous draft had fewer details and only general connections between the descriptions and the controlling idea.

In my end note and in a conference with Robert, I praised the changed organization, most obviously the new opening paragraph — which, Robert told me, had been the last part of the paper to be written. (I had mentioned in class that writers often write their openings last, after they see what their best ideas have turned out to be.) I did mention that the tone of the opening did not match the rest of the paper, but I tried to keep the emphasis on what it accomplished. Because Robert had decided to make connections between the exploration of outer and inner space, that controlling idea had to be kept alive throughout the paper — not an easy task. Further, in both drafts the paper takes us through a troop meeting from beginning to end, so the organizational changes had to occur in the development of the idea — not in the chronological order of events. In both drafts, the closing paragraph presents the writer's analysis of the meaning of what has been described, but they are entirely different. In fact, I decided (with Robert's permission) to duplicate his essay to illustrate for the class the ways in which well-structured papers used opening and closing paragraphs to set tone as well as topic.

Here is what I wrote at the end of the paper:

> Robert, this is an excellent revision of your earlier draft — which was good work to begin with. You have focused your details on your new controlling idea, which is more convincing and satisfying to me than the condemnation that ruled the previous draft. You have also used the controlling idea to control the organization of the paper, to focus its elements.
>
> As you prepare this paper for your portfolio, you might want to see if you can harmonize the tone of the opening paragraph with the rest of the paper and if you can develop your idea of exploration more fully. Can you give us more details about the "self-exploration" you only suggest in this draft? I am impressed at the way you have improved your writing and look forward to what you might do with this interesting essay.

Because I require further revision of second drafts for certain assignments, I include some suggestions for improvement even on the best papers. Indeed, I find that most people are more interested in improving their best writing than their worst. Despite its insufficiencies, Robert's second draft remains well written and interesting, with a defined thesis about an interesting topic. Some writers might consider this draft only a first step on the path to a publishable essay, but most American college instructors would be very pleased to see work as good as this early in the school year. My response in conference to the student (who was, after all, a first-year student) was "Bravo!" and a grade of 6 on the 6-point scale. Then we spent some time in conference talking about all that was well done in the paper and how he could duplicate the process for other papers. In fact, I asked for a reflective letter on his writing process for this paper to be included in his portfolio at the end of the term, as a way for him to have a record of his successful procedure.

COLLABORATIVE WRITING

In one sense, all writing is collaborative: every writer needs some kind of audience, some conversation, some reading, and some responding. The peer groups that are now part of many writing classes serve as sounding boards for initial ideas, responders to drafts, and even editors for presentation copies of final drafts. The picture of the writer as a solitary genius holed up in an attic, emerging on occasions waving a manuscript that expresses their inner self, has not been a useful one for writing instruction. Far better is the wry comment that Hemingway is supposed to have made when asked about his times of greatest inspiration: "Nine to five on weekdays." Writing takes place all the time, among or even with other people. In fact, much of the writing done outside of the university (and, increasingly, in the university) is now actually accomplished by teams; collaboration in the writing of reports and papers has become more and more common. We see this concept in physical form in the newer configurations of computer writing laboratories, where groups of computers and collaboration software impose collaboration as a matter of course.

Collaboration offers special challenges and possibilities to the writing class. Some instructors regularly establish teams to produce papers: the teams allot portions of the tasks involved to their members, compile the drafts, and submit a single paper for evaluation as written by the team. Those who espouse this procedure claim that student involvement is much higher than in more traditional writing classes and that the results are much more satisfactory. Classes using the computer as a normal means of text production slip naturally into the collaborative mode, as an extension of networking and regular commenting on electronic texts. In some fields, such as business or science, collaborative writing is becoming so much the standard that writing courses that ignore team production seem old-fashioned. But establishing a curriculum and writing assignments for collaborative groups requires a complete rethinking of the writing course and may pose insuperable problems for commuter campuses.

Responding to collaborative writing offers challenges that have not yet been well resolved. Is the writing workshop approach, with teams going about their writing and responding to the work of other teams, too unstructured for college writing courses? Will students leaving such a class be well prepared for the individual production of term papers, theses, or other college work? Is it fair to give a high grade to each member of a team if only some of its members actually did the writing, be it ever so excellent? Is it fair to give a low grade to each member of a team if some excellent writers on the team have been insufficiently influential in determining the quality of the paper? Can the team members themselves give differential grades to their own members?

We also need to take account of a certain leveling result of collaborative writing. Such writing not only helps weak writers produce better work but also, less positively, tends to restrict the opportunities for expression of strong writers. Sometimes the best writers will resent submitting their work to other students, who may (for instance) be insensitive to metaphor or irony, and who will seek to remove individual turns of phrase or unusual points of view.

As with other innovations in writing instruction (such as portfolios), collaborative writing offers unusual opportunities to inventive teachers. In the course of the next decade, accumulated experience with this mode of teaching will help us find ways to meet the challenges of a shifting emphasis from individual to group writing, challenges only now emerging. The increasing use of computers for writing makes it likely that we will see more and more collaborative writing in all composition classes as time goes on.

Using Student Response Groups

Whether or not we choose to allow or require collaborative writing in class, we might well consider using student response groups as a way of expanding the audience for student work beyond the teacher's desk. When the teacher is the only audience, students inevitably personalize the response; instead of working to improve their writing, they work to please the teacher — a much less valuable goal. And instead of internalizing writing standards, they will wait for the teacher's judgment before assessing their own drafts.

Although the basic reason for establishing student response groups is to provide this additional audience, other reasons also make the use of student response groups valuable in class. The social nature of a small group adds to the trust and comfort of the class; students enjoy working in small groups and getting to know one another. They also learn more from one another than we suspect. Students may be used to hearing, and ignoring, teacher complaints about mechanics, but they have to attend to some of their peers saying, "This is really a mess; I just can't read it." As they explain their ideas and their evidence to a small group, they find themselves understanding and changing preliminary views; as they tell each other why they like or don't like drafts, they are forced to use the vocabulary of writing assessment in an active way. Even large lecture classes profit from some small group work, which enforces the importance of active rather than passive understanding.

As some students will find group work initially uncomfortable, we must establish the goals and procedures of student response groups in advance. And we cannot assume that students from all cultures will respond to group evaluation as positively as many students in American colleges do; students from some cultures find group work threatening, even bewildering. Furthermore, students from any culture without experience in assessing their own work and who expect the teacher to provide all judgments may simply transfer that expectation to the group, thereby intensifying their writing apprehension. Simply asking groups to read and respond to each other's work may lead to useless ("I really like this") or destructive comments. Most students will follow the patterns they have learned in school unless instructed otherwise, and will focus on mechanics or other real or perceived mistakes. They need to be instructed to focus on positive and useful responses (for example, "What is most successful?"), and you should provide models. Also keep in mind that students cannot do too many things at once ("Attend to these three questions"). These issues require that the teacher think through just what the groups can be expected to accomplish and how.

Different teachers with different teaching styles will use small groups in different ways. For example, for teachers using collaborative writing, small group work begins with the assignment itself, as the group parcels out different tasks for its members. The group is itself at the core of the writing process and must meet regularly to assess the progress and quality of its own work. When the assignment is completed, the group receives the grade.

Other teachers will use student response groups as part of a force for what literary theorists call reader-response criticism. This theory assumes that readers create as well as respond to a text. Thus it is essential for writers to hear what a variety of readers perceive as they make their way through the text. The writer must not be defensive or argue for his or her intentions; the writer's job is to be silent and take notes as members of the group detail their movement through the piece of writing and their reactions. If the writer would like to produce a different set of reactions, revision is called for.

Still others ask student response groups to function descriptively: to describe to the author what they see as the controlling idea of the piece of writing, what its assumptions and arguments are, and how they understand it to be organized. Yet other teachers focus on evaluation, with the group emphasizing suggestions for revision. And still other teachers use the group simply as a means of socializing students into the college community of writers.

Here is an example of using groups for a limited purpose, to give a response to the writers of a personal experience essay. Though the example only suggests the wide range of possibilities for group work, it shows that student response groups can be an important part of the response to writing that all authors need.

The first placement or diagnostic essay in this book (see Chapter 6, page 121), calling for the description of a character from childhood using detail that will convey an emotion, is ideal for group discussion. The groups, which should not exceed five students (four is ideal), can be instructed to read or listen to each person's paper and to write down the emotion that the writer evokes; each student should identify one part of each paper that evokes the emotion most clearly. After everyone has read or heard the papers, each writer calls for a discussion of their paper, writing down the responses of each member of the group to the two tasks at hand without being defensive. The group should not spend much time hearing what the writer "really meant to say"; the writer needs to hear what the group has heard the paper say. The inevitable comparisons and dissonance in the group give the writer a clear sense of the relative success of the paper and of possible revisions.

Each assignment and each draft lead to different possibilities for group work. Sometimes, instead of a group of four, you will want to use pairs of students. You may want to reshuffle the groups so that patterns of response do not become fixed or too personalized, or you may want to maintain groups that are working well to cement their supportive function. And you may well want to develop a sensible mix of group work with full-class work, just as you will probably rely on groups more heavily for drafts than for presentation copies of student work. If you have a heavy student load, you may want to use group responses for early drafts that you will not read so that you can devote your reading time to more finished work. If your campus is computerized, you may use computer groups as well as class groups, and you may be able to insist that drafts be subject to spell checkers or group editing before you read them.

Teachers unaccustomed to writing groups sometimes imagine that students will be unwilling to share their work with others or that they will value only the teacher's comments. Rare is the student who cannot work in a group because of personality difficulties, and though students from some cultures may present special problems, faculty who have begun to use groups find that most students are more willing to revise and to meet deadlines if they know that other students will read their work. Student responses may not be professional, but under professional guidance they can be helpful and less threatening than teacher responses. And students are less tolerant of inflated or pretentious language than many teachers are; a student comment of "Cut the bull" can serve as a healthy check on the usual student perception of "what English teachers like to read." Most important, the student response group offers a range of responses to the student paper, making it seem more significant and more worthy of attention. These responses dramatize our message about sensitivity to audience, offering a "real" audience in addition to the teacher, and also reinforce the ultimate responsibility of each writer to make appropriate revision decisions. Students almost invariably report that the most valuable activity in class is the group work they regularly undertake.

Fostering Self-Assessment

Writing groups work powerfully to help students develop the ability to assess their own work, to understand that readers respond more positively to some portions of the text than to others, to see what works and what does not, and to help them read their own writing (not merely what they intended to write). But we must be aware that self-assessment is a painful and difficult process for students — as it is for teachers, whose resistance to evaluation is legendary. And yet without self-assessment, students will not revise or will do so reluctantly and without the requisite personal involvement. What else can teachers do to foster self-assessment?

One place to start is the writing log or journal, a place for thinking and discovering but not for finished work. The writing log becomes not only a mine for writing ideas but also a place for writing that is not fixed in form, including discovery drafts. One important difference between the working habits of skilled and unskilled writers is that unskilled writers hate to discard anything from an early draft, whereas skilled writers are always cutting and rearranging their work. The writing log, unlike a more finished draft of a paper, will not trap students into thinking that the writing is carved in stone; indeed, if the log is kept on disk, it is as evanescent as electrons. The more experience students have with less fixed forms, the easier it is for them to think of early drafts as material to be reworked, reshaped, and revised. The basis of their revisions must be self-assessment, but the very idea of revision is supported by the existence of the writing log.

More direct support for self-assessment comes from work in class using scoring guides and sample student papers. A writing class will enjoy ranking a set of papers, such as those given in Chapters 6 and 7, according to a scoring guide. The exercise is more successful if the writers of the papers are from some other class, but it does work with class assignments as well. The central ingredient in such work is the scoring guide, which some teachers develop through class discussion to emphasize group ownership of the standards. Most students, in their heart of hearts, believe that teacher evaluation of writing is mysterious, subjective, unaccountable, and arbitrary. (Research on the subject supports the students' assessment.) Such a belief devalues revision, for there is no way to know if the revision will lead to a better grade even if the new draft seems better to the writer. But a public scoring guide, used consistently by the instructor and by the class as a whole, fosters self-assessment as well as group assessment and encourages revision. A student with an essay scored 4 can see why it is better than a 3 and why it is not as good as a 5; if asked to revise the essay so that it can be scored 5, most students will succeed in doing so. The next chapter will focus on some of the ways to use scoring guides and class involvement in scoring to foster self-assessment and revision.

Further, writing groups can serve as evaluators as well as support groups. Some instructors use class grading extensively, asking groups to grade the work of writers outside of their own group. This separates the support of one's own writing group (which provides coaching for revision but no grading) from the grading of papers from a different group (which provides assessment alone). But these valuable activities depend on clear public standards, which students not only understand but also agree with and enforce; when they apply those standards to their own writing — when they ask the same questions about their own writing that they do about the other papers they are grading — we get genuine revision.

Finally, there should be space in every writing course for writing that is not evaluated so that students can use writing to explore ideas, feelings, memories, and creativity without worrying about others' judgments. Whether that space is in writing logs, early drafts, proposals for papers, or even oral reports, such opportunities emphasize that the most important audience for all writing is the author, whose thinking is temporarily fixed on paper. When revision takes place to please that audience and seeks to meet internalized high standards, the writing course has done its job.

HANDLING THE PAPER LOAD

There is no point in denying it: teaching writing courses or using plentiful writing in any course requires a substantial investment of time. Whatever devices we may use to reduce the paper load, we must from time to time sit down and go through piles of papers (or a long list of computer files) and try to respond as sensitively and intelligently as we can. While we must grant the inevitability of such work, we are also entitled to try to reduce the paper load. The teacher who regularly works a ninety-hour week, spending every waking moment grading papers, is a grim cliché; such teachers eventually either leave the profession in despair or lose the humane perspective a writing teacher should have. We, no less than our students, need to "get a life," and we must preserve some time for ourselves.

Briefly, here are a variety of methods for handling the paper load without overwork:

- Require student writing logs, which you can skim and respond to without editing or grading.
- Design writing assignments with care, present them in written form, and distribute samples of excellent responses so that students will hand in better work requiring less response time.
- Include assessment criteria along with assignments so that you can more easily point out to students where they are successful or not.
- Use student writing groups to give responses to early drafts or even to grade later drafts.
- Assign writing — such as journal entries, five-minute writes, or freewrites — that you will not need to read.
- Resist overmarking, proofreading, editing, and red-marking, particularly on drafts.
- Use scoring guides, the 6-point scale, and class discussion of sample papers to develop student self-assessment and reduce the need for extensive comments on individual papers.
- Focus written comments on papers to a few main points, raising questions rather than proposing solutions and locating some passages for praise.
- Designate a limited number of papers for presentation level and grading.

Teachers of writing will continue, I am convinced, to work longer hours than most other faculty and to spend more time with their students as well as with student work. Most of us do the job because we genuinely enjoy such work and the intangible rewards such human contact brings. We have the means to keep our working hours within reasonable limits, however, and the suggestions in this book will, I hope, help on the practical end.

PRESENTATION COPY

Not every piece of student writing need be revised and edited to a high level of polish. Some students will have little trouble editing their final drafts to near perfection, but most students find this an onerous and frustrating task — particularly if they did not grow up in homes speaking the school dialect. If we have many students for whom the preparation of final drafts is a major task, we may want to specify the level of polish necessary for each assignment. After all, most of us are content with less than top performance in many aspects of our lives, even though we might be able to do a first-rate job when absolutely necessary. Some teachers feel that every essay should demonstrate the highest level of polish and that such a demand shows high standards, even though few students will meet the demand. But I think it is equally demanding, and more sound pedagogically, to identify certain essays as requiring high polish and then to insist on it; other essays, particularly drafts, can be submitted in less perfect form.

If we can be content with some work from each student that never enters final draft, work that we could grade for stated criteria that do not stress high polish, we can be particularly demanding on the work that will reach presentation level. Our students need to know just what is involved in presentation-level work, including standard citation form and clean mechanics, and they need enough practice in producing work at this level so that they — and we — know that they can turn it out when needed. But they also need to know that writing is much more than editing and that clean copy is not equivalent to good writing.

When the essay is to reach the presentation level of polish, we can use all of our editing skill to work with students: our responses will be detailed in every way. And we will ask students to keep producing drafts until the writing has achieved a high level of polish. I will do this on a few essays per semester but resist asking that every paper be brought to presentation level; we have so much to do, and writing offers our students so much beyond editing, that I am content to know that they can do high-level work, even if they do not do it all of the time.

CONCLUSION

The challenge of responding to student work is not only in rendering fair judgments (as we have learned through the paraphernalia of essay testing) but also in coaching and fostering the process. Most faculty have not thought much about the wide range of responding options they have, and so they repeat the patterns they experienced as students. But many of those patterns are useless or counterproductive, and other ways of responding can be extremely valuable to students, as well as less time-consuming for teachers. Thoughtful responding to student writing begins with a careful written assignment discussed thoroughly in class, perhaps with examples and scoring guides. As the student essay moves through prewriting and drafts, the teacher must keep responsibility with the writer, even as student groups and the teacher respond to the sequence of drafts. Editing for high polish and grading of final products may occur, but responding to student writing includes the entire range of support that teachers, acting as coaches more than judges, can give students. The result of such teaching will be students more ready to revise, more willing to see writing as a form of critical thinking, more aware of internalized assessment criteria, and more ready to be responsible for their own learning.

SELECTED REFERENCES

Anson, Chris M. *Writing and Response.* Urbana: National Council of Teachers of English, 1988.

Curzan, Anne, and Lisa Damour. *First Day to Final Grade: A Graduate Student's Guide to Teaching.* Ann Arbor: U of Michigan P, 2000.

Freedman, Sarah W. *Response to Student Writing.* Urbana: National Council of Teachers of English, 1987.

Gere, Anne R. *Writing Groups: History, Theory, and Implications.* Carbondale: Southern Illinois UP, 1987.

Glenn, Cheryl, Melissa A. Goldthwaite, and Robert Connors, eds. *The St. Martin's Guide to Teaching Writing.* 5th ed. Boston: Bedford/St. Martin's, 2003.

Lawson, Bruce, Susan S. Ryan, and W. Ross Winterowd. *Encountering Student Texts: Interpretive Issues in Reading Student Writing.* Urbana: National Council of Teachers of English, 1989.

Lindemann, Erika. "Responding to Student Writing." *A Rhetoric for Writing Teachers.* 4th ed. New York: Oxford UP, 2001. 222–51.

Newkirk, Tom. "Directions and Misdirections in Peer Response." *College Composition and Communication* 35:3 (1984): 300–11.

Spear, Karen. *Sharing Writing: Peer Response Groups in English Classes.* Portsmouth: Boynton/Cook, 1988.

Straub, Richard. *The Practice of Response: Strategies for Commenting on Student Writing.* Cresskill: Hampton, 2000.

Straub, Richard, and Ronald F. Lunsford. *Twelve Readers Reading: Responding to Student Writing.* Cresskill: Hampton, 1995.

White, Edward M. "Poststructural Literary Criticism and Responding to Student Writing." *College Composition and Communication* 35:2 (1984): 186–95.

CHAPTER 4

ISSUES IN GRADING WRITING AND USING SCORING GUIDES

GRADING AND STUDENT MOTIVATION

Most students hate to be graded. Most teachers hate to give grades. Everyone hates to talk about grades. Pat Belanoff, in her preface to the best book we have devoted to grading (Zak et al.), calls grading "the dirty thing that we do in the dark." Some writing teachers ascribe to a romantic view of student writing: that it is so imbricated in student personality and development that to impose external definitions of quality on individual expression is both intrusive and paternal. The best writing (according to this view) is a voyage of discovery, both of the topic and of the self, and the only audience that really matters is the self. Certainly, if you are committed to that view, your responding style will be nonevaluative and you will resist any kind of assessment. My experience with teaching from that perspective — and most of us give some assignments based on this theory — is that a few students flower in such an environment, but most find themselves at sea, uncomfortable with such a subjective and unaccountable view of writing. So, as problematic as it might be, grading student work is necessary. Our concern in this chapter will be to relieve some of the curse of grading from our lives, at the same time considering ways to integrate it sensibly into our responding and to use the power of grades to support the improvement of student writing.

The most important problem with grading student writing is that it tends to discourage students from taking creative risks with their writing. For some students, a grade is a measure of self-worth; for others, of teacher approval. The external and internal pressures on students to get good grades are so powerful that student concern for grades tends to reduce any assignment to some version of "what does the teacher want?" Unless the teacher is able to align the grading system with the demands and options of the assignment, students' concern for grades can encourage them to retreat to formulaic writing, safe forms (such as the five-paragraph theme), and cautious revision (fixing only what the teacher has marked as needing improvement).

We do not need to assess every piece of writing that students give us. Sometimes an encouraging word or a simple check mark indicating satisfactory work is more appropriate than a grade. But encouragement and praise are only part of teaching; it is a self-deceiving illusion to imagine that we can avoid judgment as part of our work. We are required to inscribe grades for students at the end of the term, and those symbols are a powerful response to students about the quality of what they have done. And most students are concerned enough about how they are doing to keep asking if we try to put them off until the end of the term. We should not condemn them for this; it is a perfectly professional and sound question for any diligent learner to ask. If we are wise teachers, we do not allow student concern for the grade to replace the drive to express oneself and to improve; the assessments are means to an end, not ends in themselves. Judgment is tough to do and tough to take, but unless we do it we are not professional; it comes with the territory. The reading of student writing always awaits us, and the way we do it to some degree defines us. The problem is to find ways of assessing student work that are fair, consistent, public, clear, and responsible — grades that support teaching and learning rather than substitute for them. If we can combine such responsible assessment with useful and supportive responding to student work, our students will learn that essential aspect of all learning: self-assessment.

One of the most effective ways to do this is to use scoring guides. Scoring guides make grading criteria public, so students do not have to guess why they received the grade they did. Also, students who are clear about the tasks assigned and about what standards the teacher will be enforcing are likely to produce better writing and learn how to improve their writing than in less focused environments. Further, if the assignment is clear enough and the scoring guide focused enough, it will encourage the students to assess their own work, which is the most important educational outcome of giving grades. Thus grading is best dealt with head-on: by making it an integral part of the teaching of writing. Chapters 6 and 7 will give four sample topics for short papers, suitable for in-class writing and for use in class, with scoring guides and sample student writing.

USING SCORING GUIDES TO IMPROVE ASSIGNMENTS AND TEACHER GRADING

Scoring guides, developed originally for large-scale assessment of writing, have unexpectedly become a powerful teaching tool as classroom teachers have adapted them for responding to student writing. The scoring guide describes with some detail the textual features that lead to particular scores or grades. A good scoring guide will open up possibilities of writing for students, not close them down. If the focus of the discussion, and of the creation of the scoring guide, is on the writing task and its creative possibilities, the guidelines in the scoring guide do not become formulas or restrictions; they wind up describing the ongoing work of the class. Thus they actually become liberating, since students can see what excellent work will accomplish and they can aim for it. A poorly developed scoring guide, on the other hand, can force student writers into narrow patterns, such as the five-paragraph theme or other formulaic ways of meeting goals. For example, one scoring guide in use by a school district actually defines a well-organized paragraph as one containing three complete sentences, regardless of whether or not those sentences have anything to do with each other or make any sense. Teachers need to use scoring guides to help students discover and shape meaning, not to establish patterns that all students must follow.

Here is an example of a scoring guide that has been widely used for grading essay questions:

Scoring Guide

Score of 6: Superior

- Addresses the question fully and explores the issues thoughtfully.
- Shows substantial depth, fullness, and complexity of thought.
- Demonstrates clear, focused, unified, and coherent organization.
- Is fully developed and detailed.
- Evidences superior control of diction, syntactic variety, and transition; may have a few minor flaws.

Score of 5: Strong

- Clearly addresses the question and explores the issues.
- Shows some depth and complexity of thought.
- Is effectively organized.
- Is well developed, with supporting detail.

- Demonstrates control of diction, syntactic variety, and transition; may have a few flaws.

Score of 4: Competent

- Adequately addresses the question and explores the issues.
- Shows clarity of thought but may lack complexity.
- Is organized.
- Is adequately developed, with some detail.
- Demonstrates competent writing; may have some flaws.

Score of 3: Weak

- May distort or neglect parts of the question.
- May be simplistic or stereotyped in thought.
- May demonstrate problems in organization.
- May have generalizations without supporting detail or detail without generalizations; may be undeveloped.
- May show patterns of flaws in language, syntax, or mechanics.

Score of 2: Inadequate

- Will demonstrate serious inadequacy in one or more of the areas specified for the 3 paper.

Score of 1: Incompetent

- Fails in its attempt to discuss the topic.
- May be deliberately off-topic.
- Is so incompletely developed as to suggest or demonstrate incompetence.
- Is wholly incompetent mechanically.

(White, 298–99)

This example illustrates many features common to all scoring guides. It uses numerical scoring rather than letter grades, a useful shift in symbolism for students carrying a burden of self-doubt from years of more or less arbitrary alphabetic assessments. It employs the 6-point scale, now the most commonly used one, with its generally acceptable upper-half scores centered around the 5 and its generally unacceptable lower-half scores centered around the 2. Each score descriptor follows a similar pattern, listing a set of criteria in order of importance.

Here, the first descriptor has to do with the content of the response, in relation to the question asked; the second deals with depth and complexity of thought; the third with organization; the fourth with development; and the last with correctness. To be sure, some readers will inevitably have a different order of importance, an issue that leads to much debate during large scoring sessions. But perfect agreement on this matter is not necessary, since the score is based on an overall impression of the student writing as a whole (thus, "holistic" scoring) with an understanding that strengths in one of the criteria will compensate in part for weaknesses in another. However, this scoring guide is probably more useful for proficiency exams than for classroom assignments, since it is so general in nature.

Creating a scoring guide is much more complicated than it seems. The scoring guide is a kind of test of the writing assignment, which too often has unclear purposes. You cannot create, or work with your students to create, a scoring guide until you are yourself clear on what the assignment is asking students to do and what it will be teaching them. Furthermore, no class assignment exists without a context of class discussion, reading assignments, papers already completed and to come — that is, the assignment is part of the class curriculum. Thus the assignment in question needs to fit in with overall course goals and the particular goals for that time in the course. If it does not, the vagueness of the assignment's purpose will become glaringly evident when you attempt to put together a scoring guide.

Consider the assignment below:

Some people think schools do not encourage students to be creative. Why do you suppose the critics of the schools take that position? Locate some sources arguing for or against that view and analyze what they say. (Be sure to cite your sources properly.) Finally, think about your own schooling and whether it was or was not creative.

If we wait until we have received the essays students will write to this assignment, we will have a difficult time deciding how to respond. We are also likely to be disappointed in the quality of the writing, which is likely to be disorganized and superficial. But if we attempt to devise a scoring guide before we give the assignment, we discover how confused and confusing it is. The creation of a scoring guide forces us to ask a number of questions: What will distinguish the best papers from those that are weak? What will we focus on and value enough for commentary? What are the papers supposed to accomplish, and what is the process that the writer should go through to accomplish those goals? And how will we know if they have learned whatever the assignment is out to teach?

As we start to write the scoring guide, we notice that there are five major tasks the assignment is asking students to accomplish: first, they must select, understand, and (at least in part) summarize sources arguing whether or not the schools teach creativity (which, in turn, needs to be defined); second, they must use that understanding of the sources and quotations from them to figure out "why" they say what they do — a formidable and perhaps impossible task; third, the students are cautioned to use correct citation form (a sure distraction at early stages of writing, better left for the editing stage); fourth, they need to "think about" their own schooling, describe and analyze it, all in relation to what the sources have said; and, finally, they need to develop their own ideas on the same topic — which means that the students must understand the difference between *asserting* ideas or referring to the chosen authors' ideas, on the one hand, and *developing* their own ideas, on the other. There may be a few students in a typical class who will be able to rewrite the assignment so that it can be answered in a coherent way, but most of the writing elicited by this assignment will be unsatisfactory to both writer and teacher. How could it be otherwise? We're also left to wonder if the teacher who composed the assignment was aware of the many different kinds of demands it makes on the student writer.

At this point, we need to decide what we really intend to teach. If the goal is principally the first I listed above — to help students learn to make use of outside texts — we'll have to set aside class time to practice these activities. Some work in locating appropriate material, writing a summary, using quotations properly, and accurately referring to positions that one disagrees with would all be useful as part of the teaching and learning involved with this essay. Citation format and plagiarism issues might well enter the curriculum at this point. If another important goal is to teach the importance of definition, some dictionary work might be called for that focuses on how differing views of "creativity" can emerge from the same word. But perhaps the assignment seeks to help students examine the meaning of texts. If so, the class might focus for some time on ways to analyze argument, so that students can evaluate the arguments in the articles they have chosen. Without such instruction, students are likely to simplify or distort the arguments presented, say they are right or wrong without much consideration of why, and then assert their own views without giving contrasting evidence. But perhaps course work in both those matters has taken place and the fifth goal is what matters for the assignment: development of one's own ideas. If so, then, the class may need instruction in the difference between asserting (and reasserting) ideas, on the one hand, and developing ideas using argument, definitions, and evidence, on the other. Or, perhaps, if we are looking at the critical thinking issues in the assignment rather than the rhetorical ones, we need to engage the class in some discussion of the arguments for and against differing versions of creativity in education. It is difficult to construct an argument without much information.

Is it reasonable or fair to expect students to know enough in the five areas I have just outlined to be able to accomplish the writing task set out? I don't think so. This assignment is in fact asking for superficial arguments and analysis; it is asking for the poor writing that it surely will elicit. By speaking in a casual and superficial way about its very complex demands, the assignment suggests that an equally casual and superficial response is good enough. Until we attempt to compose a fuller, more detailed writing assignment and devise a scoring guide for the assignment, its complexity and difficulties are not apparent; we might be tempted to blame the weak writing on the laziness of our students, or perhaps on the schools, which never teach their students as much as we wish. But as we start to unpack the various tasks the assignment demands and notice how many advanced skills are needed for the task, we see that an entire curriculum is adumbrated by the apparently simple task. In this way, the creation of a scoring guide demands that we articulate our criteria and goals for the assignment and understand how it fits into the purposes of our course as a whole.

We could profitably spend class time and preparatory writing assignments on each of the five major tasks involved, and then, more reasonably, have high expectations for the completion of the larger writing task. The writing assignment then would be a natural part of the class work and the class goals, and everyone involved would be well aware of these connections. Because the teacher had made clear the various components of the assignment, the students would be able to work on each and on bringing them together coherently.

If we wanted to use this assignment, after some genuine instruction in the various rhetorical and research skills it involves, we could put together a scoring guide for it. All we need at this point is a set of criteria for the scores of 5 and 2:

Score of 5

These papers will demonstrate an ability to construct and develop an argument in response to several articles from a professional journal. Specifically, they will

- Clearly and fairly summarize the articles on a controversial topic.
- Analyze the argument of the articles to demonstrate their strengths and weaknesses.
- Respond to the articles by showing how and why the writer of the paper differs from the views expressed in the article.

- Develop the views of the writer of the paper in an organized way, using personal experience and other sources, to demonstrate a conclusion.

Score of 2

These papers do not accomplish the five tasks set out in the assignment or they do so in a superficial and unsupported way. Specifically, they will

- Select weak or superficial articles and/or fail to summarize them with clarity and fairness.
- Instead of analysis of the article, present quotations or summaries without much discussion.
- Allude casually or not at all to the articles in presenting the opinions of the writer of the essay.
- Present assertions of opinion without organized development or evidence.

Again, it would be easy enough to develop the additional score points through elaboration of the criteria already set out. As the students work through a series of drafts moving toward completion of the assignment, the clear set of criteria becomes a yardstick for them to use on their own work, especially if the teacher will respond to drafts using the scoring guide. The result of this use of a scoring guide, as any teacher who has followed this process will attest, is remarkable. Once students see and understand what is expected, they can usually produce it — given enough time and support. Instead of encouraging superficiality and failure, a carefully developed scoring guide helps students work toward and achieve success.

Here is a well-conceived first-year composition assignment, designed to teach analytic reading and writing as well as use of sources (see the discussion in Chapter 1, pages 19–21), for which a scoring guide will be very helpful:

> *Write a short essay examining what the anthropologist Jules Henry means in the following passage and showing the extent to which the passage applies to your own schooling.*

> Another learning problem inherent in the human condition is the fact that we must conserve culture while changing it; that we must always be more sure of surviving than of adapting — as we see it. Whenever a new idea appears, our first concern as animals must be that it does not kill us; then and only then can we look at it from other points of view. In general, primitive people solved this problem simply by walling their children off from new possibilities by educational methods that, largely by fear (including ridicule, beating

and mutilation), so narrowed the perceptual sphere that other than traditional ways of viewing the world became unthinkable. . . . The function of
education has never been to free the mind and the spirit of man, but to bind
them. . . . Schools have therefore never been places for the stimulation of
young minds.

—From Jules Henry, *Culture against Man*

It is worth exploring why this is a particularly good assignment to teach research skills. It has a clear purpose (to help students learn to use a source as
evidence for an argument) and will help students understand a new idea and
test it, combining personal experience writing with analytical writing. Even
though it is accessible to everyone with memories of schooling, it contains challenges for the best writers: to understand an unconventional idea, to examine
the evidence for it (some teachers will want to distribute the book chapter from
which the passage is taken), to narrate and examine personal experience in relation to a source's ideas, to control point of view and tone, and to understand
the relative power of evidence from research and from personal experience.
Discussion of these matters in class will help students understand the complexity of the assignment, despite its clear demand and focus. Although the assignment does not state that quotations from the passage must be quoted and
examined for meaning, its definition of the goal of the paper ("showing the extent to which the passage applies to your own schooling") in fact requires use
of the source. Thus one clear pedagogical goal of the assignment is to help students see that they cannot merely insert quotations into their own writing, like
raisins in a pudding, but rather need to introduce and discuss quotations as
part of their argument.

If the class is unusually worried about grades and relatively inexperienced
with this kind of assignment, all that may be needed is a 2-point scale, reflecting satisfactory or unsatisfactory work depending on whether the assignment is
fulfilled. But we might choose to call those score points 5 and 2, with the intention of developing a 6-point scoring guide. A writing class will be ready, after
some discussion, to come up with something like the following:

Score of 5

These papers show clear understanding of Henry's point about schools in general and also give clear evidence from the writer's experience about the degree
to which that point described their own schooling. Quotations from the
source are well integrated into the essay. The writing has a developed idea and
its conclusions have been supported by evidence. Writing errors do not distract the reader.

Score of 2

These papers show little understanding of or respect for Henry's evidence and argument. The focus may be almost entirely on a defense of the writer's school and personal experience; the language may lack convincing detail or argument; and quotations from the passage (if they appear at all) are inserted without introduction, analysis, or connection to the paper's controlling idea. Editing is needed to deal with surface matters that distract the reader.

It would not be hard to expand these descriptors or to fill in the scores on either side of them. For example, the 6 paper would be able to show how schools must manage a series of sometimes conflicting goals. The 4 paper would accomplish the job but in a minimal way — that is, with a relatively superficial reading and analysis of the passage and little detail for the personal experience. Again, the 3 paper might have just a bit of detail and an unclear attitude toward the central argument of the passage, while the 1 paper just doesn't understand or address the task, or perhaps is a mechanical disaster. The score of 1 will mean different kinds of writing for different classes, depending on the backgrounds and abilities represented by the students.

USING SCORING GUIDES IN PEER GROUP ASSESSMENT

Once the criteria for grading have become clear enough to the teacher and to the class, they become a natural part of the writing assignment itself. The students will know from the outset the standards by which their work will be judged. Some teachers make sure to involve the students themselves in the *creation* of the scoring guide, so that they can see the quality standards as partly of their own devising. Teachers who use scoring guides in this way spend more time working constructively with students as they write their papers, since the standards for performance are clear and public and the students are more ready to seek help in meeting them.

This application of scoring guides opens new possibilities for the efficient use of student and teacher time. Since the standards for judgment are out in the open, and since they have at least in part been developed by the class, the teacher can now ask the class members to respond to and even grade the papers written by their peers. Since the students now have both a vocabulary and a scale to use for discussing and evaluating the writings they examine, they need no longer deliver only the vague and unhelpful comments common to unstructured peer groups. Instead, they can (and in fact do) hold the other students' essays to the standards set out in the scoring guide. Moreover, by learning how to read and evaluate the papers written by other students, they learn how to read their own.

This procedure has the magical value of increasing student learning while at the same time decreasing the teacher's paper load. Although few teachers will want to use peer evaluation and response for final drafts or for crucial decisions on course grades, many teachers find it a constructive and economical way to help students read and assess their early drafts.

Some writing teachers are beginning to use computer programs to assist in peer review, and the best of these programs have the additional advantage of allowing writing and writing assessment to take place in very large classes. A good example of such a program has been developed by the chemistry department at the University of California at Los Angeles, with assistance from the National Science Foundation. The program, called "calibrated peer review," is available at cpr.molsci.ucla.edu/. It includes the full presentation of a writing assignment, a scoring guide, a training program to help students "calibrate" their responses to given examples of writing to the assignment, a way for students to then respond to and grade writing done by others in their peer groups, and an assignment to use that background for self-assessment. In other words, it presents the advantages discussed in this chapter in such a way that students can perform all the activities within their peer groups, with the aid of computers, and without personal intervention by the teacher. It is not a computer grading program (with all of its problems) but rather a program to assist students in using assessment to improve the writing of other students and, as a result of that practice, their own drafts.

At the same time, the program presents its material with an air of authority that many writing teachers will resist, most particularly its assured distinctions of right versus wrong responses to the assignment and to others' writing. Perhaps that attitude is more appropriate in the sciences than it may be in other fields. Yet the program is flexible enough to offer writing teachers teasing possibilities for use in peer groups without increasing their already too high workload. No doubt other such programs will evolve rapidly.

USING SCORING GUIDES TO HELP STUDENTS ASSESS THEIR OWN WORK

One of the paradoxes of teaching writing is that the most experienced and professional writers will revise time and time again, sometimes with dozens of drafts, while the least experienced writers are usually perfectly happy with their first drafts. Teachers nowadays speak of the necessity of revision as part of the process of writing, but we are notoriously unsuccessful at convincing our students to undertake genuine revision. Diligent students will edit their work, particularly if we have marked up their drafts, in accordance with teacher demands. But a genuine revision, one that reconsiders and changes in substance what has been said in an early draft, is rare indeed. Why is this?

There are, of course, many reasons, including simple laziness and more interesting competing activities. But even diligent and serious students rarely revise their work, and the tyranny of the first draft undercuts most teacher efforts to help students improve their work. One answer to this persistent problem is related to the absence of public assessment criteria: students do not revise their work because, in their heart of hearts, they don't really think there is anything wrong with it. All writers have some difficulty reading their own drafts, and the least experienced writers have the most trouble of all.

This is at heart an assessment problem. If students could learn to assess their own work, they would be much more likely to adopt the work habits of professional writers — who usually consider the first draft as working copy to get them started, not the end of the line. The difference is not that professional writers turn out wonderful first drafts (though all writers occasionally do), but that professionals are good enough at assessing their own work to know how to delete, move text, change direction, and turn out new drafts. If we can help our students assess their own work, we will be helping them develop writing habits that will lead to better and more satisfying work throughout their lives.

The class work with scoring guides that this chapter describes has as an underlying purpose this change in the way our students produce texts. Instead of producing a draft the night before it is due and praying that the teacher will be kind, the students will have a set of clear criteria before them from the time the assignment is given. They will be expected to participate in drawing up those criteria and to apply them to the drafts they and their peers turn out well in advance of the due date.

CONCLUSION

Scoring guides help teachers teach more effectively: first, by helping teachers review and revise their assignments in the light of pedagogical goals; second, by supporting simple fairness in teacher grading; third, as a means of restoring credibility to grades by making grading criteria clear and public; and, finally, as a way for students to internalize standards for their peers and themselves. We need to be cautious and thoughtful in our use of them, however, for they can easily become formulas for text production instead of liberating influences for writers. But as part of a thoughtful curriculum with well-conceived writing assignments, scoring guides offer teachers ways to help students understand revision and make distinctions. They can relieve the teacher's workload by making peer response groups helpful and productive, at least for early drafts. They form a link between general statements of what constitutes good writing and the power of grading particular assignments that can lead to much improved student writing. As writing teachers, we need all the help we can get, and scoring guides are a particularly helpful classroom device for us.

SELECTED REFERENCES

Anderson, Rebecca S., and Bruce W. Speck, eds. *Changing the Way We Grade Student Performance: Classroom Assessment and the New Learning Paradigm.* San Francisco: Jossey-Bass, 1998.

Belanoff, Pat. "The Myths of Assessment." *Journal of Basic Writing* 10.1 (1991): 54–66.

Crank, Virginia. "Chasing Objectivity: How Grading Rubrics Can Provide Consistency and Context." *Journal of Teaching Writing* 17.1 (1999): 56–73.

McNenny, Gerri, ed. *Mainstreaming Basic Writers: Politics and Pedagogies of Access.* Mahwah: Erlbaum, 2001.

White, Edward M. *Teaching and Assessing Writing: Recent Advances in Understanding, Evaluating, and Improving Student Performance.* San Francisco: Jossey-Bass, 1994.

Zak, Frances, and Christopher C. Weaver. *The Theory and Practice of Grading Writing: Problems and Possibilities.* Albany: SUNY Press, 1998.

CHAPTER 5

USING WRITING FOR PLACEMENT AND ASSESSMENT

Most entering college students encounter writing testing and evaluation well before they appear on campus, in the form of the SAT, the ACT, Advanced Placement (AP) tests, or the local placement tests offered by many campuses. We will look at each of these ways of using writing evaluation for high-stakes sorting of individuals, since all of them have been called into question for various reasons. The theories behind these assessments are more complex (and more problematic) than most teachers realize, and the ways the assessments carry out these theories — particularly when time and money are in short supply — can be unreliable and even harmful to students.

IS PLACEMENT A GOOD IDEA?

The first English placement test for entering college students was given at Harvard University in 1874. The test seems to have had two major functions: to blame secondary schools for failing to prepare students adequately for the most selective of universities, and to maintain the class structure at Harvard by humiliating students who did not show upper-class linguistic manners (see Berlin for the history of the test [20–31] and see Brereton for key documents). As Berlin makes clear, the test also played a role in shifting the teaching of writing from the university faculty, who had traditionally spent much of their time working with student writing, to a temporary (and less well paid) teaching staff. The test sent an important message: that writing was now to be considered preparation for college work, not a substantial part of college work. The faculty at the time, of course, did not see the test that way at all; they felt it was a crucial means of maintaining standards and of helping students succeed.

Placement testing — and "remedial" courses for students who did not perform well on the tests — spread rapidly as American higher education changed its nature from genteel general education for the wealthy and the clergy to an institution with strong research and vocational functions. Although experience showed that the secondary schools could not teach college-level writing effectively to most college-bound students, it became convenient and economically useful to assume that the schools could and should. Thus student writing was perpetually someone else's responsibility. As colleges and universities reluctantly continued to teach writing, they recognized its fundamental importance for learning. At the same time, the labor-intensive and nurturing nature of writing instruction did not fit well into a curriculum increasingly based on professionalism and conveying knowledge.

These contrasting views are evident today in the continuing controversy over student placement. Some faculty and administrators regard placement testing as indefensible negative labeling that segregates some students from regular college work, while others consider placement as the most effective way to keep standards high in the required first-year English course and to help poorly prepared students gain the skills they need if they are to make it through the first year and successfully complete degree requirements. Still others see placement, and indeed the entire writing program, as a waste of scarce resources on elementary mechanics that should have been mastered in some other, lesser, enterprise. Some institutions go through regular cycles of introducing and then abandoning placement as one or the other view predominates. American higher education as a whole has gone through such a cycle in the past four decades, with many colleges abandoning placement testing (along with part or all of first-year English) in the 1960s, reestablishing the programs during the last third of the twentieth century, and now in the twenty-first century again contemplating the abolition of placement.

Each college and university should consider the question of placement in light of its own student body and its own writing curriculum, and teachers should ensure that the placement policy is consistent with the curriculum and the needs of students. Placement makes sense if two conditions are present:

- a significant number of students are failing the first-year course because their entering-level skills are inadequate and
- a basic or developmental program exists with sufficient funding and staff to help those students succeed.

When those two conditions prevail, as they do in many public institutions, placement into appropriate courses and the provision of support programs will in fact dramatically increase the number of poorly prepared students who succeed in college.

If these conditions are not present, placement may not be worth the price. With all students placed in regular first-year writing courses, teachers using classroom diagnostic testing can identify those needing special help, which may be provided by a writing lab or tutorial center. When very weak students are present in the regular first-year writing class, they demand a disproportionate amount of teacher time and lower the overall expectations of the course. On the other hand, there is surely a price to be paid in the low morale of students — not to mention teachers — assigned to a basic writing class because they scored poorly on a diagnostic test. Furthermore, all too many developmental programs are poorly funded, out of date, and inadequately staffed, and consequently cannot provide adequate support to the students who need it most.

Nonetheless, most American colleges and universities attempt to place students into an appropriate writing program, expecting that it will enhance the quality of the first-year course and help low-scoring students succeed over time. When done properly, placement wins the assent of most students, for this form of institutional caring places them where they can learn the most and be successful. This chapter will assume that your institution has reviewed the issue, that it has decided to institute a placement system of some sort (including some impromptu writing), and that it has established a program to help students who need additional support.

CRITERIA FOR A PLACEMENT OR DIAGNOSTIC TEST

When you serve on a committee responsible for a placement test, you want to know if each student has the skills to profit from the course in question, usually first-year composition. Because every college is somewhat different, you need to create a list of skills appropriate for your course and institution. A highly selective school, for example, might ask entering first-year students for considerable background in reading, control over sentence and paragraph structure, an extensive vocabulary, and a developed writing process. Such a background would allow the first-year course to assign complicated reading assignments, writing assignments that ask students to demonstrate (rather than merely to assert) ideas in a variety of ways, and individualized research projects. An open-admission community college, by contrast, would design its placement test differently, perhaps testing to see if students are familiar with the differences between oral and written dialects, have become accustomed to meeting assigned topics, have enough self-confidence to write with their own voice, and can construct effective sentences.

In American higher education, there is no consistent definition of remedial, basic, or developmental English; every institution must define for itself what constitutes readiness for freshman English. In every placement decision, you will want to be alert for students whose writing abilities have been cramped by over-attention to correctness in early stages of the writing process, or who feel that writing is only a matter of adhering to a pattern, or whose skill at composition is partly obscured by inappropriate use of a spoken dialect in school writing. The basic question you are asking is, "Is each student sufficiently ready for what the first-year course will be teaching that success is both possible and probable?"

It is especially critical, if a placement test is to be effective, that teachers of first-year composition agree on the specific goals for the course and on what they can reasonably expect of entering students. If every instructor has an independent curriculum and individual goals — as is sometimes the case — placement testing makes no sense. But if the goals of the first-year writing course are determined by the faculty and standards are reasonably consistent from section to section, some kind of placement procedure will benefit the students (who are more likely to succeed) and the teachers (who will have more homogeneous classes to teach).

If an essay test is decided on, there are many difficulties ahead. For instance, a single essay score is not by itself reliable enough for placement; at least two writing samples, with different kinds of questions, are essential for a responsible judgment. Some students will do much better or much worse than usual on a particular topic, and even the mechanics of writing will sometimes depend on the student's involvement with the material. The first two chapters of this book speak to other practical matters related to the development of clear and appropriate writing topics. But devising an appropriate essay test that reliably measures what is important is only the beginning of the problems related to such a placement device.

For instance, scoring essay tests for placement purposes usually requires a large-scale holistic reading that ranks students from high to low scores so that those at the low end of the scale can be placed in a developmental course. Diagnostic testing might take place in conjunction with either a focused holistic or a primary-trait essay reading, or (if resources for a large essay reading are not available) it might be done by the teacher of each class, depending on the use to which the scoring will be put. For example, if the assessment will determine which students receive tutorial or writing lab assistance, a reliable test score from an essay reading will be most appropriate; it is an institutional judgment. But if the results will be used to guide special writing assignments and conferences with the teacher, a teacher's grade is most appropriate.

If you are teaching a developmental writing course, you have a special problem: developmental students are accustomed to thinking of themselves as inept in English classes or even stupid. They expect the diagnostic test to prove that they don't know grammar (and never will), and they envision the course as a discouraging grind. Perhaps you do, too. The placement test and the course should focus on writing and thinking. If either the test or the course becomes a mechanical exercise, the course will not help students.

DIRECTED SELF-PLACEMENT

In recent years, a number of concerns have been raised about the validity of placement tests and the assumptions that underlie them, the effects of institutional tracking and negative labeling, and the use of university resources for those defined as not prepared for university work. Part of the attractiveness of Directed Self-Placement (DSP) is that it proposes a way through this tangle, one that might maintain the advantages of placement yet avoid its disadvantages. The idea is deceptively simple. While scored impromptu writing samples may be part of the information a college may gather and provide for placement, the institution puts its major efforts into informing students about the demands and expectations of the composition courses available to them and how they can meet the writing requirement. Then the student makes an informed choice, and takes full responsibility for that choice — instead of just grudgingly accepting test results and institutional placement.

DSP assumes that students will be mature enough to choose the course that is right for them, if they have enough information. DSP also assumes that there may be valid reasons beyond test performance for students to choose more or less demanding writing courses in their first year of college, such as self-confidence, time available, enjoyment of reading, and past experience with writing. However, DSP relies on the institution's clearly defining the requirements and proposed outcomes of its different writing courses, maintaining consistency in those definitions, and then communicating them to entering students. For DSP to be effective, the institution must develop some way to make that information clear to young students — who are generally bemused by the mass of lectures, warnings, greetings, and exhortations offered in the weeks before the opening of classes. While small colleges are likely to focus almost entirely on enhanced advising, large institutions are starting to combine all the useful information they have on students and offer tentative placement to their entering students. For instance, the University of Arizona, with about six thousand new students a year, has devised a complicated index including high school English grades and various test scores — but no writing test — to place its students into over a hundred different course sections. However, the University of Arizona suggests that some of them, after becoming well informed about the various options within the writing program, may well want to change that placement. Those who feel that they have been placed too high or too low are asked to bring writing portfolios to orientation, where they will meet with an adviser who reads through their portfolios and (after some discussion) will be able to place them in a different class. Most students accept the initial placement, and most students are placed, as one would expect, into regular first-year composition, so the individual advising system at orientation is not overwhelmed. But every student becomes responsible for accepting or challenging that placement.

Thus DSP is no panacea, though it is encouraging. Like many other solutions to educational problems, it offers new problems in place of the old. Yet the new problems are those that postsecondary education should be meeting anyway: helping students take responsibility for their own learning, replacing more or less reductive placement testing with sound counseling, developing clear curricular guidelines and outcomes, and becoming less paternal and more (shall we say) avuncular. DSP is an answer to those who unwisely call the writing requirement unnecessary in light of the modern technological and vocational revolution. DSP maintains the first-year writing requirement as an essential introduction to college-level writing, thinking, and problem solving, but at the same time DSP proposes a radical solution to the persistent problems of overtesting, negative labeling, and student alienation from required coursework.

Will it work? At this point nobody really knows. Maybe entering college students are not really able to make wise course decisions; perhaps communicating with entering students about their choices is too difficult; maybe the curriculum is in such disarray that it is impossible for students to navigate it. To make DSP possible, many institutions will need to revamp their counseling procedures for new students, and such change is sometimes difficult. All kinds of unforeseen problems lurk behind the implementation of DSP, including a general shift in the perception of who should be responsible for academic decisions. The concept is promising enough for widespread trials, and we need to gather information about what happens as the concept becomes procedure at different kinds of institutions. When we have the opportunity, teachers of writing who distrust the usual placement procedures — that is, most writing teachers — should try to move their institutions toward some version of DSP.

Dan Royer and Roger Gilles have recently edited the first book to seek to pose, and perhaps answer, many of the questions raised by DSP. Appropriately, the book seeks to document the experience of institutions rather than force agreement about the answers — or even the questions. They, and many — but not all — of the contributors to the book, are clearly in favor of DSP and seek to promote its use. It is not surprising that this innovation has attracted passionate converts. DSP is the most creative and exciting development in placement since teachers began trying to replace the dreary multiple-choice usage tests. If DSP fulfills its promise, we may be able to maintain the benefits of placement while dispensing with the huge expense, in time and money, of placement testing.

THE NEW "WRITING" PORTION
OF THE SAT AND ACT

When both the College Board and the American College Testing Program announced some years ago that they would begin offering actual writing on their admissions tests, many of us in the field of college composition were modestly optimistic. We had been asking for decades for a writing test to emphasize that writing was not the same as filling in little test bubbles. With great fanfare and a blaze of favorable publicity, the new tests appeared in 2005 — but alas, they fell far short of their promise. They turned out to be the same old multiple-choice tests that had been so inadequate in the past, with a very brief (half an hour or less) impromptu essay attached. The impromptu essay score, with its unreliability and artificiality, was combined with the fill-in-the-bubble score (which counted much more heavily) for a total "writing" score. A student could achieve a quite good score without writing a word.

The testing firms say, very quietly, that the so-called "writing" score is an aid to the admissions process and should not be seen as a placement test, nor should it be used by itself at all. I take it that means the new test is basically a public relations gesture, particularly aimed at the large public universities that had threatened to abandon the SAT unless it evaluated writing. Since the professional disappointment has been so fully articulated, perhaps the "writing" tests will be improved. But until that occurs, faculty should be careful to guard local placement procedures against incursions from the national tests, which are bound to tempt those not informed about their weaknesses to use them for student placement.

TRANSFER CREDIT, ADVANCED PLACEMENT,
CLEP, AND DUAL ENROLLMENT

Teachers of writing, particularly those who take their turn as writing program administrators, will sometimes be called on to advise college admissions offices about these four methods of receiving credit for first-year composition requirements without taking the first-year course. A teacher's first reaction is usually an uncompromising negative: how can we grant credit for a course so based in process, so central to the college curriculum, to students who have not had that course experience as our own college defines it? The use of these substitutes appears to embody that offensive phrase used by many college advisers about general education courses: they should be "gotten out of the way," as if these courses were simply an impediment to something important.

But then the complexities of the situation begin to make themselves felt. Certainly, students who have passed the course at other colleges as good as ours should not be required to take the course again; transfer of credit is reasonable and fair. Advanced Placement (AP) credit, based on a "college level" high school course plus a demanding examination, is a little less clear. Most students taking the test score at the 3, 4, and 5 levels — those recommended by the College Board for credit — and the 3 level is just too low a score for some institutions to award credit. If you are asked to give advice on the matter, you should consult some of the scholarship on the subject (see the end of this chapter) and look for campus studies evaluating the transcripts of students who have received credit for a 3. But most faculty seem content to accept AP credit at some level as another form of transfer credit.

The most problematic of these methods of meeting writing requirements without taking the writing class are the College-Level Examination Program (CLEP), a less-demanding version of the AP test without the AP class; and dual enrollment, a less demanding version of the AP class without the AP test. The CLEP offers a wide variety of tests of varying quality, only a few of which call for the student to write, so many faculty distrust its results and try to avoid awarding credit to students attempting to "CLEP out" of writing courses. If you become responsible for this issue, you must get to see and evaluate the particular CLEP test the student took, in terms of the goals for your own composition program. Again, many faculty distrust the grades of the "dual enrollment" classes some students take in high school; unlike AP classes, these classes often have little resemblance to college writing classes (despite their name) and there are no outside assessments to check on the level of student achievement.

EXIT AND PROFICIENCY ASSESSMENTS

Two kinds of institutional writing assessments often occur on campus:

- exit assessments for multisection courses, which may determine or affect students' final grades; and
- proficiency barrier assessments at the sophomore ("rising junior") level or at the upper-division level, which may determine whether or not a student will be allowed to continue toward the degree or graduate.

Because these are institutional rather than classroom assessments, we are usually involved with committees that represent a variety of views. Because writing faculty are usually asked to participate in or even coordinate these assessments, this section is designed to assist faculty in this situation — which many find awkward or even repellent. As many faculty have discovered to their surprise, each of these assessments is much more complicated than it appears to be, so complex that instructors sometimes feel that testing professionals or other administrators should handle all the details. Yet the effects of the assessments are profound for students, teachers, and the curriculum; writing teachers must be present, informed, and vocal when decisions are made, or else crucial matters slip away from the faculty and into the hands of administrators and clerks who may know nothing about the teaching of writing. I urge writing teachers on campuses with assessment programs to insist on playing a role in them.

Procedures for Developing Assessments

An assessment is, in one sense, a means of gathering information. This suggests that we should be clear about what information we want and how we will use it before we decide about the means of gathering it. In most cases, however, the method of assessment is the first issue decided instead of the last; the answer is sought before the question has become clear. Typically, some influential campus figure or group presses for a particular test (often heavily promoted by a testing firm) or a new type of assessment (such as portfolios). But it is wasteful and intrusive to gather more information than we can use, and it is unconscionable to use instructional funds to gather information that has no instructional purpose. Furthermore, it is dishonest to use a test designed for one purpose (college admission, for example) as if it provided information for another (writing placement), even if student scores are already on hand. Before we decide on any assessment method, we must insist that it respond to clearly articulated goals.

This means that the first job of developing a writing assessment is to establish its purpose and determine what information is needed to accomplish that purpose. And as faculty, we should also consider — and require that the committee consider — how the assessment will affect the students and the programs being assessed. Only after those decisions have been made does it make sense to choose a particular assessment instrument. For example, if we want evidence about the improvement of student writing that occurs as a result of a year's work in first-year composition, we cannot just choose one of the many commercially available multiple-choice tests that purport to give scores for "writing." We need first to ascertain just what has been taught in that writing course, consider how it may reasonably be measured, and keep in mind how our decision on an assessment device might ultimately affect the course. Again, if the course has focused on development of argument and evidence, use of the library, and discovery of individual voice, we need to find ways of measuring those matters.

Sometimes assessment goals are clear and straightforward: which students write well enough to pass first-year composition? At other times, the goals are complicated and political: which students write so badly that they should not receive a college degree despite passing grades in their courses? But every assessment program needs stated, preferably written goals, for everything that follows depends on them. For example, one placement testing program set out its goals as follows: (1) identify students lacking the sentence construction and reading skills required for entry into first-year composition; (2) deliver support services to these students before entry into the first-year class, increasing their passing rate in first-year composition by at least 50 percent; and (3) upgrade the first-year composition curriculum by removing elementary sentence and reading skills and replacing them with a new focus on developing and supporting ideas. The interweaving of assessment and curriculum goals in this series is typical of goals developed with heavy faculty participation.

Once the goals have been clarified, assessment specifications can follow. If a goal is to discover which students write well enough to pass first-year composition at the end of the course, the specifications will list just what is required to do so — for example, "Students must provide evidence of ability to integrate library research into an expository essay" or "Students must be able to produce on demand a coherent and developed essay responding to a given text." The specifications for a course exit exam normally emerge from the course syllabus, and they usually require a series of faculty meetings to reach consensus on what is or should be going on in class. By contrast, specifications for a more general goal (such as to discover which students write well enough to receive the college degree) may call for a much broader consensus by the entire college community. The specifications cannot be so general that they lack real meaning ("Students should write at the college level"); they must be precise enough to lead to an assessment device.

Once the assessment specifications have been made clear, decisions must be reached on the criteria for their measurement. What level or levels of performance will the assessment seek to determine? Is the assessment to judge minimal competency (however that may be defined) and thus focus on a failing cut score? Or is it to reward the topmost group and thus pay the most attention to definitions of excellence? What criteria will allow a university to assert that only competent writers are receiving the bachelor's degree? In some cases, the criteria can be set only tentatively, to await the results of the actual assessment; the performance of real people on an assessment often surprises its designers.

We also need to balance the expense of assessments in time and money against the information we need. Most writing instructors are partial to portfolio assessments these days and so are likely to argue that portfolios should be used for any writing assessment. But if all that is needed is, say, a pass/fail decision based on sentence and paragraph construction, an essay test calling for two short writing samples may provide that information at a small fraction of the cost of a portfolio assessment.

Most commercial tests for the purposes we are considering will fail to measure what campus committees regard as most important. It is unlikely that the general criteria for a commercial test will fit the particular needs of a local assessment, that the usual multiple-choice format of those tests will be able to measure the active generation of text that most writing programs teach, or that the norm group used by the commercial test firm to establish the meaning of scores will match the local population. The temptation to accept a commercial test that claims to measure what the campus is looking for is hard to resist, as it is both convenient and cheap to adopt an existing measure. But no matter how economical such a choice may appear to be, it can become extremely costly when the information it produces is not the information needed.

Exit Assessments

On many campuses, students must achieve a particular score on an exit examination to pass a course (in this case first-year composition), regardless of their performance in the class. A more flexible version of the exit assessment is the coursewide assessment that is advisory: the class instructor must take the student's score into account (perhaps as some specified percentage of the final grade), but the instructor is ultimately responsible for that grade. In all cases, the exit examination attempts to mandate coursewide standards for classes that may be taught by as many as two hundred different instructors.

There are strong arguments for exit assessments, particularly when the teachers are relative beginners or graduate students. The assessment — which may be a test, an exchange of papers among instructors, a portfolio review, or some variety or combination of measures — requires that instructors agree on common goals, specifications, and criteria for the course. Though no one would expect perfect uniformity from section to section, and though considerable latitude in reaching the goals is customary, students are entitled to approximately the same kinds of requirements and standards regardless of which section they may be in. The assessment not only encourages this communality but also fosters continuing discussion of the curriculum and ways of teaching. Finally, the exit assessment lends credibility to the course in the eyes of the administration, the faculty, and even the students.

There are also strong arguments against such assessments, particularly where the number of sections is relatively small and where the faculty are more experienced. Experienced faculty are better positioned to evaluate their students, because of their repeated reading and responding to the students' writing, than any single assessment could be. Where there is a wide variety of course goals, reading assignments, and philosophies of instruction, no assessment will satisfy all needs.

A campus that can use the advantages of an exit assessment while avoiding its disadvantages has much to gain. A faculty member and a committee asked to develop such an assessment have a delicate balancing act to perform, calling for wide consultation on goals and criteria as well as broad participation.

After the goals, specifications, and criteria have been discussed and a reasonable consensus has been achieved, it is time to consider the assessment instrument. In most cases, the choice will be between an essay test and a portfolio assessment (a multiple-choice test contradicts the very notion of writing performance). In making that choice, practical and theoretical concepts collide, with portfolios theoretically more satisfying but essays more practical.

An essay test can be managed efficiently and relatively inexpensively, and the scores generated by such a test correlate highly with other writing performance for many students.

But the disadvantages of an essay test are also clear. Most obviously, it usually asks only for first-draft writing, whereas many writing courses insist on revision as essential to the writing process. The test also necessarily restricts writing to at most two kinds, which are assumed to stand for all the writing in the course. Furthermore, it defines writing as test writing to external demands, a partial definition offensive to educators with visions of the expressive and cognitive possibilities that writing can offer students.

A portfolio assessment can preclude most of these essay test objections but presents special problems of its own. However, the recent developments in portfolio grading have not only begun to resolve these problems but have added new dimensions and possibilities to portfolio assessments (see Chapter 8).

Any assessment will deliver flawed information; enormous expenditures of time and money can give the most accurate data, but then that time and money is no longer available for instruction. We might well adopt the "good enough" notion from sociology, in which some scholars argue that excellent parenting yields about the same results as parenting that is "good enough." An exit exam needs to be good enough to bring the faculty together on goals and standards but not so authoritative as to interfere with the creativity or individual teaching styles of teachers. The scores yielded by the exit exam ought to be good enough to be useful to teachers grading their students but not so arbitrary as to determine student grades all by themselves. We need to balance our trust in the scores we have worked hard to make useful and reliable with our confidence that teachers usually have thoughtful and repeated experience with assessing their students' work. We should resist the temptation to rely on a single exam or portfolio assessment to the exclusion of teacher evaluation — which in a writing course is usually based on multiple drafts of many assignments. But under the right conditions, an exit assessment can support and enhance the teaching of multisection writing courses by requiring the teachers of the various sections to talk to each other about goals and standards and to consider the views of those who differ from their own approaches.

Proficiency Barrier Assessments

Writing proficiency is one of those slippery terms that hide an even more slippery concept. Consider the variety of performance measures now in use. Some over-achieving tots pass proficiency tests on alphabet blocks to win certificates at kindergarten graduation ceremonies; second-graders in some school districts must be able to identify punctuation marks and write their names to make it into third grade; many high school graduates must be able to fill in a job application and write a paragraph with three complete sentences before the school board gives them a diploma; college students seeking to demonstrate that they need not take the required upper-division writing course at the San Bernardino campus of the California State University must write a three-hour documented comparison/contrast essay based on readings assigned in advance. On some college campuses, the proficiency test that certifies student writing as sufficient for the bachelor's degree is actually less demanding than the freshman placement test; the proficiency test is in fact a minimal competency test of mechanics designed only to weed out the students most likely to embarrass the institution whenever they set pen to paper. Prospective teachers in California and Oregon must complete two impromptu essays to set topics in an hour before they may begin their teaching careers. Although it is hard to imagine a single description that would apply to these various tests, they are all comfortably known as "proficiencies," and everyone seems to accept them in both theory and practice as authenticating writing ability. And their role as barrier tests, which must be passed if a student is to proceed, is generally accepted and endorsed as appropriate.

In many instances, the term *proficiency* seems merely to replace the workaday term *skill* — on the well-established bureaucratic principle that long words for simple concepts are more dignified than short words. But an additional sense of adequacy, sufficiency for a particular purpose, is conveyed by the word *proficiency:* a person who is *proficient* is demonstrably capable. The fact that some people who pass their "proficiencies" are *not* particularly capable — in fact, are at best minimally functional at a few skills — sometimes makes the terminology of proficiency testing seem pretentious.

Because colleges and schools vary widely in their curricula, students, and faculty, it is not possible to suggest here the kinds of proficiencies appropriate at various levels. Indeed, one sensible law — now replaced, unfortunately — requiring proficiency testing for high school graduation in California specifically demanded that each school district develop, define, and administer its own proficiency tests. In all instances, however, if proficiency tests are to be useful to the students, instructors, and institutions who must cope with them, they must be carefully developed along the lines I have been suggesting.

Goals of Proficiency Assessment at the University Level

The extension of writing proficiency testing to the university level represents a relatively new phenomenon on the American educational scene. Comprehensive subject-matter examinations are traditional at the graduate and undergraduate levels, and placement testing has been common since Harvard began examining entering students in 1874, but only in the past thirty-five years has a special writing proficiency certification begun to be added to course requirements for a college degree — no doubt as a reflection of general discomfort with university educational standards.

To people outside the university community, it might seem odd that the bachelor's degree should need the support of additional certification in writing skill; if a college degree does not in itself certify a high level of literacy, one might well wonder if it means anything at all. Nonetheless, in recent years, such upstanding members of the university community as the City University of New York, the Georgia State University system, and the California State University system have felt it necessary to protect the quality of their degrees with a writing certification requirement. Two particular aspects of university admissions have a great deal to do with this new requirement: the expansion of college opportunities to previously excluded groups and the expansion of community college programs that satisfy university requirements for the first two years of study leading to the bachelor's degree.

Responses varied. Some institutions made few changes in the curriculum, well aware that inexperience with the conventions of prose did not necessarily reflect an inability to learn; they simply expected their new students to make rapid adjustments, sometimes with minimal support. Other institutions instituted a wide range of basic writing courses (with placement testing) and support services, well aware that inexperience with the conventions of prose presented a serious handicap to students who would have to write papers for a traditional faculty. Meanwhile, a dramatic decline in entrance test scores meant that in addition to these new populations entering the university, a sizeable group of traditional students also lacked experience with academic writing. For these reasons and many others, it became much more difficult to enforce high academic standards in first-year writing courses.

At the same time, more and more students were beginning their university work at community colleges; after graduating from these colleges and receiving certifications that they had completed all general education requirements, including writing proficiency, these students transferred to four-year colleges. Although the two-year colleges tended to take seriously their responsibilities for writing instruction and general education certification, many of their composition classes were occupied by large numbers of students who were not likely to proceed to four-year institutions. It became difficult for these community colleges to maintain standards, and the four-year institutions receiving their transfer students with writing requirements fulfilled became increasingly uncomfortable with such certification.

While these forces were threatening the standards and the credibility of first-year-level writing certification, the universities were experiencing an increasing fragmentation of their curricula. Fewer students were majoring in the humanities and other liberal arts disciplines, and increasing numbers were pursuing majors that they felt would lead more directly to jobs in business and technology. Except at a few highly selective institutions, there was no longer a consensus among faculty that writing well was important in all fields. Teachers who assigned term papers or essay exams found increasing numbers of advanced students for whom such work was new and surprising. And employers began to complain more loudly than ever that degree recipients could not write as needed on the job.

Thus the new writing proficiency requirements at the university level result from a widespread belief that a student can complete course requirements for a bachelor's degree and still be unable to write at an acceptable level. The new certification requirements also assume, with somewhat less justification, that colleges can and should define a level of writing proficiency appropriate for all graduates and that such an achievement can be certified.

TYPES OF PROFICIENCY ASSESSMENTS IN USE

Various institutions have been implementing policy on the writing proficiency requirement in recent years, and it is instructive to review the procedures that are in use. As always, the assessment problems have turned out to be much greater than they were imagined to be, and every method of implementation has shown both strengths and weaknesses.

Multicampus Testing

The principal advantage of a large-scale proficiency test is its overall efficiency. Substantial resources are available for its development, administration, scoring, and analysis; participating campuses can realize the benefits of the test without incurring much cost. Such long-standing programs as the New York State Regents Examinations (for high school subjects) have demonstrated the advantages of establishing statewide standards of proficiency in various fields. Yet large-scale proficiency testing in writing is fraught with special problems. The statewide examinations for college students in Georgia and Texas, for example, have aroused substantial faculty opposition from those who find them insensitive and inappropriate for their particular campus or students. Because any definition of writing proficiency must be developed through discussion and consensus, and because a campus's standards for writing are a major component of that campus's educational quality, proficiency testing in writing perhaps should not be conducted on too large a scale.

Of all writing tests, the proficiency test is the most political, the hardest to agree on, and the most dependent on instruction. The large-scale test grants a uniformity of standards and is economical, but it has no relationship to classroom instruction, which is the only thing that gives the concept of college writing proficiency a meaningful context. Many faculty will argue that the best method of demonstrating writing proficiency is through the completion of a demanding course requiring a substantial amount of writing and rewriting, with some sort of coordination and assessment beyond the classroom to confirm consistency of standards. If such an instructional program cannot be instituted, another strong option is a portfolio assessment with wide participation by faculty from a range of disciplines. A writing proficiency program ought to encourage such methods of certification, for a series of writing samples will provide more reliable measurement than any one test can, and careful response and instruction during the course or after the portfolio review will lead to improved writing overall. A test can be the weak link in assessment and is generally an unsatisfactory alternative to instruction. The further removed a test is from instruction, the more problems it accumulates — and large-scale writing proficiency testing is no exception.

Campus Testing Programs

An individual campus faced with implementing a writing certification requirement is likely to turn first of all to a single test. Particularly when the campus is large and complex, a test offers many advantages: a single standard, sometimes imagined to be "objective"; an addition to the quality control of the campus without the effort of reviewing or changing the curriculum; and a simple funding apparatus, a test fee. The test provides the answers, so there is no need even to raise the questions; everything looks deceptively simple. But the test is the beginning of problems, not the end of them. The extremely high stakes of a barrier proficiency test — which will deny some students the opportunity for further education or even the degree — makes the test into a major enterprise in itself. Special attention must be given to continuous test development, to student advisement both before and after testing, and to test security and cheating. Fly-by-night outfits are likely to appear in town the weekend before the test with expensive materials and cram courses in test taking. Students who have failed the test several times become increasingly desperate and, with only the test between them and their degrees, may tend toward increasingly desperate measures. Meanwhile, pressures to lower the standards of the test or to provide exemptions for an increasing number of special cases become almost irresistible.

At the same time, students who do not pass the test after one or two attempts and who seriously want to improve their writing will make continued requests for the establishment of a course to teach them the skills they lack. The result of such requests has been a new and appalling course: the upper-division "remedial" English course. Such courses are never called "remedial," as no one is willing to admit that the institution enrolls juniors and seniors who lack writing proficiency; hence, they are given a wonderful variety of pseudonyms: intensive English, grammar review, proficiency test preparation, and the like. With the exception of a few heroic and responsible senior faculty, the instructors of these difficult and unpleasant courses are generally those with the least experience, status, and knowledge.

Some administrators and faculty members claim that a single proficiency test, despite its problems, is still the most effective way to raise literacy standards on their campuses. As large numbers of students with particular majors fail the test, the faculty in those fields must recognize their responsibility to teach writing in their courses, and only the test can convey that message. But it is extremely difficult to include substantive matters on such a proficiency test, and the standards for scoring tend to become very low; after all, the test is an absolute barrier to the degree for a wide variety of students, and it is politically unwise to fail too large a percentage of graduating seniors. In addition, some inept students (unwilling or unable to take additional writing courses) may wind up taking the test repeatedly, hoping that some miraculous event will allow them to pass. The test poses special problems not easily dealt with for students for whom school English is a second language or a second dialect, and such students often cannot pass a timed essay test without special consideration. Essays turn up written by students taking the test for the ninth or tenth time. Not only is there an air of desperation in the exams of such students, but their recurrent papers serve to lower disproportionately the overall quality of test performance.

These examinations violate an essential general principle of testing: no single test score is sufficiently reliable to be depended on, by itself, for a major decision about students. A second proposition is almost as important: when assessment becomes separated from teaching, both teaching and assessment suffer. And when passing a test begins to seem unrelated to learning, we ask our students to become cynical about learning itself.

Course Certification

The foregoing arguments are so compelling to some faculty committees and administrators that they decide to omit proficiency examinations entirely and depend wholly on certification by the course instructors. Students who pass particular courses will be presumed to be proficient writers, and that is the end of it. But that procedure is no more an end to problems than a test is. Again, new difficulties present themselves. Where is responsibility for the certification course to reside? Some campuses will decide to remand certification of writing proficiency to the department of the student's major. History majors should write well enough to please historians, engineers to satisfy the engineering faculty, and so on. But that decision tends to work out very badly, as many of these instructors know little about the teaching and measurement of writing, and some of them may be less than adequate writers themselves. Thus results tend to be so uneven as to diminish the requirement; some departments become very demanding, requiring a disciplinary writing course with high standards, while others become cynical and designate a course that may have no more than a single essay examination, if that. On one campus, a course in musical composition and a course in computer programming were supposed to satisfy writing proficiency requirements.

In an attempt to make such course designations more consistent and fairer to students, some campuses will establish guidelines for writing proficiency courses and even faculty committees and administrators to enforce the guidelines. (Such procedures sometimes lead to writing-intensive course requirements, a variation I take up next.) Unfortunately, with no common assessment or strong coordinator to hold together such a program, the centrifugal forces usually become too strong to resist. In departments with little or no training or interest in the teaching or assessment of writing, the program will relax into a series of departmental courses that may or may not involve writing and are taught by new faculty members. Therefore, some campuses with experience in this area no longer expect the academic departments to certify writing proficiency. All students must pass an English department writing course or a course administered by the English department. Although such a procedure reduces the problems of administration and inconsistency, it tends to confirm the destructive myth that only the English faculty need be concerned about student writing. In addition, it puts an immense strain on English department staffing (which usually must accommodate first-year composition as well) and diminishes the emphasis on the study of literature, which most English departments wish to maintain. The proficiency course becomes a burden to be borne by unwilling literature instructors, the English department alone is responsible for denying degrees to students approved by everyone else, and the rest of the faculty (whose lack of concern for student writing has spurred the demand for proficiency certification) are free to continue business as usual.

Writing-Intensive Courses

A popular variation on the course certification requirement is the establishment of an institutional "writing-intensive course" requirement. Every graduate must complete a certain number (usually two or three) of "W" or "WI" or "M" (for "Writing in the Major") courses, so designated in course listings; sometimes one or more of those courses must be taken outside the area of the student's major.

The "W" program often begins with a strong vote of confidence from the faculty and the administration, for its advantages are many and obvious. Faculty from throughout the university will be teaching the certification course, so responsibility for student writing is disseminated as it should be; faculty teaching the "W" courses will become so attuned to the power of writing as part of learning that they will carry that pedagogical understanding over into all of their teaching, even spreading the word to their colleagues; the writing course helps induct students into the discourse community of the major, an often neglected but important task; students will understand that writing is often required in courses that are taught outside the English department; instead of creating a new testing program or a new curriculum, the institution simply has to adjust existing courses to fit the "W" requirements. A simple adjustment of general education requirements takes place, and a cadre of enthusiastic faculty from a variety of disciplines volunteer to offer the opening set of "W" courses.

But the "W" program is filled with pitfalls. For example, in the mid-1980s, a large state university in the East launched itself into writing across the curriculum in a well-publicized attempt to improve the thinking and writing of its graduates. The university senate required "W" courses to be instituted in each department; three "W" courses were required for the degree. The administration promised four kinds of support: a consistent faculty development program, an improved and supported writing center, enrollment caps of twenty for the "W" courses, and a long-term effort to support formative as well as summative assessment of the program.

Five years later, as evaluator of the program, I found the shambles of what remained of the ambitious and laudable design. None of the four administrative promises had materialized. The faculty development program and the writing center had been sacrificed to a budget cut, a new administration had felt no obligation to the assessment program, and the enrollment caps had been made the responsibility of each department chair — whose budgets depended on high enrollments.

At a meeting of the teachers of the courses, I heard that so few "W" courses were offered that enrollment pressures caused by the requirement had led to an average class size over fifty, that the faculty were angry and frustrated at being asked to teach writing with no support under such conditions, and that very little writing was going on in the (ironic laughter) writing-intensive courses. From the department chairs, I learned that the weakest instructors and the least attractive courses had been designated "W," as the requirement ensured survival for both.

In a devilish twist, faculty teaching non-"W" courses had sharply diminished their writing requirements because their "W" colleagues were now supposedly teaching and requiring writing, thereby relieving them of that time-consuming responsibility. Even the most dedicated "W" teachers were doing more harm than good, as they had received no training in ways of using writing to assist learning. One physicist took me aside to tell me that he was devoting many class sessions in his "W" course to spelling and punctuation (though he himself had only the dimmest understanding of them), despite the demands of the class material and the lack of time to read student writing. I tried hard to praise him for his goodwill, but when I asked him if he had found a way to teach revision to his students, he looked surprised and puzzled, so I changed the subject.

I was not surprised to find, at a meeting with students, that some of them did not know what the "W" requirement stood for ("Work in Class"?). No assessment of the "W" program had been conducted and none was contemplated — and it was just as well. Recently, over a thousand graduating seniors had the requirement waived because insufficient "W" courses were offered for them. Net result of the new writing program: less writing throughout the curriculum, cynical faculty, mocking students, and graduates even less prepared to do critical thinking and writing than before.

But I have also seen a "W" program still effective after ten years — indeed, becoming more effective as it matures. The University of Missouri (UM) in Columbia began modestly, with a single required "W" course, and in 1993 expanded that requirement to a second "W" course. As opposed to the eastern university, UM saw to it that the necessary support structures for the "W" program were protected and developed. The writing center is well funded — with professional direction, excellent facilities and staff, and a budget for tutors. Although UM does not require small classes for the "W" designation, classes that surpass twenty are budgeted for trained teaching assistants to help with the writing instruction. A powerful campus committee oversees the program, reviewing course curricula and insisting that its list of course requirements be included in the actual curriculum of each "W" course; these requirements include a minimum number of words for students to write, a minimum number of revisions, and a paper that debates issues in the field of the course. Most important, the university has continued to sponsor well-reputed seminars in writing, attended not only by the faculty but by various administrators as well.

Despite the high morale, continued support, and favorable reputation of UM's "W" program, it is not free of problems. As the program expands, it is unclear whether the faculty will continue to volunteer a sufficient number of "W" courses to meet enrollment demand. And the program has not yet encountered an entirely new administration that may have different priorities. Nonetheless, universities like UM that take writing seriously can make a writing-intensive program work successfully. But no one should minimize either the difficulties or the expense involved over the long term.

Test with Course Option

Some campuses have tried to combine the advantages of certification through a test with those of a certification course. For example, students who fail the campus test are not required to keep retaking it until they pass; they might be certified as proficient despite a failing score on the test if they receive a passing grade in, say, "Intensive English."

The advantages of this procedure are clear. Most students will presumably pass the test and receive certification. Only the weakest students will need an upper-division writing course, so the staffing burden and expense for such a course are no longer overwhelming. If the test is responsibly run and the course well staffed, the quality of the college degree is protected without the necessity for every department to review its curriculum and without the elaborate structure of the "W" requirement.

However, this procedure ends up combining the worst aspects of both test and course certification. Because the test is the primary means of certification, all the pressures on the test will urge a higher passing rate and lower standards; the test will generally be seen as a minimum proficiency test, to be failed only by dumbbells. Thus all the problems of the single-campus test procedure will remain, with the one important exception that adequate writers who do not test well will now have a more appropriate route to the degree.

Meanwhile, it is hard to exaggerate the negative effects on the course that must be taken by students who fail the test. The resentment felt by the teacher assigned to teach the upper-division remedial class is usually matched or overmatched by the resentment of the students forced to take it. No one expects it to be a substantive class; some simulacrum of minimum competency is bound to be the goal. The (usually young and inexperienced) teacher is solely responsible for upholding university literacy standards, under great pressure from students who have managed to get by until now despite poor writing ability.

Thus the test with course option tends to be a depressing method of certifying students' writing proficiency. Both the test and the course behind it tend to be public embarrassments, euphemistically titled and attended with reluctance by everyone involved. One major urban university now lists between sixty and seventy-five sections of an upper-division remedial writing course each term and hires a trained corps of graduate students to teach this pedagogical oddity each year. The people involved argue that the course is well taught and essential, particularly for the large numbers of able students for whom English is a second language. Nonetheless, the test is exceedingly elementary, and the course hardly rises above the high school level despite its upper-division designation. One wonders whether the proficiency program in fact protects university standards or rather protects faculty throughout the university who neglect their own responsibilities toward their students' writing.

Portfolio Assessment

Peter Elbow and Pat Belanoff gave great impetus to portfolio assessment in writing when they began to publicize the proficiency program begun at the State University of New York at Stony Brook. In two articles, they demonstrated how a portfolio assessment team could replace test scoring for proficiency assessment at a good-sized university. The students were required to prepare a portfolio from their work in the composition class; the class instructor was involved, but not predominantly so. In evaluating these portfolios, the assessment team was able to maintain consistency and reasonably high standards, with sensitivity to the differences among both students and faculty. The advantages of portfolios were made evident (see Chapter 8), and the enhanced validity of the entire operation seemed clear. The Stony Brook program demonstrated that relatively large-scale portfolio assessment could be practical and enormously advantageous to the teaching program; it also demonstrated how difficult such an assessment is to maintain. Many other institutions — including New Mexico State, the University of Cincinnati, and Alaska Southeast — have developed portfolios for proficiency assessments, adapting the Stony Brook model to their own programs. Not all of these programs have survived — or survived in their original form — but portfolios remain the most powerful and valid assessment device available for proficiency assessment. An institution that is willing to support portfolio assessment and has devoted leadership can develop a power-ful and meaningful barrier proficiency assessment that supports the teaching of writing.

I encourage institutions that have decided to institute a writing proficiency barrier requirement to attempt portfolio assessment if the faculty leadership is willing to give a major effort for some years to the project — and if dependable resources are available. Crucial to the assessment will be a large and diverse cadre of faculty trained and willing to take their turns scoring the portfolios and who are aware of the implications of their scoring on the curriculum.

Certification through General Faculty Involvement

Because student writing proficiency (however it may be defined) is a result of consistent attention to student writing by the faculty in general and because the call for certification outside the curriculum reflects dissatisfaction with faculty standards, any truly effective certification program must involve the faculty as a whole. I am not speaking here of altering existing courses to form "W" courses but rather of establishing a separate course — as part of a university's general education requirements — to be taught by faculty from various disciplines. Such a certification program must assume regular and well-supported faculty development activities as well as an effective student writing center.

Most of the other methods of certification avoid the painful and political process of involving the faculty in fundamental curriculum change. Yet a felt need for a barrier proficiency assessment — the assumption on which we are proceeding here — ought to be seen as a demand for such change. Testing pro-grams extraneous to the curriculum have problems because they treat symptoms and actively avoid dealing with root issues. Although a writing certification pro-gram that does not involve many faculty is relatively easy to put in place, it is also easy to dismantle when attentions or budgets drift elsewhere. Because no real changes are involved, the program tends to be more cosmetic than actual, despite the energy expended by the people committed to it. Even the "W" course program is largely extrinsic in that it involves additions to ordinary courses, and these additions can easily be dropped by the next teacher to be as-signed the class. Furthermore, because the only campus check on a "W" course is a curriculum review, no one can feel sure that students passing the course have demonstrated much writing proficiency.

An effective way to certify student writing proficiency at the college level is to require of all students a passing grade in a significant general education writing course at the upper-division level, a course with clear, common, and public stan-dards. If such a course becomes an accepted requirement, no one will consider it remedial, and all the pressures on the course will urge substance and quality.

What appears to be the major disadvantage of this procedure turns out to be a substantial advantage: the faculty must be willing to include the certification course as part of the required general education program at the upper-division level. Woodrow Wilson once complained that it is easier to move a cemetery than a university faculty, yet without such movement a writing proficiency program is bound to be an empty gesture. If the faculty as a whole is willing to assume responsibility for student writing, and to demonstrate that responsibility by adding and respecting an upper-division general education requirement, the pressure for proficiency certification outside the curriculum is bound to disappear in time. The greatest success that a writing proficiency program can achieve is to become unnecessary; if most faculty members decide to require writing in their classes and demand high-quality work, so large a proportion of students will pass any barrier assessment that it will wither away.

Once a writing proficiency course is part of the required curriculum, many of the problems we have been describing become manageable. Staffing demands need not fall only on the English department but can be spread throughout the institution, with all the advantages of widespread concern for student writing. Coordination of the program remains necessary and difficult, but each institution can draw on its tradition of coordination, common course requirements, and common exit examinations for multisection general education courses. Most important, neither teachers nor takers of the course will have any incentive to debase it; it will in fact seem more like a senior honors seminar than a remedial writing course, and students as well as faculty will bring inventiveness and interest to it. One by-product of such a course may well be more important than the course itself: course instructors — which over time should include most of the faculty — themselves learn the power of writing as a means of learning and begin to incorporate writing into the rest of their courses. Students end up with repeated opportunities to write and revise their work throughout the curriculum, the ideal toward which all of these programs seek to move.

Experience has shown that a common essay examination or portfolio assessment is absolutely necessary if the specialized content and content-oriented assessment for departmental advanced courses are to be subordinate to advanced writing instruction and assessment. If the staff teaching the proficiency course each term must meet to plan, discuss, select, and grade a common examination or the portfolios of all students taking their classes, there will be a built-in corrective to the tendency to diminish the importance of writing. The assessment should be under the purview of a faculty committee that monitors the required course as well, a high-prestige committee that will help maintain the quality of the program through regular oversight of staffing, training, curriculum, and assessment.

Some students will be able to test out of the required course by demonstrating a high level of proficiency on a difficult written examination or through an expert portfolio. Such an examination or portfolio can be unabashedly demanding — requiring, for example, analytical skill and a substantial ability to use sources; knowledge of how to organize, demonstrate, and connect ideas; and the capability to revise one's work. Because the standard means of certification is the required course, the pressures to depreciate the assessment will not be difficult to resist. As long as the course is seen as the basic certification device, the challenge assessment can be appropriately demanding, designed for the relatively few special students who clearly do not need the course. Perhaps those who pass can form a special honors seminar or in some other way build on their demonstrated writing ability. Failing the assessment is no disgrace, for few students pass and most do not even attempt it. Most important, the challenge assessment now sinks in importance and prominence to its proper place, subordinate to instruction. Though the test or the portfolio will, of course, call for several kinds of writing and show careful concern for validity and reliability, it need not carry the entire burden for institutional standards.

This procedure for certification, involving the introduction of a new general education requirement at the upper division and requiring assent from most of the faculty and participation by many of them, requires more than most universities are willing to give. Establishment of the program is likely to take years of committee work, debate, and compromise, and its maintenance calls for substantial resources and attention. Most of the university administrators and faculty concerned about the writing ability of their graduates do not want to confront the issue if it entails so much trouble; they will prefer instead to complain (often about English teachers or the high schools) or to think that a test will make the problem go away. Some administrators and department chairs will neglect to ask how students can complete some courses of study without competency in writing. Others will point out and genuinely believe that writing is an outmoded or minor matter compared with the real business of the university (whatever they take that to be). Still others will allege that certification of writing proficiency should be in the hands of the first-year English staff or the admissions office. Some may even regard the concern about writing ability as a passing fad, even now being replaced by worries about computer literacy and science training. For all these reasons, and many more, the stopgap and halfway measures I have been describing seem on many campuses to be a more reasonable response to pressures for certification of writing ability than the thorough reform that the required general education advanced writing course represents.

It is idle to imagine that the need for institutional certification of students' writing proficiency will disappear in the near future. Indeed, the democratic promise of expanded opportunity for less privileged populations and the renewed vigor of community colleges should continue to provide most colleges in the United States with unconventionally trained upper-division students; there also seem to be no signs that specializing majors in the college curriculum will ask their advanced students to return to the core of the liberal arts. Further, there are no signs that elementary and secondary education will be able to make significant changes in the writing instruction or standards now in use, nor do the teacher training programs in the colleges and universities suggest that the needed improvements are even contemplated. Thus the demands for the certification of students' writing proficiency outside the curriculum will probably continue and increase. The people responsible for such programs would do well to build on the experience summarized in this chapter. In this area, as in most others, the close linking of assessment to teaching produces the most constructive solution to educational problems, which are never as simple as they appear to be.

WRITING ASSESSMENT AND SPECIAL NEEDS STUDENTS

As American higher education becomes more diverse, various nontraditional populations are appearing in our writing classes. For some of them, the usual assessment devices do not apply or apply in different ways.

Language Issues

ESL.   International students, often defined as those who attended schools where English was not the language of instruction, have received the most attention. These students are often fluent in their first language, resourceful, and capable — though they may not speak idiomatic English, or may have some second language interference. The assessment of choice, offered to most foreign students in their native countries, is the Test of English as a Foreign Language (TOEFL), given nine times a year. Seven of those administrations also allow a written portion as an option, the Test of Written English (TWE) — an impromptu essay to a set topic, scored holistically in ways similar to the examples in the next two chapters. If the American college requires good scores on both of these tests (TOEFL 550, minimum 500; TWE 8, minimum 7), most international students will be able to hold their own, more or less, in regular writing courses.

Sometimes these students are placed in developmental courses along with native English speakers who write badly. This is a serious mistake, for these populations have quite different needs and abilities. Some institutions with large ESL populations have separate writing tracks for these students, staffed with ESL professionals. There is considerable disagreement among ESL specialists about whether this kind of segregation is helpful (many students are more comfortable in special ESL classes) or harmful (mainstreaming coincides with the students' purposes in studying in America). Whatever the course of study, there is general agreement that ESL students need to demonstrate adequate English writing ability by the time they have completed their studies.

There is also general agreement that either essay tests or portfolio assessment can evaluate ESL English writing proficiency fairly, as long as two special conditions apply: they will need additional time for editing their work, often half again as much as native speakers; and the grading system should not penalize them for writing with a foreign accent — trivial and unavoidable errors are to be expected in most ESL writing, and they should be accepted in writing as they are in speech.

Generation 1.5. Increasingly, we are seeing another nontraditional population: students who are immigrant U.S. high school graduates still in the process of acquiring English. This group is growing rapidly and is quite diverse: some students may read, write, and speak in both English and their first language; others read, write, and speak only in English. Unlike international students, who are new to American educational culture, assignments, and expectations, Generation 1.5 students have been exposed to the U.S. educational system to varying degrees. As such, placement for this group is quite difficult to do well. Some students prefer ESL classes because they feel more comfortable there, while others identify with their American peers and do not consider themselves ESL students. For these students, placement into an ESL class causes great harm. Generation 1.5 students are, fortunately, typically placed in regular first-year writing courses because they are U.S. high school graduates and have no obvious indications of special problems on their records. But that also means that, without some kind of placement procedure, they may not have the opportunity for special programs or assistance.

However, basic writing placement is also problematic. While some students would benefit from a basic writing curriculum, these students also need some linguistic support — which many basic writing instructors are not trained to provide. If an essay placement exam is in use, readers must be trained to recognize the difference between superficial, lingering second language features in an otherwise proficient essay and an exam that demonstrates a student's lack of proficiency in written English.

In the mainstream classroom, Generation 1.5 students may need time to develop responses to readings instead of being put on the spot; likewise, they (and all students) would produce better feedback for peers if allowed to study the peer's draft outside of class, prior to discussion. These students will need varying levels of support and instruction in academic discourse and English grammar; direct instruction in weak areas works well for Generation 1.5 students, who often cite a desire for instructors to push them to excel in English grammar and argumentation styles. For more discussion of these issues, consult the Schwartz dissertation listed at the end of this chapter.

Physical Disabilities

Federal law mandates fair treatment of students with physical disabilities, including special accommodations in assessment; recent advances in technology (such as talking computers) have opened doors to college for a new population. Those of us who have had blind, deaf, or wheelchair-bound students in class have become aware of how much they add to class discussion, and we welcome them. We have become accustomed to the signer who accompanies a deaf student, the Seeing Eye dog curled beneath the desk of the blind student, the friend who interprets the motions of the student in the wheelchair with a pointer chart. Almost every college has special offices to assist such students, and campus regulations in relation to assessment are designed to level the playing field for them, without lowering standards or disrupting class procedures. Each student is different. For example, a student deaf from birth may well experience written English as a kind of foreign language, while a student who became deaf after some language experience as a child will have internalized much grammar and some complex sentence patterns. By the time students have passed through all the hurdles necessary to appear in our classrooms, they know what they can and cannot handle, and they will be eager to fulfill course requirements. The teacher's task, in comparison, is rather simple: to communicate with the student in question, learn from the student about what kind of assessment will be fair and appropriate for the class, and incorporate the student as fully as possible into the class activities. For more information on teaching students with physical disabilities, see the Selected References at the end of this chapter.

Learning Disabilities

We tend to be less sympathetic to students with hidden disabilities than we are to those with more obvious ones. But we will be seeing more and more of such students in our classes, some of them with problems difficult indeed to overcome. Students with various forms of dyslexia, for instance, may be unusually intelligent and talented, but convinced by years of insensitive schooling that they are stupid. One such student appeared in one of my graduate classes and, working very hard and slowly, turned out a splendid master's thesis — on dyslexia. We can expect to see an increasing number of students with learning disabilities (yet untapped abilities) in our classes in the future — a challenge to our teaching and assessment patterns. Theoretical and practical research on this matter is just getting under way (Barber-Fendley and Hamel, for instance) and we can expect to learn much more about constructive teaching and assessment in the near future. For more information on teaching students with learning disabilities, see the Selected References at the end of this chapter.

COMPUTER SCORING OF WRITING

This section on the controversial use of computers to score writing is derived from the opening chapter, written by my colleague Ken McAllister and me, of *Machine Scoring of Student Essays: Truth and Consequences,* edited by Patricia Ericsson and Richard Haswell (Utah State University Press, 2006) — a book every writing teacher should consult.

The close relationship of assessment to teaching has been brought home in the early twenty-first century by the increasing use of computer scoring of student writing — using the seductive yet specious argument that if computers take care of the great burden of grading student papers, teachers will have more time for teaching writing. This argument has great appeal for college faculty in many fields of study, since they normally have no training or experience in teaching or assessing writing and find it a relief to relegate that responsibility to a machine. But the absurdity of such a position — not to speak of the utter inadequacy of present computer grading programs — is apparent to most teachers of writing, who well know that assessing and responding to student work is the most powerful way to teach writing. The notion that a computer can deliver aesthetic judgments based on quantifiable linguistic determinants is so foreign to our vision of writing as a complex and deeply personal human communication that it is sometimes hard to take the enormous interest in computer scoring seriously. But most teachers who do not teach writing are baffled by these reactions. The well-funded public relations and promotional campaigns for such programs as E-Rater, Intellimetric, WritePlace Plus, or the Intelligent Essay Assessor promote their wares as time-saving tools that get grading out of the way so that teachers have time to teach. Since we are now starting to see some essay writing programs on the Internet — just input the topic and out will come an essay, including an all-purpose graph and fake bibliography — we can foresee a time when essays will be written, read, and graded by computers without ever passing through the mind of a human. It seems perverse to see that as an educational advance.

Yet we sit back and mock these efforts at our peril. For decades, serious computer scientists have been working on artificial intelligence and its primary component — "natural language processing." Lavishly funded during the cold war, these efforts attempted to accomplish machine translation from one human language into another. In 2004, the Natural Language Software Registry listed no fewer than 171 computer applications to analyze written text and listed dozens more in areas such as "spoken language understanding," "corpus analyzers," and "multimedia information extractors" (registry.dfki.de/). The researchers are investigating the way thinking itself takes place and are seeking ways to make computers function similarly to the human brain (and vice versa?). But the researchers do not make company policy, and the marketing divisions of these enterprises have targeted schools and universities as prime markets well before the claims they make can be substantiated. Make no mistake: huge sums have been and are being spent on this effort, and one place the companies sponsoring such work expect to recoup expenses is from college faculty and public schools seeking to evaluate student writing.

The first job for writing teachers confronted with the prospect of computer scoring of student writing is to become informed. No one will listen to objections based on emotion rather than information. The second job is to look for ways that computer assistance can in fact help us teach and assess writing. For instance, spell checkers have largely removed spelling as an issue in the writing of students with access to good word processing software. Grammar checkers are still not adequate and most editing programs are at best problematic. Programs, such as the "calibrated peer review" programs discussed in Chapter 4, allow teachers great flexibility in presenting assignments and criteria to students, and offer many of the advantages of scoring guides for the teaching of writing. And computer programs offer a prospect of student papers with most of the common mechanical problems already taken care of and with organizational issues highlighted. We should keep an open mind as claims for computer grading are made, and we should be ready to accept computer help with our work, if it can be depended on. Such a stance will allow us to resist the substitution of machine counting of features for a human response to writing.

SELECTED REFERENCES

Belanoff, Patricia, and Marcia Dickson, eds. *Portfolios: Process and Product.* Portsmouth: Boynton-Cook, 1991.

Belanoff, Patricia, and Peter Elbow. "Using Portfolios to Increase Collaboration and Community in a Writing Program." *WPA: Writing Program Administration* 9.3 (1986): 27–40.

Berlin, James A. "The Nineteenth Century Background." *Rhetoric and Reality: Writing Instruction in American Colleges, 1900–1985.* Carbondale: Southern Illinois UP, 1987. 20–31.

Brereton, John C. *The Origins of Composition Studies in the American College, 1875–1925: A Documentary History.* Pittsburgh: U of Pittsburgh P, 1996.

Elbow, Peter, and Patricia Belanoff. "Portfolios as a Substitute for Proficiency Examination." *College Composition and Communication* 37 (1986): 336–39.

Faigley, Lester. "Ideologies of the Self in Writing Evaluation." *Fragments of Rationality: Postmodernity and the Subject of Composition.* Pittsburgh: U of Pittsburgh P, 1992. 111–31.

Haswell, Richard, and Patricia Ericsson, eds. *Machine Scoring of Student Essays: Truth and Consequences.* Logan: Utah State UP, 2006.

Royer, Daniel, and Roger Gilles. *Directed Self-Placement: Principles and Practices.* Cresskill: Hampton, 2003.

White, Edward M. "Change for the Worse." *AAHE Bulletin* (1990): 1–4.

———. *Developing Successful College Writing Programs.* San Francisco: Jossey-Bass, 1989.

———. *Teaching and Assessing Writing: Understanding, Evaluating, and Improving Student Performance.* 2nd ed. San Francisco: Jossey-Bass, 1994.

Williamson, Michael, and Brian Huot, eds. *Validating Holistic Scoring for Writing Assessment: Theoretical and Empirical Foundations.* Cresskill: Hampton, 1993.

DISABILITIES REFERENCES

Association of Higher Education and Disability. <www.ahead.org>.

"Auxiliary Aids and Services for Postsecondary Students with Disabilities." *Office for Civil Rights, US Department of Education.* <ed.gov/about/offices/list/ocr/docs/auxaids.html>

Barber-Fendley, Kimber, and Chris Hamel. "A New Visibility: An Argument for Alternative Assistance Writing Programs for Students with Learning Disabilities." *College Composition and Communication* 55.3 (2004): 504–35.

Brueggemann, Brenda Jo. "Partnership Grant." *Fast Facts for Faculty: Writing in the University.* <telr.osu.edu/dpg/fastfact/>.

Butler, Deborah L., Cory L. Elaschuk, and Shannon Poole. "Promoting Strategic Writing by Postsecondary Students with Learning Disabilities: A Report of Three Case Studies." *Learning Disability Quarterly* 23 (2000): 196–213.

Chase, Geoffrey. "Accommodation, Resistance and the Politics of Student Writing." *College Composition and Communication* 39.1 (1988): 13–22.

"Complexity of the Writing Process." *Assistive Technology for the Classroom.* Landmark College. <www.landmarkcollege.org/institute/assistive_technology/writing_organization.html>.

Hodge, Bonnie, and Jennie Preston-Sabin, eds. *Accommodations or Just Good Teaching? Strategies for Teaching College Students with Disabilities.* Westport: Praeger, 1997.

Kaiser, Paul. "Suggestions for Helping Learning Disabled Students to Write." *LD Resources* (2005). <www.LDresources.org/?p=274>.

Policastro, Margaret. "Metacognitive Attributes in College Students with LDs." *Success for College Students with Learning Disabilities.* Eds. Susan Vogel and Pamela Adelman. New York: Springer-Verlag, 1993. 151–75.

Rodis, Pano, Andrew Garrod, and Mary Lynn Boscardin, eds. *Learning Disabilities and Life Stories.* Boston: Allyn and Bacon, 2001.

Rose, Ernest. "Faculty Development: Changing Attitudes and Enhancing Knowledge about Learning Disabilities." *Success for College Students with Learning Disabilities.* Eds. Susan Vogel and Pamela Adelman. New York: Springer-Verlag, 1993. 130–50.

Schwartz, Gwen Gray. "Vietnamese Students Who Cross Over: An Ethnographic Study of Generation 1.5 Students in Mainstream Composition." Diss. U of Arizona, 2006.

Strothman, Stuart, and Lynne Shea, eds. *Teaching Writing to Students with Learning Disabilities: The Landmark College Guide to Composition.* Putney: Landmark College, 2001.

Vogel, Susan, and Pamela Adelman, eds. *Success for College Students with Learning Disabilities.* New York: Springer-Verlag, 1993.

CHAPTER 6

EVALUATING IMPROMPTU WRITING BASED ON PERSONAL EXPERIENCE

THE VALUE AND LIMITATION OF IMPROMPTU WRITING

Portfolio assessment has become the writing measurement device of choice as it has developed over the last two decades. Portfolios have obvious advantages over essay testing for evaluation of student writing: they contain a number of student papers, sometimes in several drafts, so we can see the writer's process of composition as well as multiple products; they emerge naturally out of class writing and so support teaching in a way that impromptu writing does not; they require students to reflect on and write about their writing, so portfolios incorporate self-assessment naturally into the external assessment. The obvious value of portfolios does not mean that we should ignore the value of impromptu writing in class, or of short essays to be written out of class. We cannot teach everything at once, and the very limitations of short writing tasks let us focus attention on just a few important matters. Besides, as our students move through college and into the world of work, they will encounter many classes and other situations that call for short, focused, organized, and otherwise competent writing under severe time constraints. We should use common sense and caution with grades from impromptu writing; much research has demonstrated that student performance on such writing tasks will vary, sometimes greatly, from one kind of assignment or circumstance to another. But the kind of short writing assignment typical of essay examinations is a powerful way to help students understand some of the quality differences that distinguish successful writing from unsuccessful writing.

WRITING ABOUT PERSONAL EXPERIENCE

Some teachers feel strongly that students should not be asked to write about their personal experience. Such writing, these teachers feel, is not sufficiently challenging for college students — its content and organization tend to be obvious, and it opens the way for simple narratives instead of more reflective writing. In addition, the self-revelation that personal writing invites can be intrusive (even an invasion of privacy), may tell teachers more than they want to know about the students' lives and families, and can be hard to evaluate. If the student reveals criminal acts or intentions, teachers have legal obligations to pursue the matter — at least with college administrators such as the dean of students; we do not have the confidentiality rights of an attorney or the clergy. And, at heart, such writing suggests certain emotional aspects to the teacher-student relationship that make these teachers uncomfortable.

These are not trivial matters. Yet other teachers feel that, with care in assigning and sensitivity in responding, personal writing offers important advantages for teaching writing. It draws on immediately accessible material and detail, and can be engaging to students in ways that more abstract topics are not. Using the experience of the writer as evidence, these teachers will argue, is an effective way of teaching students how to use evidence to draw conclusions. By engaging in personal writing, students learn to integrate their emotional and rational sides into their writing, and they gain access to their experience in new ways.

Studying British schools some decades ago, James Britton and his team of researchers found little personal writing; most school writing was to set abstract topics that failed to engage the students and was terribly dreary. He recommended more personal writing to infuse some vitality into school writing. Today in America, some researchers are finding that the reverse is the case — too many students enter college with little experience beyond personal writing. I try to reap the benefits of personal writing by opening my college writing courses with personal writing and then moving by stages into more abstract and reading-based work (see Chapter 1). But every teacher who has the option should experiment with a mix of personal and reading-based writing assignments to find the combination of assignments appropriate to their own teaching style.

The following two assignments based on personal experience have several benefits, particularly at the start of a writing course. Because they ask students to draw from and reflect on their personal experience, every student should have plenty to write about and should be interested in the topic. Even very weak writers can accomplish some description, and very good writers will have a chance to manage tone and point of view for subtle effects. Personal-experience topics are also good preparation for expository writing because the use of concrete detail as evidence for what the writer has to say reinforces the need to demonstrate ideas, rather than just assert them. In addition, you can see if the student is accustomed to understanding and fulfilling writing goals and if the student has a writing process that they can describe. (These topics offer a starting point for entries into students' writing logs.) Editing problems are sure to appear, particularly if you limit the time available; the student samples below are from forty-five-minute essay tests, which don't allow for much revision or even editing. But as we will demonstrate in our discussion of the unsuccessful papers, the editing problems are part of an entire process that requires attention.

If you do not want to use personal experience papers in your writing class, you should skip ahead to the next chapter, which gives two examples of text-based topics.

ESSAY TEST 1: PERSONAL-EXPERIENCE ASSIGNMENT 1

Describe a person you knew well when you were a child. Your object is to use enough detail that your readers can picture the person clearly from the child's perspective and at the same time understand from the tone of your description and from the particular details you choose how you felt about the person you describe.

If you are using this assignment as a test, you will (of course) print it for all students taking the test. Many teachers will be more casual about their assignments in class, but it is generally good practice, and most efficient, to duplicate and distribute all class assignments. If you merely tell students what the assignment is, many of them will not take notes and will misremember or misinterpret the assignment. If you assign the paper to be written at home, you should also spend a considerable amount of time discussing the assignment with students and reminding them to take notes on the sheet you have distributed so that the information they need will be at hand when they start writing.

Your discussion of the assignment should focus on the key words, as we noted in Chapter 2. *Describe* suggests concrete detail, for example; you may want to help students see the difference between vague and telling detail — "Her crooked smile never left her lips" is much more effective than "She was a friendly person." Some students will ask how old the child in the assignment is expected to be. You might reply that any age will do, as long as there is some distance from the present; the student will need to choose a specific age, stick with it, and be sure to give the reader sufficient clues. You should also point out that you do not want the child's language, merely the child's perspective. And the challenge of the assignment should be stressed: can you let us know just how you felt only by description, without telling us directly? Depending on your class, you might want to let that instruction stand as a kind of game, or you may want to press further into the concept of *tone*.

Tone (or mood) is a product of the relationship among the writer, the reader, and the topic. The concept is not complicated; it insists that all writing is an act of communication and hence involves some kind of relationship. Your students know about tone in conversation. They might describe their friends as "husky" or "chunky," whereas people they don't like are "fat." They may have studied something called "connotation" and "denotation" in school. But the tone of writing is set in many ways besides the use of metaphors and connotations: such matters as abrupt or leisurely sentences, direct or indirect quotation, and even punctuation help determine the relationship of writer to reader. The issue here is that students select actively (rather than passively) the right words and sentences, with the right tones, to express the relationship they have in mind in the assignment.

If you use this first essay as a timed diagnostic test, you will probably not be able to have the prewriting discussion described here before the test; you will be testing to see if the students can go about these procedures on their own. But you may want to give the students an opportunity to revise their work after you return it to them, scored, as a springboard for instruction in such matters as tone or revision. I suggest that you duplicate and distribute the scoring guide and the sample papers illustrating it on the next pages in this chapter, if you use them to guide your scoring; they will help demonstrate differences in quality, illustrate the clarity and fairness of the grading, and reinforce the need and possibilities for revision. The discussion can then be particularly rich and fruitful.

Though you may not wish to grade the essay for class purposes, sometimes it is necessary to do so for other reasons; you may be using the results for placement or be giving a pretest/posttest to your students to evaluate how much they learn by the end of the term. That is, you may want to give the essay test again at the end of the term to see if students have learned how to write this kind of assignment more effectively. If so, you will need to compare student scores. If you are giving the diagnostic essay to a large group (the entire entering first-year class, for instance), you will want to conduct a holistic scoring session to obtain the most reliable test scores for rankings. The sample scoring guide for this question that follows can be used by a group of instructors, or even students, as well as by the individual instructor; it is based on the kind of scoring that many large-scale testing programs use.

The holistic scoring guide is based on several principles. At its core, it assumes that writing is best judged as a whole rather than as a series of discrete skills. We need to teach separate skills, of course, and to notice which aspects of writing a particular class may need to focus on. But for scoring purposes, holistic theory says that the whole is greater than the sum of its parts and that readers respond to overall quality.

Holistic Scoring Guide

Students should be rewarded for what they do well in response to the question. In timed impromptu writing, every writer will make a few errors. Patterns of errors, such as repeated failures to predicate sentences or to relate ideas, will usually indicate a lower-half essay (scored 3, 2, or 1), but occasional errors are likely to appear in even the best writing. Evaluate the essay as a whole, without giving undue weight to any single aspect.

For Personal-Experience Assignment 1, the student is asked to describe a particular person, using detail, so that a reader can understand the nature of the relationship. Essays that do not select a particular person or that are so general in their descriptions that we must guess at the relationship should be scored in the lower half, as they fail to understand and respond to the question.

6. A **superior** response will not only define and describe the person in detail but also provide vivid and particular descriptions arranged for a clear purpose. It will have a personal voice and use words with attention to their tone as well as their meaning; it will have a discernible organization and be focused.

5. The **strong** response will be less vivid, detailed, and focused than the superior one and may explain the relationship as well as show it. But the writing will accomplish the task strongly; the paper will use words with care and be orderly.

4. The **competent** response will accomplish the task in a minimal way: the descriptions will be clear enough to convey a relationship, but not in a particularly distinct way; the writing is likely to be marked by minor but frequent errors.

3. The **weak** response does not accomplish the task, for a variety of reasons: it tells about, rather than describes, a person; it features minimal or muddled detail; it loses track of its purpose; it shows patterns of error.

2. The **inadequate** response is likely to show patterns of serious error, to misunderstand or confuse the question, to use superficial and stereotyped language, to include oral structures with the written language, or otherwise demonstrate serious problems.

1. The **incompetent** response conveys ineptness at handling the assignment: it reflects failed attempts to begin the task, inability to produce the written dialect, unwillingness to undertake the writing assignment, and the like.

If you were to use this scoring guide for the sample essays that follow, you would have to adapt it somewhat for your particular situation. The scores should represent reasonable levels of accomplishment for your particular school, and those levels of accomplishment should reflect the kind of writing your students normally produce. Successful essays will probably fit into the 6–5 range; marginal essays, in the 4–3 range; and unsuccessful essays, the 2–1 range. You should have enough representative papers on hand to allow you to make decisions about the scoring scale and about the applicability of the various levels for the sample essays before you begin grading.

Sample Student Essays

Score of 6

A Fourth-Grade Memory

Looking back, practically the first thing I think of when I remember her is her behind. It was a ponderous specimen to the fourth grader that I was; always an impossible obstacle thrust out into the aisles of our desks as she leaned on her elbows, absorbed in the smudgy penciled work of one of her students. I would stand contemplating it, wrapping one white knee-socked leg around the other, waiting. It was not that she intimidated me — she that sat in the dirt of our playground as if she were one of us — I could have made my need to pass known, but where, where to poke or tap her? Her shoulders were bowed over the desk, her face beaming not two inches away from her pupil's.

Her face was an entirely different matter. The precision of her nose brought to mind the image of a pert little bird, a sparrow perhaps. Her eyes were a crisp blue, literally framed by scholarly brown glasses. Her hair might have reminded a student or two of the pictures of the thatched roofs in Norway that she enthusiastically waved at us during geography hour. (She once confided to me that she looked in the mirror but once a day, exclaiming, "God, you're gorgeous!" and then abandoned vanities for the rest of the day.)

Despite her decrepitude — she must have been over forty years old — she was a real Bohemian, complete with bean bag chairs and tie-dyed blouse. She had a deep affection for my father. She was widowed or divorced, I suppose, with three teen-aged children, and when she asked me how my father was and told me that he had the most beautiful, happy eyes, I wanted to hug her and let her move into my room with me. She must have been very lonely. She was generally a soft-spoken person, but was capable of an awesome bellow that would stop any taunting boy in his cruel tracks. How often I wanted to bury my head in her polyester lap, my friend, my protector, but she was my teacher. I respected her not only wholly, but voluntarily.

Score of 5

Someone

He was someone who sat at our dinner table and told us to "shut-up" so he could listen to the news; he told us to eat our vegetables or we would get no dessert. He was someone who caused me to cry and leave the table if I spilled some milk because I so wanted to please him. He was someone I said goodbye to at night when he went off to work. He was someone who got us up in the morning and told us to get ready for school and "Be sure to make your beds," he always said. I remember him helping me do my math problems, and how I would get upset when he would yell at me because I could not understand. He was always telling me to straighten my room, hang the clothes, do the dishes, and help your mom with dinner.

He was someone whom my mom would ask to take us somewhere on Sunday. He was always telling us kids to be quiet and not to fight while he was driving. He once stopped at a wreck and showed us what might happen if we did not behave while he was driving. He was someone who broke my arm by shaking me and swinging me on the ground when my younger sister and I were fighting. He was someone who gave us an allowance so we could go to the show on Saturday.

He was someone who worked hard for our food and clothes, and who on Sundays at my mom's request took us somewhere.

I am still trying to please my father and wishing he were different than he is. He is someone whom I respect for his hard work, but I wish he would please me more with himself. Today my father and I talk of troubles in the world, but never of any personal troubles or concerns. He is still the someone who tells us, "Be quiet!" at the dinner table whenever we are home to eat. He is still the someone who furnishes us with food and a place to sleep; but now he never offers us a dime unless we ask. He no longer takes us somewhere on Sundays because our family cannot get along.

My father will always be someone whom I respect, but he will never be the dad I have always admired and wished was my own.

Score of 4

Uncle Bill

We kids loved Uncle Bill. He had a red face and a potbelly and a jolly big laugh. At Christmas time we thought he was a kind of Santa Claus, but the best kind that would roll on the floor playing with us and tickle us as we played. He liked games as much as we did and we had so much fun with him until dad would say, "that's enough, Bill," and we'd have to stop laughing and act serious again. He wasn't a real uncle, but an old friend of my fathers.

We were five kids and we got along real well, not like most families. Tina was closest to me in age, than there were Ron, Lily, Grace, and the baby Hilary. Tina and I always ran the show and the others were happy to go along. We had a big old house with lots of hiding places and we played hide and go seek for hours. Of course Christmas was our favorite time, that's when lots of relatives showed up with presents.

It's funny that I can't remember much about Mom and Dad, they just were there. They never seemed to change, even today they seem to be the proverbial Mom and Dad from TV. But I have lots of memories of the other kids. I guess we were like a TV family in lots of ways.

Uncle Bill never changed either, not even as we got older. I remember at one point telling him to stop tickling me and he didn't want to. He looked kind of hurt when I said I was too grown up for rolling on the floor and he said that growing up was no fun. Then he tried to tickle me again and I ran upstairs. After that, things were never the same between him and me, though he was just the same with the younger kids.

He never read to us at night in bed, though he was a fantastic reader and took on all the voices of the characters and made them seem real. We'd all gather around him when he read The Night Before Christmas and he could do it like nobody else. I know that as a teenager I never felt as comfortable with him as I did as a kid. It was like he stayed the same while I went on. But I had lots of interests by then and was on the soccer team and that took up most of my free time, aside from homework. I was pretty good at math and English and was trying to get a scholarship.

Now that I'm grown, I never see Uncle Bill any more and I can't get my parents to talk about him. But that's the way it goes when you grow up, as he used to say, when we were all having fun together. In some ways, I miss him, but he is part of my past. I hope when I have kids of my own they can have fun with my friends the same way I did with Uncle Bill.

Score of 3

Gramps

Gramps, we called him. My mother's father was very old, but always enjoyed seeing us kids when we came for summer visits. He lived alone in a small town in Ohio, I don't remember the name, in a small house with a garden out back.

Gramps loved to work in the garden and he always had things for us to do. How he kept his pipe going all day long while weeding I'll never know. Once he showed us how the irragation worked and I helped him cut and put in a new line. He never seemed to lose patience, though I'm sure I was not much help.

He always had a housekeeper, though I don't remember much about them. Somehow, food appeared at meal time and the house was clean. When we were there Gramps spent all his time with us, though we were always helping him do his chores. The special time of the day was walking downtown to get an ice cream cone on hot afternoons. At night he liked to read stories to us from an old dusty book.

Gramps died a few years ago, I really did not pay much attention at the time, I was busy with school and sports. But now as I write this I realize that I miss him for lots of reasons and wish I had appreciated him more.

Score of 2

Desert Home

As a child, my parents moved from Texas to California in search for a better paying job. My parents had no idea of living in the desert would be like, yet my father had high hopes because among his friends he heard that California was the place to live, and jobs were more available. As time went by, my parents soon learned that the lower desert in Southern California was a rough rugget, bold place to live. The dry climate was very hot in the summer and very cold in winter. The large stretches of land made the desert spacious. So roomy that people felt lonely when left alone unvisited by civilization.

As a rule everyone knew and respected owning a car or truck in the desert. It was a major prority or else suffer the consequences of being stranded out without transportation which made life even more miserable. On paid days, once a month, the whole community rised from the dead in an up roar of happiness. Everyone knew their destination. Some headed towards Needles, other to 29 palms, Barstow, and San Bernardino. Leaving the desert for awhile, and coming in contact with civilization again meant alot for the 15 families that worked for Santa Fe Railroad Company.

Our small community was called Cadiz, California. It had a post office a train station, a small market called Champlus, a tailer park, and eight cabins for visitors stopping off from highway 66, a gasoline station, and a restaurant that was a couple miles away. You see! route 66 was the main road to civilization.

Discussion of the Essays

I suggest that you begin responding to the assignment by asking your students to consider the importance of understanding what a writing assignment calls for. Students need to see that the central concern of this particular topic is the use of detail to meet the goals of the assignment. Many students write inadequate essays because they do not pay enough attention to the job at hand. The first successful response does depart from the descriptive goal of the assignment to discuss the relationship in its last sentence, as does the second one. But the second essay uses powerful detail to convey the distant and disappointingly harsh relationship between the writer and the father, brilliantly conveyed by the "Someone" of the title. The first essay, by a more talented writer, handles the assignment with great sophistication, managing language and point of view with skill. The writer of "Uncle Bill" also shows talent, particularly in the detailed opening paragraph and the vivid scene in the fourth paragraph. But the essay is filled with distracting material and fails to focus on what we must see as the funny uncle of the title. Indeed, by the end of the essay we wonder if the writer is really aware of what was going on with him, even though she is now an adult. The writer of "Gramps" understands that detail is necessary but gives the detail in a scattered way, not focusing on any particular aspect of the relationship.

The writer of "Desert Home" loses track of both the topic and the goal of the assignment. This student has some feel for the language of description but is not accustomed to the school dialect; at numerous places the writer uses a rough approximation of oral dialect (*rugget, paid days, couple miles*), and the student is unlikely to know how to revise or edit. What can you do to help this student without overwhelming her with everything that is wrong with the paper?

The writer of this essay needs to see that she did not meet the goal of the assignment in that she describes a town rather than a person. She must also be told that she will have to develop a writing process that will allow for revision and editing to bring her initial ideas into the school dialect. Her writing indicates a paucity of experience with writing assignments, experience that must be guided by assessment if she is to succeed.

What resources are available at your institution to help such a student? Is there a developmental program that will help her learn what she needs to know? Can she be assigned a tutor in the learning center? Regular conferences with you? A peer tutor from the class itself? Your objective as a teacher is to read this student's errors as an indication of ways to provide help, rather than merely as an indication of failure.

You will, of course, want to use this essay assignment in various ways in addition to its placement or diagnostic function. Students should begin their writing logs by describing how they went about producing the paper; if you ask them to revise the essay (always a good idea), a description of the process of revision should also go into the log. Depending on your class and your institution, you may want to deal with organization of the paragraphs and the essay as a whole, with sentence structure, or with other issues that have emerged. And you will want to distinguish this kind of assignment from the more analytical and expository essays to follow.

ESSAY TEST 2: PERSONAL-EXPERIENCE ASSIGNMENT 2

Many observers of our society claim that modern people, immersed in materialism, are "owned by their objects." Yet many of us have objects that we treasure not just for their material value but for a variety of other reasons. Describe one object that is important to you. Explain what values it represents, and comment on those values.

This topic is parallel to the first diagnostic essay in its demands. It requires detailed description, draws on the writer's experience for subject material, and moves beyond mere description into levels of abstraction. The difference between the two topics, however, may be significant for some students. Many students find it easier to describe objects than people, and such students will perform more successfully on this topic. Similarly, because a discussion of values is a more straightforward activity than management of tone, this topic will be easier for students without much control of verbal nuance. Nonetheless, the challenge of recalling human relationships may stimulate certain introspective students to write more effectively on the first assignment, despite the fact that it is in one sense more difficult. And some students may write badly on the second assignment because they may be unable to discuss values without resorting to simple sentimentalism or stock phrases.

This topic is built on the usual test demand for a well-stocked and accessible bank of memories. Even more than most, it calls for students to come up with a suitable memory, decked out with detail, before they can begin to compose. The student who came up with the music box as object (the 6 paper that follows) clearly had an advantage over the student whose memory could supply only the clichéd teddy bear. Every essay question contains this kind of hidden demand for memory and for retrieval of the right kind of memory for the writer's use. Nearly all questions — even text-based ones — will ask for details, support, or examples as part of the response.

If you choose to discuss this topic with your students before they write, you will probably want to spend time considering the most appropriate objects they might choose. Most students, particularly in a test situation, just plunge in and write about the first thing that comes to mind. More skillful students, however, will pause before beginning to write, choosing from a range of possibilities.

It is also effective to assign the topic as a diagnostic test without prior discussion and then to discuss these matters with the students after you return their first attempts, as they begin their revisions. Here is a scoring guide to use (or adapt) for this assignment.

Holistic Scoring Guide

As with the first assignment, students should be rewarded for what they do well in response to the question. For Personal-Experience Assignment 2, they are asked to describe an object important to them. They are further asked to explain what values it represents and to comment on those values. Note that the question does not ask for unusual objects. But it does require the choice of a specific object, not generalized abstractions such as life or God, and it asks for some descriptive detail as well as a more abstract discussion of values.

6. A **superior** response will not just name an object but also describe it in some detail, and the essay will not just identify the values represented but also explain and comment on them, their nature, and their source. A superior essay will be literate and orderly, despite the occasional minor error.

5. The **strong** response will both describe a particular object and explain the values it represents, but without the unusual richness and development of the 6 essay.

4. The **competent** response will select and describe an object, though less fully than the 5 essay; it will adequately consider the issue of values. Minor mechanical or grammatical errors may be noticeable but do not seriously distract the reader.

3. The **weak** response may adequately handle both parts of the assignment but will contain too many mechanical or grammatical errors to be considered competent. Or it may be mechanically competent but fail to accomplish the task — for example, by dealing with only one part of the two-part question; ignoring the representativeness of specific objects; or treating the subject in a superficial, immature, or stereotyped fashion.

2. The **inadequate** response is likely to show patterns of serious error, to misunderstand or confuse the question, to use superficial and stereotyped language, to show consistent oral interference with the written language, or otherwise demonstrate serious problems.

1. The **incompetent** response conveys ineptness at handling the assignment: it reflects failed attempts to begin the task, inability to produce the written dialect, unwillingness to undertake the writing assignment, and the like.

Sample Student Essays

Score of 6

The Music Box

We have in our living room a music box, which for three generations has given pleasure to the eyes and ears of my family. It stands about a foot high and measures about two feet in length and width. Except for a spray of flowers carved on its face, the outside is unadorned. Inside, pasted to the lid, is a turn-of-the-century lithograph of a pair of plump cherubs. There is a set of tin records, perforated here and there, that goes with the music box. It is run by winding it up and releasing the spring. Its tunes are dated; "My Gal Is A High-Born Lady" and "I Guess I'll Telegraph My Baby" haven't been among the top ten for quite a while, but this does nothing to lessen the enjoyment they give.

My grandfather was the first to own the music box. He traded a horse for it and presented the music box to my grandmother as a gift. They had been married for only six months. At first it was a very big deal. A music box in a Nebraskan farming town can cause quite a commotion, but as time went by and the popularity of "victrolas" grew, the music box passed into oblivion.

Ignored and dusty was the way my father discovered it in the cellar. He cleaned it up and got it running and showed it off patronizingly to his friends as a relic from his parent's youth. It was played at parties as a novelty, but again it lost out against the incoming rage: the radio. So back into the cellar went the music box to await rediscovery one more time.

This time it was my sister and I who resurrected it. We hauled it out into the light, dusted off its rosewood sides and listened to the songs first heard what seemed to us to be eons ago.

My grandparents grew old, and being practical people, decided to divide their possessions with their children before their death to avoid a tragic scramble afterwards. To my father went the music box, and he carefully brought it to our home and revived it one more time.

Now, despite its years, it keeps on playing its old familiar songs. I love the old music box. It can never be associated with a price tag. My grandfather acquired it with an honest trade and it has been handed down through the years. The music box symbolizes my grandfather's love for my grandmother, my father's years at home, my sister and I exploring in the dark cellar and countless fine memories. I love it for its beauty, the rich, soft red of the rosewood, the way it gleams in the sun. I love the whirr of the motor and vigorously cranking the handle. I love the corny song titles and running my fingers over the rough surface of the records. And although its value is largely sentimental, its worth stems from the fact that it has survived many years with grace and beauty; something very few *people* can claim.

Score of 5

My House

As I look back on my life, the object that I place the most value on is the house that I grew up in. For sixteen years I walked through its doors and lived in its rooms. That house became a part of me.

Now, almost nineteen years old, it stands in a middle class suburb of Los Angeles. The surrounding streets are lined with well-kept homes and neatly trimmed yards.

Children that I don't know play baseball on the avenue and cars that I don't recognize fill the driveways. My dear house is in an alien world both to me and to it.

My family took pride in that home. We bought it new, put in all the landscaping, and made it a beautiful place to live. In all the years we lived there, I never once took its loveliness for granted. I would sit and look at it and know what a wonderful home we had.

That long avenue was my world. Little playmates moved in and out of the other houses, but I was the stable one. I didn't believe we would ever leave our home.

That building saw my first step, heard my first word, and watched me fall off of my first bicycle. It stood by when I was sick and was there for all the happy moments too. It became more like a person, part of the family.

Leaving it all alone for new people to run about in was next to impossible. Is it as lonely as I am?

Our new house is bigger and more modern than that one was. Still, this makes no difference. It will never be home.

Score of 4

Objects I Value!

At this point in life, I don't have many objects which I value a great deal. The few things I do value have a sentimental value rather than a monetary value.

The first objects I value are trophies I won diving. They have a very deep sentimental value to me because it was my reward for the hours and years I practiced, working for a goal. When I look at my trophies on the shelf I think of all the joys I felt at winning and also the heart break of losing. I think of the self-control and self-discipline I gained at going to practice each day while my friends were at the beach. This, right now, is very important to me. These trophies have no real monetary value or sentimental value to anyone but me because only I earned these trophies and only I cherish them.

Another object which I value is a ring I recieved from my grandmother. This ring is also a sentimental object to me. I recieved it after she passed away and so it is my rememberance of her. This ring also has monetary value. It is a gold ring with a small diamond in it. Others would value it because of it's worth but my family and I are the only ones who value it for a sentimental reason.

My next valuable object is my wallet. My value on my wallet is very sentimental. In it, it contains all my pictures of friends and experiences which I have gone through. If someone stole my wallet or I lost it, I would rather lose my money than some of the pictures inside. Maybe this is because I am not overflowing with money at the moment but right now my pictures come over my money.

My last valuable is a watch I received at Christmas from my boyfriend. This is very important to me because it is from him. I have had watches before from my parents and they really didn't have very much sentimental value to them. But my watch contains many memories and I would really be upset if I misplaced it. Just like the ring, it is valuable to others because of the cost but to me it is the person who it signifies.

These are my most valuable objects and it isn't because of the amount of money they're worth but instead for the sentimental value of them. I don't really own anything excessively expensive so I really don't value many things for their value in money.

Score of 3

Bear-Bear

Blue body with a white tummy and round black eyes, soon to be loved. This poor little teddy bear went through so much just for me.

When I came home after my birth, I had 3 sisters and a strange new friend waiting for me. My sister Jamie had a teddy bear placed in my crib. They tell me I actually giggled when I first saw *my* teddy bear.

Well days went on and after countless washings, due to being thrown-up on or thrown into the toilet, my little teddy bear had seen his last day with those round black eyes. Yes, my little teddy bear needed some new eyes and blue buttons, so Jamie did a repair job, with some grown-up help. Now it seemed perfect. After all, blue eyes match a blue body!

Jamie decided, one day, that she would teach me how to say Teddy Bear. It was a noble effort on her part even though all I could repeat was *Bear!* The Teddy bear still didn't have a name.

The next day when I was in the living room, I realized that my teddy bear wasn't around. With the terrifying thought that he might be gone, my tiny voice piped up with; "Bear-Bear, Bear-Bear!"

There was no mistaking what I wanted. Now that he had a name, Bear-Bear would never be more than a helping hand away.

I never really pondered on why I kept Bear-Bear all these years. It's simple — I love him and I'll keep him many more years I imagine. Bear-Bear will always mean love, security, and friendship. Perhaps that's why I choose my friends carefully and value their love so greatly. My friends have been wonderfully good to me (and vise-versa) since the very first time my giggle said "Hi, let's be friends!"

Score of 2

Cars

Heat, exhaust, fumes, burning rubber and smoke are all caused by a remarkable invention that has spured our society into being one of the most materialistic in this modern age. Our society today depends on the car for transportation. We overlook the bad side of this invention for all the wonderful things the car has done for us.

No longer are people confined to one small region for their entire lives. Trips to the coast or to a distant city for a day are not unheard of now. It has actually broadened our horizons for we can meet new people, go new places. People we haven't seen in a long time are in easy reach.

Working days are shortened with the use of the car. Instead of walking many miles to work, it provides fast and easy transportation on highways.

Status is related to owning a car. Some people seem to feel that the bigger a car is, the better it is. Socioeconomic status is based on the number of high value materialistic things we own. Having four or five cars in a family tends to raise a family's status.

Cars come in all shapes and sizes. Big or small we can find one that fits the needs of everybody. Compact, economy and luxary cars are priced to fit people with even low income budgets as well as high.

There is a limit that people using cars must draw. Excessive use of a car can damage our enviornment. Taking a car into high mountain area can damage or even ruin flora and fauna. Pollution from cars cannot be stopped unless all cars are banned.

With all the good and bad sides to cars, which way can we turn? Cars can be used for destructive purposes as well as useful, meaningful reasons.

Score of 1

My Values

I am going to write on some object which are pretty important to me. The first would be my religion because I think I should put my faith in something other than "man," and worldly goods. I also believe that I as a person have that right to look forward to something bigger and better in life, I can live life better day by day. This is important because I'm a person who doesn't like to have things cramed down my throat then expected to digest it easily. I feel I have the right to choose who and what I believe in, without someone handing me 2 alternatives to chose from. I want to choose freely on my own will and judgment. I feel that I am old enough to choose and have "free choice." Another object or value which is important to me is my "Freedom." I like to do what I like, go where I want, see what I want, to a point where I do not interfere with another persons "Freedoms." My whole life is based on what I can do for me and other people. Without this freedom I could not serve to the best of my ability my fellow man. I couldn't put forth 100% because I would be restricted to do only certain things. Therefore, without my religion and freedom to do what I want I should have never have been born and with out these two basics of life I do not see how any man can live. So I have told you two of my basic values, again they are "Freedom to choose my own religion" and basic Freedom to live an everyday life.

Discussion of the Essays

"The Music Box" (scored 6, superior) exemplifies the excellent writing that some students can produce in forty-five minutes under test conditions. Its wealth of detail, clarity, focus, organization, and amplitude all attest to a student with superior writing skill. "My House" (scored 5, a strong response) is clearly less excellent, but it shows a skillful writer using personification of the house as an original way to fulfill the assignment. Some teachers may be bothered by the relative lack of detail and by the placement of the writer at the center of the essay and so may want to lower the score; others may want to reward even more highly the imaginative quality of the writing. The competent essay, scored 4, reveals a skillful writer undone by a fragmented essay; depending on the program and the institution, this paper might well be placed in the lower half of scores.

We scored "Bear-Bear" at the 3 level (weak response), despite its minimal satisfaction of all requirements of the assignment, on the grounds of its immature approach and stereotyped treatment of the subject. However, the considerable detail and consistent tone argue for a higher score under some circumstances. The generalized paper on cars exemplifies the inadequate (2) essay, which fails to come to grips with the topic and is beset by writing problems, despite a kind of focus and some sentence control. The last essay suggests a student likely to need substantial assistance before succeeding in a regular college composition program.

Although no single test of any type is accurate enough to be used by itself to make irreversible decisions about student programs, the essays presented here suggest possible courses of action. The student who wrote the essay scored 1 (incompetent) might be recommended by this test for remedial or tutorial attention, if further testing and background information support the evaluation. Such a decision might lead to success for a student otherwise heading for failure. At the other end of the spectrum, the student producing the superior (6) essay might be a candidate for credit by examination, if other evidence confirms the ability shown in "The Music Box."

ESSAY SCORING BEYOND THE CLASSROOM: USING GROUP SCORES

If you prepare carefully for a holistic scoring session, selecting sample essays to illustrate the scoring guide and following standard procedures, you and your colleagues should be able to score several hundred essays in a day (with two separate scores for each essay) with about 90 percent agreement within a point on the 6-point scale. Readers can score about twenty-five essays an hour after they have reached general agreement on sample papers in a training session. Although most impromptu essays are still handled individually by classroom instructors, more and more writing staffs are now accomplishing such group scoring. At the least, it brings the staff together to consider standards; in many cases, it leads to substantial sharing of ideas about the teaching of writing as well as to useful scores for placement. One caution is that unless collegial procedures respecting differences of opinion are followed, group scoring can backfire and exacerbate existing hostilities.

PRETESTING AND POSTTESTING USING IMPROMPTU WRITING

One way to try to measure the gains students may have made in writing ability in your course would be to give the placement or diagnostic essay again at the end of the term. The second administration would be the posttest and might show student improvement — if instruction in the course focused on personal-experience writing. (It is a common mistake to use a pretest/posttest assessment without ensuring that what is being tested is in fact what is being taught; if the curriculum asks students to do text-based writing, you should choose topics like those in Chapter 7 of this book.) You can expect that students will write better, particularly if they have had instruction and practice in that kind of writing.

To ensure that your results are trustworthy, take some precautions against unintentional skewing of the scores. For example, you might save the pretests and grade both pretest and posttest at the same time; furthermore, you could get someone else to cover names and dates and to code the papers so that you would not know whether a particular paper had been written at the beginning or the end of the term. Even more credible would be a system using two different topics. Half of your group could take each topic as a pretest, and each group could write on the other topic at the end of instruction. After coding, you and a colleague or two could grade each question carefully and then compare group pretest scores with posttest scores. Of course, you will want questions that are parallel in their demands on the students (though no two essay questions are ever of exactly the same order of difficulty), and you will have to use identical scoring guides for this purpose.

If you use a system of this sort, you will want to be clear in your mind about the difference between scoring papers for your use (to learn, say, what you have taught most or least successfully) and grading papers for the classification or education of your students. Each of these purposes is legitimate in its own way, but each of them calls for a different approach to grading. For example, if you are grading papers to help students improve their work, you need to supply comments and prepare for discussion that will help students revise subsequent drafts; scoring for a pretest/posttest study requires only highly reliable grades.

In addition, grading for the benefit of the students will tend to focus on what is best about the writing and often yield more encouraging higher scores, while a program assessment is more likely to focus on generating a reliable range of scores, with considerable concern for improving instruction in what the students do not do well.

But the cautions about the use — and misuse — of personal experience writing scores with which this chapter began are particularly important in the case of pretesting and posttesting. If the composition program focuses on this kind of writing, a difference in scores will give useful information about the outcomes of the program. If, however, the program is principally concerned with other kinds of writing — argument, research, text-based analysis, or writing in the major — then information about improvements in writing personal essays will tell you very little. In that case, you will want to find ways to measure what has been taught, as (for example) the next chapter does with text-based writing topics.

SELECTED REFERENCES

Elbow, Peter. *Writing with Power: Techniques for Mastering the Writing Process.* 2nd ed. New York: Oxford UP, 1998.

———. *Writing without Teachers.* 2nd ed. New York: Oxford UP, 1998.

Roen, Duane H., Stuart C. Brown, and Theresa Enos, eds. *Living Rhetoric and Composition: Stories of the Discipline.* Mahwah: Erlbaum, 1998.

Shepard, Alan, Gary Tate, and John McMillan, eds. *Coming to Class: Pedagogy and the Social Class of Teachers.* Portsmouth: Boynton-Cook, 1998.

Spigelman, Candace. *Personally Speaking: Experience as Evidence in Academic Discourse.* Carbondale, IL: Southern Illinos UP, 2004.

Thompson, Thomas C., ed. *Most Excellent Differences: Essays on Using Type Theory in the Composition Classroom.* Gainesville Center for Applications of Psychological Type, 1996.

CHAPTER 7

EVALUATING IMPROMPTU WRITING BASED ON GIVEN TEXTS

This chapter gives two additional impromptu writing assignments with supporting material (discussion, scoring guides, and sample papers at differing levels of performance). The assignments are based principally on a given text, so the student must begin with examination and explanation of that text. Although some personal experience may well enter the student's response, these topics require much more ability to handle abstract concepts and other people's ideas than the impromptu writing of Chapter 6. Though each mode of essay has its strengths and problems, your particular teaching situation will suggest which is more appropriate for your students.

If you use the assignments from this chapter (or Chapter 6) for an evaluation of your writing program (sometimes called an outcomes study), be careful to note that these pairs of assignments provide parallel topics — not identical topics and not necessarily topics of identical difficulty; you will want to use the procedures outlined at the end of Chapter 6 to provide meaningful results. Remember that any pretest/posttest study should use identical scoring guides and topics that in fact measure what your course teaches. Neither of these kinds of topics will tell you anything about library research skills, for instance, or the ability to revise. And finally, if (like most writing instructors) you have little experience at studies derived from social science research techniques, you might want to seek some statistical support for an outcomes study from a colleague in psychology, statistics, or education, where such studies are more or less routine.

Whether or not you are engaged in an outcomes study, you want to find out as quickly as possible how well your students write in relation to the goals of your course or program. These essay topics are designed, and have been used, as in-class writing assignments for the first day of class. Select one that is appropriate for your class, and it will give you important information you need to be able to teach effectively — as well as allow you to start the writing class with writing. Meanwhile, be sure to look at the last chapter of this book for a sophisticated way to use portfolios for an outcomes study, if you have the time and resources.

LITERATURE AND THE TEACHING OF WRITING

Since most teachers of writing have received advanced degrees in some field other than writing, they are likely to be tempted to substitute the content of those fields for writing instruction, particularly when they have had little or no training in rhetoric and think that writing instruction is a limited or even remedial activity. Further, a college course calls for substantial content and challenging reading; teachers, reasonably enough, want to teach what they know best. Yet students have enrolled for a writing course, not for one in literature or political science, and teachers and writing program administrators are concerned about truth in labeling, as are the students. While we need to maintain sufficient intellectual content in the writing curriculum, we need also to see the distinction between this material *supporting* the teaching of writing rather than *substituting for* the teaching of writing.

One helpful way to understand this distinction is by considering what sort of writing is assigned and how it is evaluated. Is writing integrated into the course as an end in itself as well as a means of learning the material? For instance, what proportion of class time is spent on such activities as prewriting, journal writing, evaluating drafts, small-group peer discussion of student writing, teacher-led discussion of sample student papers, and the like? Does the material allow reasonable scope for a variety of student interests, for a series of writing assignments with a coherent rhetorical purpose related to increasing student writing ability, for revision and development of student ideas? Do the syllabus and the evaluation procedure allow time for and reward revision of writing, and is student writing ability the main criterion for the final grade? Are student-teacher conferences about writing built into the course plan?

Or, on the other hand, is the course built around mastery of the content? Is most student writing evaluated as a product, such as a term paper that is largely the student's responsibility and is handed in at the end of the course? Are most classes devoted to lectures on or discussion of the reading? Is the course grade wholly or largely dependent on tests or unrevised papers evaluated on mastery of the content?

For example, a Shakespeare course will define a group of a dozen or more plays by date ("early") or by kind ("tragedies") or the like. The students will spend their time reading the plays, perhaps writing an occasional limited short paper on one of them (the meaning of suicide in *Hamlet,* the clothing imagery in *King Lear,* or the hidden colonialism in *The Tempest*), and probably writing a term paper on some aspect of the plays read or on some topic relating the plays to early modern England. The students may read some Shakespeare criticism, see videos or live performances, or undertake other activities to deepen their understanding of Shakespeare. There will be a final examination, and perhaps a midterm as well, to evaluate the depth of their knowledge.

Such a course should not be called a writing course, even though it may include a good bit of student writing. The writing is there to support the learning and understanding of Shakespeare (as it should), and writing instruction is incidental to the major goals of the course. But it is not hard to conceive of a writing course based on Shakespeare (or any other content area). Such a course would use the plays to provide content for a variety of writing assignments. Perhaps one sequence could move from a description of a performance to a review of the performance to a research paper on classic performances of the same play. A comparison of *Much Ado about Nothing* and *Othello* (with their similar plot lines) could lead to a series of papers comparing comedy with tragedy as artistic forms or even as approaches to understanding experience. Class time would be spent largely on the writing problems posed by the course — though, naturally enough, some attention would be given to the reading of the plays. But now the understanding of Shakespeare would be ancillary to the student writing, and the students' grades would depend much more on their writing than on the depth of their understanding of the plays within the early modern context.

The issue is not to exclude literature from a writing course but to use whatever reading is assigned to support the writing process the students are learning to pursue. Since reading and writing abilities are interwoven in ways we hardly understand, careful reading surely belongs in a writing course. Numbers of books and handbooks are available to illustrate research and other kinds of long assignments on literature and other content areas; that interesting topic is beyond the scope of this book. But the two following assignments, scoring guides, and sample papers illustrate how impromptu writing based on a given text can support and allow for evaluation of student writing.

ESSAY TEST 3: TEXT-BASED TOPIC 1

The best swordsman in the world doesn't need to fear the second best swordsman in the world; no, the person for him to be afraid of is some ignorant antagonist who has never had a sword in his hand before; he doesn't do the thing he ought to do, and so the expert isn't prepared for him; he does the thing he ought not to do; and often it catches the expert out and ends him on the spot.

— Samuel Clemens

Write an essay that explains what Clemens means by his description of the "best swordsman" and the "ignorant antagonist." Relate Clemens's concept to an area about which you are well informed.

Notice that this assignment makes very different kinds of conceptual demands on the writer than those made by personal-experience topics. Instead of requiring the writer to plumb experience for a person or an object to write about, this question demands close and sensitive reading of the passage as the crucial first step. There is no evidence to show that text-based topics are inherently more difficult than experience-based topics, though they are for some students, or that they elicit more complex thought or writing. All we can say with certainty is that the demands are different and less personal; in some ways, these topics are more "academic" than the first set and will thus have more appeal to faculty across the curriculum, though rather less to most students. The text-based questions in this chapter make complex demands on students in the areas of both reading and writing and so may be more appropriate for advanced students than for those lacking experience with complex texts.

Here is a general scoring guide that is useful for such topics and, in particular, for Text-Based Topic 1.

Holistic Scoring Guide

6. A **superior** response addresses the question fully and explores the issues thoughtfully. It shows substantial depth, fullness, and complexity of thought. The response demonstrates clear, focused, unified, and coherent organization and is fully developed and detailed. The essay demonstrates superior control of diction, syntactic variety, and transition but may have a few minor flaws.

5. A **strong** response clearly addresses the question and explores the issues. It shows some depth and complexity of thought and is effectively organized. The strong essay is well developed, with supporting detail. It demonstrates control of diction, syntactic variety, and transition, though it may have a few flaws.

4. A **competent** response adequately addresses the question and explores the issues. It shows clarity of thought but may lack complexity. A competent essay is organized and adequately developed, with some detail. This response demonstrates competent writing, though it may have some flaws.

3. A **weak** response may distort or neglect parts of the question. It may be simplistic or stereotyped in thought. It may demonstrate problems in organization. It may use generalizations without supporting detail or detail without generalizations; details may be undeveloped. The weak response shows patterns of error in language, syntax, or mechanics.

2. An **inadequate** response demonstrates serious problems in one or more of the areas specified for the weak (3) response.

1. An **incompetent** response fails in its attempt to discuss the topic, or it may be deliberately off-topic. A response in this category is incompletely developed and mechanically inept.

Sample Student Essays

Score of 6

The Expert Is Always on Guard Against Checkmate

When Clemens speaks of the "best swordsman," he brings up the trained expert, the professional who has mastered the rules of the game. This expert is ready for antagonists who play by the rules. The "ignorant antagonist" stands for the untrained or rebellious outsider who reserves the right to make up his own rules. The opposition between these two ways of fighting, playing, or living applies in many different ways.

When revolutionaries break diplomatic rules by engaging in acts of terrorism, the governments affected are often "caught out" and government leaders sometimes "ended on the spot." In today's world, the superpowers ready their defense for major confrontations with other superpowers or "second best" powers, but not for isolated and unpredictable acts of terrorism such as the taking of hostages, the assassination of political figures, or the hijacking of a plane — often for personal or even crazy reasons.

On the other hand, unconventional chess players don't have the slightest chance against an expert unless these outsiders are well beyond the novice stage. The brilliant innovations in chess have nothing to do with ignorance. No expert can lose to the novice opening with rook pawns or carelessly throwing his queen into opening positions. A brilliant amateur can win at chess, where nothing can by this time be entirely new, but the innovator cannot be ignorant. However, chess is here, as elsewhere, atypical. What Clemens says does not apply in this tight, square world, so unlike the disorderly real one.

Any proverb has a basic truth but needs to be applied with care. Maybe the very best experts are those most alert to the ways unconventional moves can work. Our swordsmen in foreign relations need to be ready for mobs, terrorists, and others who will refuse to acknowledge our rules. If the ignorant antagonist can do in the duelist, the swordsman has more to learn.

Score of 5

Uncle Fred

The Clemens passage reminds me of a saying heard often in our family: "You can't argue with an ignorant man." This line has been repeated whenever someone mentions my Uncle Fred. Fred plays the part of the "ignorant antagonist" on many subjects, but most especially in politics and religion.

Although Clemens speaks metaphorically, Uncle Fred is a literal example as well. A genuine "ignorant antagonist," he never takes the time to become informed on any one political party, candidate, or issue. He hears bits and pieces of news stories and reads headlines and political cartoons in his local small-town newspaper and then forms his opinions.

When Fred claims that the Russian leaders will always take advantage of the Americans, because they are so much smarter, we have learned not to argue. In the next breath, Fred might say, "I think Yeltsin has been sent to save the world. He is going to achieve world peace." The next day Fred declares, "Congress is so stupid, they let the state department manipulate them on everything." First, our government is not smart enough to protect us from Yeltsin, then Yeltsin is going to save us. Finally, the state department is too smart for 435 elected representatives, despite its stupidity. It isn't that Fred has a blind loyalty to any one party or that he is against all of them. He just changes his opinions as quickly as the stories change on the news broadcasts.

You can't argue with a man like Fred, just as the "best swordsman in the world" can't fence with the "ignorant antagonist who has never had a sword in his hand before," because he doesn't play by recognized rules. He changes the rules as he goes along. This can in part be explained by using Berne's Transactional Analysis theory. When an adult interacts with another person, he anticipates how the other person will respond. Things usually go smoothly when the person responds correctly, that is, according to the unstated rules of adult transactions. However, if the person responds using an unanticipated ego state (say, child instead of adult, or parent instead of child), you get a crossed transaction, which often "catches the expert out and ends him on the spot."

Score of 4

The Best Soldier

The best soldier in the world does not fear the second best soldier of any country. The soldier that he must respect and fear is the nonprofessional soldier, the one who has no set standard of fighting or long regimental traditions. The "ignorant antagonist" as he relates to me is untrained and unskilled in the latest military arts. These people have never held a rifle in their hands with the intent of killing another human being.

The unconventional soldier does not use the usual military tactics that the best soldier uses. His is the world of the underground. The expert is not prepared for this opponent.

The "ignorant antagonist" in the low intensity conflict is the soldier of his/her land. They fight a war that is unconventional and usually very deadly to the best soldier. Throughout history there are examples of such fighters besting the best soldiers. Our American Revolution is a good example of "ignorant antagonists" beating an army that was considered the best. The lines of redcoats were no match for the farmers that used what we call today cover and concealment to engage the on comming best soldiers.

The minute men, as they were called, blended in well with nature and destroyed the will of the best soldiers to continue the fight. Recently, the Afghan rebels gave the best Russian soldiers a run for their money. In Central America the contras are making it difficult for the Marxist government to expand their hold on the country. The Sandanistas are the best soldiers in that region of the world.

The "ignorant antagonist" usually has the best chance of winning the contest if the fight is short. But there is one difference that the antagonist might overlook, and that will be his undoing and the expert will "catch *him* out and end him on the spot." That difference is flexibility. What made the expert the best in the first place was the ability to reason, to understand that his way has been time proven through many trials, to adapt, to learn new ways. At that point, the roles are reversed, for the best becomes the "ignorant antagonist" and the ignorant antagonist becomes the best. Thus you have a situation that the "ignorant antagonist" does make mistakes and that buys time for the "best swordsman" to counter his blows.

The one who makes the least mistakes wins the contest. It takes 50,000 dead and wounded soldiers to train a general. Can the "ignorant antagonist" pay that price? I believe he can and does. The best wins the battle with no dead and wounded, but that is not the rule but the exception. The best must be aware and fear the ignorant for the ignorant do not know what to fear about the best.

Score of 3

The Better Man Doesn't Always Win

Samuel Clemens story about the best swordsman can best be related to that old cliché: "The better man doesn't always win."

Clemens story about the best swordsman best depicts a situation that I have experienced in basketball. My situation deals with a basketball game I was playing in, when I was in High School. When I was in High School, I thought of myself as being a fairly good basketball player. This feeling soon changed when I was matched up against a person who I felt I was better than. This person was terrible in the game of basketball. This individual couldn't dribble, shoot, or even walk for that matter. But, there was one thing he could do very well, and that was guard me. Like the antagonist in the best swordsman, this individual was awful. His defensive play was like none I had ever seen before, it was awkward and unorthodox. This individual was so bad that after a quarter of play, he made me look bad. I couldn't understand it, every move I used to fake him out wouldn't work. Every time I would put a move on him to get past him, he would be right there to stop me. After a quarter of this, I became frustrated and got benched, much like the best swordsman's end.

In conclusion, I feel this story about the best swordsman best depicts my situation. In my situation, the awful defensive man is much like the antagonist in the best swordsman. In that, like the swordsman, anything I did to the antagonist to beat him, wouldn't work. Consequently, I was sent to the bench, much like the best swordsman was put to his end.

Score of 2

Freshman Coach

The passage by Samuel Clemens reminds me of a Junior College basketball coach, and his Freshman athletes. Here, like the "best swordsman," is the Coach: a man who knows his craft but fears the ignorant antagonist; the Freshman athletes. Why? because the basic skills of dribbling, passing, rebounding and shooting that his Freshman athletes should of learned in High School; the majority of these Freshman athletes don't possess. Because practice time to teach those skills one on one is short, this puts fears in the coach who feels these Freshman athletes should already be prepared.

By lacking these skills the Freshman athletes, like the ignorant antagonist dosen' t do what the coach expects from him, because the Freshman figure they already know from their previous basketball experience what to do.

Because the Freshman athletes have their own preconceived notions that their prepared with these skills, this makes the Coach who is the expert feel not prepared. The Coach now feels like he must start all over teaching the basic skills to young adults who should have learned these skills from their adolescence to teen-age lives.

This passage shows us how the best "the Coach," can be fearful of the ignorant antagonist "the Freshman athletes," because when the Coach is not prepared for the ignorant antagonist "the Freshman athletes" he finds himself pushed to be the best.

Score of 1

The Best the Stronger

The passage tells us about the best swordsman, and the first thing we find it to know who is the "best swordsman," but this would be different from genration to genration, and from surroundings to surrounding. The swordsman usually like to fight, like to tell the people around him, he is the stronger. In the other hand the ignorant antagonist does not like to fight and has never had a sword in his hand. Why he never had sword, because he hate to be enemy to be agrassion. The swordsman often does not know Clemens's concepts. He hate the people and fight them maybe because he is not want to see any body more healthy or welthy than him. In my home country I know, both the swordsman and the ignorant antagonist. Therefore some of swordsman different than other depends where is he live what kind of his invironment, some of the people who leave in desert, and mountain area. Those are often agressive, and like to fight the people with reason and with out reason. I think the motive for the that only to be the best the stronger the first man, but some of them to struggle to sarvive. The swordsman with the new life became less enemy than before. They became to have Clemens and let the people to live. The ignorant antagonist those people in the area which I live in had never had sword to kill the people or to make anything for the people. Those persons like the people to have good life with out any problem with out fighting let the people to have wonderful time in their life. They know exactly what Clemens means, and why it's important for the people and for their life. The swordsman should be live, and let the people to live. They should go around him and see what the people do, and do as the people. The compassion is very important to compassinate the children and the elderly people. This is the life, and this is the good way in this life.

Discussion of the Essays

The superior response exemplifies the description in the scoring guide. The writer begins by defining terms, accomplishing the task of explaining what Clemens means by using terms that can be applied "in many different ways."

For this writer, the opposition between the "trained expert" and the "rebellious outsider" works in foreign relations — and the writer shows just how — but does not work in the "tight, square world" of chess, "so unlike the disorderly real one." Though the response is necessarily brief given the time limit, the writer does explain the meaning and apply it in two other areas; throughout, the writer is clearly thinking about meanings and applications. The demonstration that the quotation works on some occasions but not on others shows complexity of thought, and the tight focus of the essay shows careful organization. The essay includes such details as the taking of hostages and chess openings with rook pawns. Finally, the writer shows accomplished control of style, diction, and other aspects of writing.

The essay on Uncle Fred was scored 5, even though the discussion of the quotation appears only in the last paragraph. This writer began immediately with Uncle Fred, as a way of exploring the meanings of the quotation, using dialogue and detail; the writer sees Uncle Fred as the "ignorant antagonist" that no expert can handle. The paper is focused and responsive to the question, though it lacks the depth and writing skill of the 6 paper.

"The Best Soldier" opens with four strong paragraphs connecting the quotation to military history, using details from a series of wars to exemplify the meaning. Unfortunately, the last two paragraphs wander off the subject and do not seem to connect with either what has come before or the quotation. Nonetheless, the strength of the first four paragraphs shows the competence of the writer and justifies the score of 4.

The essay scored 3 (weak response) reflects a common mistake in approaching essay tests. Instead of attending to the meaning of the text, this writer glanced at it and moved to a personal-experience narrative. But unlike "Uncle Fred," the experience here seems vague, lacking in detail, and not altogether related to the quotation. The opposing basketball player, we are told, was "terrible" but nonetheless succeeded in outplaying the writer with unorthodox moves. Most readers were unconvinced by this essay because the assertions that the opposing player was an ignorant antagonist are contradicted by his success, and the writer presents himself as anything but expert. The writer clearly knows how to proceed, but the unsupported generalizations and simplistic view of the quotation move the paper into the lower half of scores.

Nonetheless, the weak response shows an understanding of the passage that the inadequate response (scored 2) does not reach. Here we are told about the coach and the unwilling freshman, but the meaning of the quotation is lost. In addition, the problems with sentence structure indicate a weak writer who may, depending on the institution, profit from special tutorial or developmental instruction before or during a composition class. Finally, the incompetent response (scored 1) betrays severe problems with reading comprehension and language use, probably a sign of inadequate skill in English as a second language. Without special support services of some kind, this student will not be able to succeed in first-year work in college.

ESSAY TEST 4: TEXT-BASED TOPIC 2

The following assignment differs somewhat from the previous one by using two quotations and requiring a comparison/contrast response. If you are using it with the first text-based topic, in a pretest/posttest study, you should probably use only the first quotation (which works well by itself) and prepare directions for writing that are parallel to those for the Clemens passage. In addition, you should use exactly the same scoring guide, revised appropriately for the abilities of your students and for the specific skills taught in your course. I present the question as an example of a difficult essay assignment with complex demands.

This question requires that students (1) understand two passages, both of which are metaphorical and in part ironic; (2) recognize the attitude each passage reflects toward the role of science in human affairs; (3) conceive and present an imaginary argument between the protagonist of one passage (the scientist) and the deceived "some" who speak in the other; (4) speculate on the views of the authors of the two passages; and (5) organize and present this material in an orderly and literate way under time pressure. Clearly, such an assignment requires substantial academic preparation. If you have many students such as those scoring in the lower ranges on Text-Based Topic 1, this question will not yield useful information for diagnosis or anything else. But this assignment, or one with even more extensive reading passages, may be just what you need if you are teaching students who have had the benefit of rigorous academic preparation.

Read the passage and the poem; then write an essay as directed following the poem.

This is a story about one of our great atomic physicists. This man, one of the chief architects of the atomic bomb, so the story runs, was out wandering in the woods one day with a friend when he came upon a small tortoise. Overcome with pleasurable excitement, he took up the tortoise and started home, thinking to surprise his children with it. After a few steps he paused and surveyed the tortoise doubtfully.

"What's the matter?" asked his friend.

Without responding, the great scientist slowly retraced his steps as precisely as possible, and gently set the turtle down upon the exact spot from which he had taken him up.

Then he turned solemnly to his friend. "It just struck me," he said, "that perhaps, for one man, I have tampered enough with the universe." He turned, and left the turtle to wander on its way.

— Loren Eiseley

"The path of life," some say, "is hard and rough
Only because we do not know enough.
When Science has discovered something more,
We shall be happier than we were before."

— Hilaire Belloc

Explain each writer's attitude toward the relationship between science and human happiness. To what extent do the scientist in Eiseley's passage and the "some" in Belloc's poem agree or disagree? Do the two authors seem to agree more with the scientist or with the "some"?

Holistic Scoring Guide

6. **Superior** responses will be well-organized essays that address the three parts of the assignment. They will accurately explain each author's attitude, discussing directly or implicitly the irony in the poem, showing where the two selections are similar and how they differ, and indicating how the authors seem to agree more with the scientist than with the "some." Generalizations will be supported with appropriate details. The superior essay will display a high degree of competence generally but may have slight flaws in writing, consistent with timed, first-draft prose.

5. **Strong** essays will address all parts of the assignment, display good overall interpretations of both selections, and clearly demonstrate strong reading and writing. However, they may be less fluent or thoroughly developed than the superior papers, may reveal some inaccuracy in interpretation, or may contain minor grammatical errors or occasional awkwardness.

4. **Competent** essays will adequately address all parts of the question but may lack the development of higher-scoring responses, may perceive similarities and differences somewhat less accurately, or may contain some errors in sentence construction or usage. They may deal with one aspect of the assignment by implication rather than by direct statement.

3. **Weak** essays may show signs of strong writing but respond to only one or two parts of the assignment, may contain misinterpretations of both selections or a radical misinterpretation of one, may show evidence of serious deficiencies in writing, or may lack sufficient details to support their generalizations.

2. **Inadequate** responses may show serious problems in reading and understanding the selections, reveal serious patterns of faults in writing, display considerable irrelevance, or be simplistic.

1. **Incompetent** essays will reflect almost no understanding of the question or the selections, and the writing will display ineptness in sentence construction, usage, and idiom.

Sample Student Essays

Score of 6

Science Is No Panacea

In the first passage, the writer is illustrating by the anecdote that science is not necessarily a good or beneficial thing to human beings. The inventor of the atom bomb seems somewhat regretful that he used his scientific knowledge to invent something so destructive to people and the earth. This regret is illustrated by his reluctance to tamper with even the simplest laws of nature; that is, the progress of the turtle in the woods.

The second passage takes a more ironic, mocking tone. It is saying essentially the same thing as the first, even though it looks different, by using a poem and the phrase, "some say." Who are "some"? The author makes us doubt seriously the quote from the "some" by deliberately leaving it vague. All we know is that they have a blind belief in the virtues of science: "When Science has discovered something more, we shall be happier than before." This is very insubstantial and illogical. It does not follow that science will change life from being "hard and rough" to something better; maybe (as with the Industrial Revolution) many people will be even worse off.

The "some" in the second passage don't agree with the scientist in the first. The "some" have no scientific knowledge; just a hazy idea that more scientific discoveries will make life easier. The scientist knows that this is not necessarily so because he has ample facts on which to base his knowledge. The development of the atomic bomb did not make life easier or less rough. In fact for a lot of people in Hiroshima there was no more life, period, because of this "scientific discovery." The "some" in the poem have no specific data to back up their claim — it is a generalized statement based on lack of specific knowledge of anything scientific.

The two authors seem to agree more with the scientist than with the "some." The scientist in the first passage has found out what the "some" in the second passage still don't know. Science needs to be handled with care; all scientific progress, discoveries, and work do not necessarily lead to health, wealth, and happiness. The "some" in the second passage are truly ignorant of this, and they are probably the very people who pay for scientists to work on anything bigger or more advanced in the hope that it will bring them "true" happiness.

The author of the second passage, by spotlighting this glaring ignorance, is mocking the "some," and is in agreement with the first author that science is not the panacea for all human ills.

Score of 5

Fear of Science

Throughout history, people have debated the usefulness of science for the betterment of human life. Sometimes research threatened religion, and religious leaders raised voices in protest; sometimes scientific remedies were viewed as the path to human salvation.

These passages from Eiseley and Belloc illustrate the logical fear of the human hand interfering with nature. Eiseley relates a story, almost a parable, about a designer of the world's most devastating weapon, the atomic bomb. This physicist was overcome with joy at finding a tortoise to bring home to his children. But some small respect for nature or a pervasive guilt from creating the atom bomb causes him to put the creature back, as near to where he found it as possible because he fears that he has tampered with the universe enough for one man.

Of course, his major "tampering" has already been accomplished by the time he discovers his conscience. Eiseley is illustrating the human burden of responsibility that comes with scientific experimentation.

One doesn't know the effect that an invention can have on fellow human beings.

Invention of the machine did give leisure time to many, but also damned others to a life of drudgery and boredom, destroyed eardrums, and bad backs. Creation of mechanized factories caused city crowding, which led to crimes, pollution, and other urban problems.

Belloc, in capitalizing "Science," seems to banish the idea that "Science will bring happiness" to the realm of myth. The rhyme, simplistic and childlike, makes those who espouse this belief seem silly.

Belloc's "some," trusting and naive, rely on the wisdom of scientists, not realizing that they are human, prone to act on ego or for other human but less than humanitarian reasons. They equate intelligence and knowledge with wisdom, not realizing that scientists (or "Science" — "The Force") can have regrets like Eiseley's scientist coping with his guilt in a token way.

Both authors seem to agree with the scientist that humans must be cautious in their tampering and must think of all of the possible effects of what they are creating.

Score of 4

Science Makes Things Worse

In the passages, Eiseley and Belloc seem to agree in most areas. It is my belief that Belloc's passage is written with sarcasm and that this is the factor which tends to unite the meanings of the two passages. I feel that both Eiseley and Belloc believe that science is ultimately destructive although it may seem to be a way to positive progress.

The final decision of the scientist, in Eiseley's passage to leave the turtle in its natural surroundings shows symbolically that the world should not be tampered with. Also, Eiseley demonstrates in his passage that the scientist has some regrets for creating something as destructive as the atomic bomb. I feel these are expressions of Eiseley's personal opinion on the subject of science and its negative effects upon nature.

I feel that Belloc, also, would agree that the scientist made the proper decision by letting the turtle remain in the woods. My reason for this opinion is that Belloc's use of the word "some" is outright sarcasm and is used to represent others besides himself. Yet another example of Belloc's sarcasm is the part of the passage which says happiness comes from scientific discovery. Illustrating how far-fetched this idea is, the scientist in Eiseley's passage was not happy after his discovery of the atomic bomb but, instead, he was regretful.

Although scientific innovation seems to be a synonym for progress, I find myself forced to agree with Eiseley and Belloc. To me, science only tampers with nature in such a way as to worsen our natural conditions. Belloc and Eiseley, I'm sure, would be proud to here me state such an opinion.

Score of 3

Science and Human Happiness

Loren Eisely and Hilaire Belloc express different views toward the relationship between science and human happiness. Their attitudes voice the contravercy between the need for the knowledge which science offers and it's conscious limitation to avoid the possible destructive ends it sometimes promotes, such as the atomic bomb mentioned in Eiselely's passage. The extent to which the scientist in Eiseley's passage and the "some" in Belloc's passage agree or disagree is the manifestation of this contravercy.

In Loren Eiseley's passage their is a very concerned attitude expressed toward the relationship between science and human happiness. Eiseley views science as being destructive to human happiness through it's creation of atomic warfare. His protagonast replaces a turtle to it's natural habitat in a symbolic gesture of not further "tampering with the universe" as he had previously done as one of the architects of the atomic bomb. Eiseley obviously believes that science can go beyond a reasonable limit, that it can and has been a destructive force in human happiness. The very least which it has done is to cause one man (Eiseley's protagonist) to question the morality of tampering with the universe in any way, even such an apparantly insignificant act as removing a tortoise from the wild. Eiseley's expressing through his protagonast his concern for the need to restrict the tampering with the universe and thus with human happiness. Science has the power to do this.

Hilaire Belloc expresses a somewhat different view of science than does Eiseley. Belloc observes the hardships in life and their relationship to ignorance. Science is knowledge; it discovers new things which conquor the ignorance and thus the hardships in human life. He places his foundation on the relationship between happiness and hardships, deducing that a decrease in hardships will produce an increase in human happiness. The validity of this foundation may be questionable, but Belloc uses it as a premise to indirectly saying that science has a direct bearing on human happiness. We need science, science will make us happier by removing our hardships. This is a very different view than Loren Eiseley's.

The extent to which the scientist in Eiseley's passage and the "some" in Belloc's agree or dissagree is the voicing of the contravercy between the need to promote or to limit science. The scientist and the "some" are not in agreement. Eiseley's scientist feels that science interferes with the univers, that it tampers with things which should be left alone. His tortoise is a very symbolic representative of this. Belloc's "some" feel that science promotes knowledge and ends hardship, thus helping people in their strive for happiness. This is a complete disagreement; a contravercy between the limits and morality of science.

Both Loren Eiseley and Hilaire Belloc side with their protagonasts in their views concerning the necessary limitations of science. The argument between the scientist and the "some" is the same as between Eiseley and Belloc, both presenting different views on the limits and morality of science.

Score of 2

Different Attitudes

Attitudes of Loren Eiseley and Hilaire Belloc toward the relationship between scince and human happiness are different in the following way.

Loren Eiseley, in his passage about one of our great atomic physisists, shows that this man who challenged nature in the most vialent way by taking the atomic power from it still thinks that there are some things that a man should not touch in order to be happy. This is described in the scientists's words when he was walking in the woods with his friend and picked up a tortoise but put it back after giving it some thought: ". . . perhaps, for one man, I have tempered enough with the universe."

Hilaire Belloc, however, describes in his passage about what "some" say about science a significantly different attitude. "Some" say that ". . . life is hard and rough only because we don't know enough" and that scientists should temper with nature as much as possible and that "when science has discovered something more, we shall be happier than before."

Score of 1

Agreement on Science

When the great atomic physicists saw the tortoise he was full of excitement. He had thought he could have had fun with it at home with his family. As soon as the tortoise stuck him he realized that it would be happier if it was left to wander its own way. Belloc says "We say the path to life is hard and rough only because we don't know." Personally I think Eiseley and Belloc agree to the fact that there is a lot of things we don't know, thus we say its rough or hard simply because we don't know. Sooner or later when things get discovered and we start knowing things life will be easier and we will be happier than before.

Both of the authors seem to agree on science. Eiseley feels that he has already tampered anough with the universe and doesn't feel like dealing with the tortoise. He'd rather leave it alone and let it wander whereas Belloc feels that it's only because enough things haven't been discovered so as to let us know what will make us happy or what is good from what is bad. In a way I agree with what Belloc says because the more things are discovered through science or technology the happier humans are because life gets to be easier and we wouldn't have to be wandering all the time. A solution or conclusion has been reached. The passage and the poem disagree at the point where the physicists chooses to let the tortoise wander the way it wishes to and Belloc says it's only because it doesn't know what is good or bad for it. The tortoise could be happy under the physicists care than it would be just out in the woods. So more discoveris have to be done to make even the animals as happy as humans. It seems like both authors look at human rights scientifically and logically according to the way they feel or they define human rights in relation with science.

Discussion of the Essays

Both the essay rated 6 ("Science Is No Panacea") and the essay rated 5 ("Fear of Science") demonstrate careful and incisive readings of the two selections, answering all parts of the question and showing good control of organization, diction, and mechanics. The major distinction is in the depth of the superior paper's reading of Belloc. These papers show extraordinary ability to handle a complex reading and writing job under time pressure.

The essay rated 4, "Science Makes Things Worse," also answers all parts of the question and understands the reading, but at a comparatively superficial and undeveloped level. Shadings of meaning that the better responses describe pass this writer by; for example, whereas the essay rated 6 notes Belloc's "more ironic, mocking tone" and the essay rated 5 points out that Belloc's "some" are "trusting and naive" and his rhymes are "simplistic and childlike," the essay rated 4 sees only "outright sarcasm." Nonetheless, this paper accomplishes the task adequately and with clarity.

Despite poor spelling, the essay rated 3 ("Science and Human Happiness") recognizes that the issue of the comparison/contrast has to do with the values, limitations, and dangers of science. It presents a clear reading of the Eiseley passage. But, in common with the other lower-rated (2 or 1) essays, the Belloc poem — with its ironies — poses unsolvable problems for this writer. The essay shows that the assignment is to a large degree a reading examination; without the sophisticated reading skills that give access to the Belloc poem, no writer can handle this question.

The response rated 2, "Different Attitudes," summarizes the Eiseley passage with limited accuracy and then quotes several chunks of the poem. But the question goes largely unanswered, and its separate sections are ignored. It is better than the paper rated 1, "Agreement on Science," for it goes through the motions of comparison/contrast, but all it does is assert that the selections have "a significantly different attitude" without explaining what that difference is or what it means. The incompetent (1) response demonstrates only the dimmest awareness of the meanings of the selections, with writing that seems to go in a variety of directions at once.

CONSTRUCTIVE NOTES ON IMPROMPTU WRITING FOR ASSESSMENT

You will notice some common characteristics among the essay topics given in this chapter and Chapter 6. Each of them was initially developed for a testing program; that is, each has been refined over a long period of time to make sure that it works as an essay test question. Essay test developers conclude that a question works if (1) it is clear enough in its demands that graders can tell if the question has been answered or not and can thus score the papers consistently; (2) it leads to a range of scores that reflect the range of abilities in the group (instead of clumping scores in the middle, as many questions do); (3) it allows all students in the test group to write something and is interesting enough to stimulate genuine responses; and (4) it is free of bias and does not place any group members at an advantage or a disadvantage.

The underlying role of essay assignments such as those I have supplied is to help students see that there are real differences between papers of high and low quality; students are much more apt to revise their work (as are professional writers) when they themselves can see what needs to be improved. Thus the scoring guides and sample essays have an important teaching function: they can help students learn to evaluate their own writing and to see what they must do to make it better.

At the same time, teachers and administrators need to be cautious in interpreting the results of essay tests, even precise and clear ones that have been shown to work. Students can perform badly on an essay test for a wide variety of reasons, from a headache to lack of preparation for a specialized task (such as the reading of ironic poetry such as Belloc's). In particular, students for whom English is not a first language are likely to require time for revision and editing that is not usually allowed on timed impromptus.

The quality of essay test writing has a strong correlation to the quality of writing done under less pressure, so it is surely worth examining. Further, it does provide a useful way to show students important differences between successful and less successful work. But one test score is best interpreted in a limited way: the student wrote in a certain way on the particular question at a particular time under test conditions. The score suggests certain abilities that may or may not show up under other conditions. It is unwise and unprofessional to generalize about a student's abilities on the basis of one test score without other evidence. But that score may draw the attention of faculty to students who need help if they are to succeed in college.

SELECTED REFERENCES

Beach, Richard W. "Evaluating Students' Response Strategies in Writing about Literature." *Evaluating Writing: The Role of Teachers' Knowledge about Text, Learning, and Culture.* Eds. Charles Cooper and Lee Odell. Urbana: NCTE, 1999.

Collins, James L., ed. *Vital Signs 1: Bringing Together Reading and Writing.* Portsmouth: Boynton-Cook Heinemann, 1990.

Elbow, Peter. "Reflections on Academic Discourse: How It Relates to Freshmen and Colleagues." *College English* 53.2 (1991): 135–55.

Salvatori, Mariolina. "Conversations with Texts: Reading in the Teaching of Composition." *College English* 58.4 (1996): 440–54.

———. "Reading and Writing a Text: Correlations between Reading and Writing Patterns." *A Sourcebook for Basic Writing Teachers.* Ed. Theresa Enos. New York: Random House, 1987. 176–86.

White, Edward M. *Teaching and Assessing Writing: Recent Advances in Understanding, Evaluating, and Improving Student Performance.* 2nd ed. San Francisco: Jossey-Bass, 1994.

CHAPTER 8

USING PORTFOLIOS

A portfolio is a folder or binder containing examples of student work. For years, some faculties in the fine arts have been using portfolios for assessment and grading; the final examination in a class in drawing, painting, or architectural design, for example, will often consist of a portfolio of the student's work — which will be displayed, critiqued, and graded. Many writing teachers have used portfolios in the same way in their writing classes, and in recent years some writing programs have done the same. Because the use of portfolios for assessment is very attractive, many schools and colleges have begun using portfolios for all kinds of purposes: screening students for advancement, assessing general education program outcomes, evaluating instructors, providing students with employment dossiers, and so forth.

The great advantage of portfolios for writing assessment is that they can include numerous examples of student writing produced over time and under a variety of conditions. Unlike multiple-choice tests, they can show a student's actual writing performance; unlike essay tests, they can showcase several kinds of writing and rewriting, without time constraints and without test anxiety. Whereas most evaluation instruments provide a snapshot of student performance, the portfolio can give a motion picture. Some programs enhance the meaning of the portfolio by allowing (or requiring) revisions at the time of submission so that students can appear at their best and can demonstrate to themselves as well as to their readers what they have learned to do. And if one requirement of the portfolio is a self-assessment or reflective essay, students wind up taking responsibility for their own learning.

The problems with portfolios as measurement devices emerge from their sheer bulk, the uncontrolled conditions under which they are produced, and the difficulty of achieving consistent scores. The mass of portfolios can be daunting. Even twenty or twenty-five portfolios at the end of one writing class form a formidable pile of papers, over one hundred thousand words to read. Several classes or an entire first-year composition program multiply the quantity, of course, and some institutions require each student to compile a portfolio throughout the college years, the reading and evaluation of which is a truly massive undertaking. The uncontrolled conditions for portfolios pose another set of problems. Because it is difficult and inappropriate to supervise closely the production of the portfolio contents, several validity problems are inevitable: a weak student with no outside responsibilities will be able to produce a more substantial portfolio than a better writer who happens to be a single parent supporting a family (a timed test evens out the measurement conditions); and students are likely to get help of various sorts (from consultations in the writing center to purchased papers from unscrupulous commercial firms), so it may be hard to know just what we are assessing. If we are assessing portfolios that show responses to a variety of assignments from other instructors, we may not understand the context of some classes or the assumptions behind the particular work (although we might ask students to provide this information); we may also be evaluating the assignments as well as the responses, as better assignments tend to elicit better writing. The scoring of portfolios has been particularly vexing for many reasons, including the expense, the variable quality of the components, and the inherent complexity of most stated criteria; until very recently (see below) portfolio scoring has been the largest deterrent to widespread use of portfolio assessment.

The problem for teachers in using portfolios, then, is to maximize the advantages of this method of assessment while minimizing the disadvantages. If you can perform this balancing act, you will find that portfolios are the most valuable means you have of combining evaluation with teaching.

A BRIEF HISTORY OF PORTFOLIOS AND THEIR EVALUATION

Assessment of writing by portfolios has gone through several developments since it emerged in the early 1990s after publication of several essays by Peter Elbow and Pat Belanoff describing the program at the State University of New

York at Stony Brook and a volume of descriptive essays by Belanoff and Marcia Dickson. As with most innovations in writing measurement, it began with a great sense of enthusiasm and discovery, despite its long history of use in the fine arts. Portfolios appeared to resolve many of the problems that had become evident with essay testing: the validity problem of using only one (or at most two) impromptu writing samples; the absence of opportunities for the writer to reflect and revise; the lack of context or audience for the writing; inappropriate or banal writing prompts, and so on. Portfolios supported teaching, fostered revision, and offered much increased validity by using multiple writing samples over an extended period of time. Teachers who hated grading welcomed portfolios as a way to delay or even ignore that unpleasant task, although there was nothing inherent in portfolios opposed to paper grading; teachers committed to teaching writing as a process rejoiced to find an assessment tool that welcomed drafts as well as final copies.

The next development began with the questions raised at the writing portfolio conference at Miami University in 1993 and contained (or at least mentioned) in the book from that conference (Black et al.). After the first year or two of uncritical use, portfolio problems were beginning to emerge. By the mid-1990s, several articles and book chapters had continued to raise questions — for example, Richard Larson in the MLA book *Writing Assessment* (White, Lutz, and Kamusikiri) and my *College Composition and Communication* article arguing that portfolios are essentially a much expanded essay test rather than a writing assessment panacea (White, "An Apologia"). But portfolios have proved to be a robust methodology, and these questions have on the whole been met by particular assessments in special ways (e.g., Yancey and Huot; Yancey and Weiser; Haswell). The advantages of portfolio assessment have overridden its problems, and as we move into the twenty-first century, portfolios have now achieved standing as the writing assessment method of choice. When time and resources permit, and leadership is well informed, a writing assessment today will usually be a portfolio assessment. (For a much more detailed history, consult Hamp-Lyons and Condon, particularly Chapter 1.)

Problems with Holistic Scoring of Portfolios

One underlying and intransigent problem with portfolio assessment has diminished its value until now, despite all the advances in portfolio theory and practice: almost all such assessments have been scored holistically, using the system developed for essay testing by the Educational Testing Service in the 1960s and illustrated in Chapters 6 and 7 of this book. This assessment method has worked well enough for single essays (as we have seen), indeed well enough there to have been imported without much question to become the standard method of portfolio scoring. But the problems with scoring portfolios holistically are many, much more than for single essays, and they are not readily resolvable. Indeed, many aspects of holistic scoring work against the principles behind portfolio assessment. We have from the start needed a scoring methodology that responds to and reflects the nature of portfolios, not merely an adaptation of essay scoring.

Holistic scoring was developed by the Educational Testing Service in order to solve the twin problems historically undermining the direct assessment of writing: inconsistent scoring and high cost. Senior researcher Paul Diederich showed how to handle both problems for a single piece of writing, as he describes his groundbreaking research in *The Measurement of Growth in English*. He required his large number of essay readers, representing many writing-oriented professions, to give a "general impression" score after a quick reading, and he found that the readers could do this at a rapid enough pace to make essay scoring financially feasible. But the range of scores given to each piece of writing was so great that the scores were not meaningful. He attacked this second problem by a statistical operation called factor analysis, through which he discovered that the readers divided into five different groups, each using a different set of intuitive scoring criteria. Within each grouping, the scores were sufficiently consistent. If somehow all readers for a particular essay would use the same set of defined criteria for their general impression scoring, then (he posited) we would have reliable essay test readings at reasonable cost.

From this research came the familiar apparatus of holistic essay scoring described in Chapters 6 and 7, designed to keep all readers of an essay using the same set of scoring criteria: controlled essay readings, preceded by training sessions designed to inculcate the same set of scoring guidelines for the particular essay topic assigned; sample papers illustrating the various score points; public discussion of the ways in which the sample papers illustrated those score points; and record keeping to see to it that readers generally agreed on scores and did not dilly-dally during the time set for the reading. As Diederich predicted, these methods produced quick and reliable essay scoring and swept the country in a remarkably short time — promoted mainly by English teachers (like me), convinced that we could replace the ubiquitous multiple-choice usage tests then in general use with real writing by students, scored by real writing teachers. And, for perhaps a decade, it did.

This story has been told before in considerable detail (Williamson and Huot; White, *Teaching and Assessing Writing* 270–87), and I only summarize it here to point out how far from its base holistic scoring has wandered when applied to portfolios. To be sure, the very success of holistic scoring quickly led to its misapplication and overgeneralization. Note that the methodology was designed for the scoring of a particular essay assignment, often with criteria that were question specific: "Were all three parts of the question answered?"; "Did the student notice the ironies in the given passage?"; "Did the student notice that the words 'some say' define 'some' in an unflattering way?" Further, the reliable scoring of the particular student response applied only to that particular piece of writing and might — or might not — reveal anything about the student's ability to write to other questions or in other modes of discourse. But almost imperceptibly and very quickly holistic scores began to take on much larger meanings and importance than its developers imagined.

Before long, holistically scored impromptu essay responses were being used for all kinds of measurements: to certify high school or even college graduates; to place students into college writing programs; to evaluate the quality of entire writing programs; even to influence admission into graduate business, medical, and chiropractic schools. The results were mixed but the value of direct measurement of writing overrode many psychometric concerns. However, the expansion made many teachers and administrators uneasy. A scoring methodology that worked well for defined essay questions, when applied sensitively and collegially by a coherent faculty group, had expanded into a one-size-fits-all scoring system, delivering reliable grades for many — sometimes quite inappropriate — purposes. It is no surprise that professionals began questioning the validity of scores so derived for such a wide variety of uses. Nonetheless, its ability to deliver reliable scores is so powerful that it has remained the methodology most commonly used for any student writing evaluation, including portfolios. (See, for example, the portfolio scoring guide from Miami University, one of the best of its kind, in the appendix to my *Teaching and Assessing Writing* [300–303].) Other well-known portfolio programs, such as the one from Washington State University (Haswell) and the current program at Carleton College, wrestle with the problem of consistency or inconsistency across different pieces and genres, but the final scoring represents at best an uneasy compromise of values. Which genres are the most important and hence have the most weight? What does a passing score really represent?

Regardless of how it is adapted, holistic scoring is fundamentally unsuited for evaluation of portfolios. How can a scoring system designed to record a reader's "general impression" of a single essay, guided by a question-specific scoring guide, apply to two or more different pieces of writing of different genres, purposes, and quality? Do we attempt to average the high quality of a personal narrative with the low quality of a research paper? What do we do with the terrible sonnet included after the competent short story? And what about the lab report we cannot understand or even the analysis of a novel we have not read?

Until now, there have been two ways of dealing with these problems, both quite unsatisfactory. Either we have graded the entire portfolio by averaging evaluations of the different components, more or less intuitively, or we have developed a scoring guide listing traits that must appear somewhere (but not everywhere) in the portfolio: reasonably edited copy, appropriate use of sources, development of ideas, and so on. Whichever system was used, problems bedeviled the reading. For instance, the surface matters that holistic scoring attempted to reduce in importance were likely to resurface with more weight as mechanical traits recurring from item to item, while the rhetorical and critical thinking abilities that holistic scoring tried to emphasize became more difficult to identify consistently. We muddled through somehow this way, though reliabilities usually were much lower than for single essays, and reported our scores with some misgivings. What else were we to do, since we valued the production of the portfolios as important for student learning and we had no other way of developing scores?

The method for scoring portfolios that this chapter describes has developed over the last few years and was elaborated in 2005 in my article in the journal *College Composition and Communication*. Phase 2 scoring allows for relatively efficient grading, where portfolio scores are needed and where time and money are in short supply. At the same time, it is derived conceptually from portfolio theory, rather than essay testing theory, and supports the key principle behind portfolios — that students should be involved with reflection about and assessment of their own work. It is particularly valuable for classroom teachers, since it focuses on the central role that reflective writing can play in portfolio scoring.

One particular strength of portfolio assessment is its capacity to include reflection about the portfolio contents by the students submitting portfolios. Most such assessments require the portfolio to open with a "reflective letter" or "cover letter" in which the owner of the portfolio comments about the products or the processes shown in it. This reflective letter, normally mentioned in passing as one among many features by those working with portfolios, has the power to turn a mere collection of materials into a unified and important document. When we think about portfolios, we cannot help but consider reflection; it is no accident that the most vigorous proponent of portfolio assessment, Kathleen Blake Yancey, has written an important book about the various definitions and educational force of reflection as part of writing instruction: *Reflection in the Writing Classroom*. When a student introduces a portfolio with serious reflection about it, the student winds up taking responsibility for the quality of work, the choices that were involved in the writing, and the learning that has occurred — or not occurred. It is a powerful metacognitive act — thinking about thinking — that no other assessment device includes. But now we have learned how to connect the power of the reflective letter to the actual scoring of portfolios, and thus we are able to connect the power of portfolios to reliable scoring.

KEYS TO PHASE 2: GOALS STATEMENTS AND THE REFLECTIVE LETTER

The Phase 2 method of scoring portfolios requires the development of two new documents as part of the assessment: first, a set of goals set by faculty for the particular course, program, or purpose for which the portfolio is submitted; and second, a reflective letter to readers composed by the student arguing that those goals have been met, using the portfolio contents as evidence. Although these do not appear at first to be particularly novel developments, when used together they completely change the nature of portfolio assessment, and for the better in every sense. Since a Phase 2 portfolio assessment requires the student to construct the reflective letter in response to the goals statement, we need to consider that document first.

Before students can write such a reflective letter, they need to have a clear understanding of the goals of the course. Two examples of such goals statements (a short one from Northern Arizona University and a long one [based on the Outcomes Statement of the National Council of Writing Program Administrators (WPA)] from Arizona State University) are printed at the end of this chapter. Your goals statement may be long or short, immensely detailed or fairly general, but the students need to understand it in order to write their reflective letters. Since the reflective letter is essentially an argument — in the rhetorical sense, using the materials in the portfolio to show to what extent the student has in fact met the course goals— a clear sense of what the goals are is crucial. When students have such an understanding, the reflective letter loses the narrative looseness typical of such letters ("I learned a lot this term and worked really hard" or "You are the best teacher I've ever had") and gains structure and purpose ("You can see how I learned to revise by comparing the first paragraphs of the first draft of my second essay on portfolio page 9 to the third draft opening on page 22"). We return to this letter on page 180.

Teacher-Graded Course Portfolios

The easiest and most direct use of portfolios is in a single writing class. The student is expected to keep all drafts, revisions, and presentation copies in a folder as a record of the term's work. Some writing programs even design their own folders, sometimes with grading criteria and a decoder for marking symbols printed on them, and require every student to purchase one — a small money-maker. The student brings the portfolio to conferences or to the writing center, and the final "exam" is to revise the most interesting papers in the portfolio and to write a self-assessment or reflective letter as a foreword to it.

You have many options for assessing the portfolio. For example, you might focus on one or two papers with multiple revisions to give a "process grade" on the student's ability to improve from draft to draft; such a grade is a responsible way to reward effort by writers who have not yet learned to produce excellent final products. Perhaps that process grade can combine with grades on the products to give a fairer term grade than one based wholly on final drafts. Again, you might allow students to focus the portfolio on a few papers they like the best, or you might define the portfolio as including several essential papers, with their notes and drafts. Or you might adopt the Phase 2 procedure described below, focusing principally on the reflective letter and the quality of the argument it makes. The point is to promote student ownership of the portfolio, despite the fact that the teacher must finally grade the work, and to demonstrate that the writing grade depends on more than a finely edited product. Indeed, to drive that point home, some experienced instructors refuse to grade the portfolio at all, though that strikes me as an unfortunate loss of a powerful assessment tool.

Because the portfolio will probably include some writing in the process of revision, the terminology for student drafts calls for some thought. Many teachers will ask for a "first draft" and a "final draft" without clarifying what those terms mean. The teacher usually wants the first draft to be what the student thinks of as the final draft — an unedited but coherent piece of writing. The student usually thinks of the first draft as a rough set of notes (which might nonetheless be a useful record of getting under way for some portfolios). Because of these problems with terminology, I suggest using more precise terms. I like the term *zero draft* for the prose that comprises the notes — which, upon revision, then becomes a *discovery draft*. Almost always, this discovery draft then requires reorganization, focusing, and development. Typically, the discovery draft will not state its principal concept until the next-to-last paragraph; the student has discovered the real topic by writing about it. An experienced writer will realize this, throw away almost everything preceding that paragraph, and produce a new draft with that paragraph as the opening. But students usually feel it a waste to throw away anything and need the help and encouragement of a professional to see that the function of the discovery draft has been fulfilled if the writer has come to discover what they really want to say.

The draft that revises the discovery draft will normally show the development and organization that a college paper needs, but this *final draft* is often much in need of editing. Some teachers will delay editing comments to this stage and, for a few selected papers, require a *presentation copy* with careful editing and a high degree of polish as a revision of the final draft.

But we do need to be careful to allow for different writing processes. Not every student — or every professional, for that matter — will follow this typical pattern. Some writers seem able to compose a series of initial drafts in their heads, and these writers turn out first drafts that need little revision; other writers may find that editing is the spur that leads to revision, rather than the tedious final cleanup stage of writing. Such exceptions — and they are rare — will define their writing process in special ways and are likely to need some flexibility if they are to meet a portfolio requirement for all stages of a particular writing task. The writing process is a concept, not a formula, and different writers (or the same writer on different occasions) may find a variety of routes to the finished paper.

The portfolio allows you to review — and perhaps grade — essays that have gone through many stages. If we do grade the various drafts, we should stay aware of the different purposes of the stages. The zero draft requires that the student collect thoughts, references, and experiences that stake out the area for the paper. The discovery draft revises the zero draft with the goal of finding out what is really interesting and worth saying about the area. The final draft focuses and develops that idea as fully as time and talent allow. The presentation copy revises the final draft for a demanding audience that expects the developed, interesting idea to be written with standard sentence structure, spelling, punctuation, and footnote form — as well as appropriate control of tone, metaphor, and diction.

Though every paper in the portfolio need not include these stages (or other possible stages in a variety of writing processes), the portfolio is the only assessment device that can evaluate a student's ability to understand revision processes. We may talk about revision, but portfolio assessment supports that talk by collecting and evaluating several papers in multiple drafts. If the portfolio were to include only a collection of final drafts, this opportunity to support teaching about the writing process with assessment would be lost. And one great virtue of portfolio assessment is that it can document the revisions that show the essential learning about the writing process that goes on in the writing course, in a single folder at the end of the term.

To be sure, the improvement in teaching and learning that portfolios bring about can weigh heavily on the instructor. Course portfolios do leave you with a great heap of folders to get through at the end of the term. But no one demands that you read every word of every draft of every paper of every portfolio. You must read selectively, and since by this time you have come to know the students fairly well, you can decide where to invest your limited time. Indeed, if you use the Phase 2 method of reading, you can focus almost entirely on the reflective letters. This is not cheating; the portfolios are part of the course, prepared so that the student will have a record of work to be proud of. "Did I really write all this?" a typical student will ask, with some bemusement. "You sure did," you and the portfolio will reply. "And some of it is really good, better than anything you have done before. Take it home and be proud of it."

Staff-Graded Course Portfolios

Recognizing the value of portfolio assessment, some colleges have used it for assessment outside of the individual classroom. A typical example is the assessment of student portfolios from the writing class by faculty who have not taught the students' writing class. Students prepare portfolios for evaluation, following certain criteria (which I will address in a moment), and present the portfolios to an assessment team. The team might be as simple as the course instructor and one outsider or as elaborate as a full-fledged review board. This team then evaluates the portfolios, and that evaluation will play an important (perhaps even predominant) part in determining the students' grades.

This procedure has several clear advantages. The most important one is that the class teacher is relieved of full responsibility for grading. This is a definite plus, for if the portfolio is to be graded by others, the teacher then becomes more a coach than a judge. The teacher will in that case be helping the student prepare the best portfolio possible for the assessment that is to come. The student comes to see the teacher as a supporter rather than as an adversary, and the standards for judgment of the portfolio become a subject that the student wants to learn. The teacher's comments and grades become valuable clues to the way others like the teacher will probably grade the portfolio. Rather than giving a failing grade, for example, the teacher can merely indicate that a portfolio with papers of this quality probably will not pass. Any system that turns the teacher into a valued coach is likely to assist in student learning and, incidentally, make the teacher's life much more pleasant.

Students will sometimes find the unknown portfolio team even more threatening than the known course instructor and resist team grading; everyone is likely to be suspicious of outside evaluators, naturally enough. And some teachers may initially be uneasy about losing some of their power of assessment. If the assessment team works in secret and if the results are handed down as law without appeal, these concerns will grow and eventually undermine the entire portfolio plan. But if the staff works together to define the portfolios and the grading standards, and the assessment gains their assent, the operation will become supportive rather than threatening. And once the staff sees the portfolio assessment team as "us" rather than "them," they can allay student concerns by their confidence in and support of the grading standards. The persons responsible for the portfolio team must carefully and regularly consider ways to maintain the genuine collegiality of the program.

Further, the imposition of a staff grade for portfolios can set standards that reflect the institution rather than the individual teacher. Though most writing programs make attempts to normalize standards, few are able to do more than influence slightly how teachers grade. Every student knows that some teachers are hard, others easy, and the rest in-between. But with portfolio grading, those unjust differences are evened out somewhat — for everyone works to achieve fair and consistent grading of the portfolios, whoever the class teacher may be. To be sure, some teachers will be more effective than others, putting their students at an advantage. But the enforcement of reliable standards for grading will help less effective teachers and their students improve, for all students will be subject to the same consistent and appropriate criteria.

Of course, that very impersonalization of standards is a disadvantage of staff grading, for it may also work some injustice in particular cases. Many instructors feel uncomfortable with grades given to their students by others, particularly by others who do not know the students they are grading. Perhaps the excellent student whose work dropped sharply in quality because of a divorce or a parent's death ought to be given special consideration. And perhaps the good work of the talented writer should not receive as high a grade as it appears to deserve because, as the teacher knows, a little revision from that student would have produced truly superior work. Every department contemplating portfolio team assessment will have to discuss and resolve the relationship between the team grade and the course grade. One way of dealing with it would be to make the portfolio grade a set percentage of the term grade, which would remain the responsibility of the class teacher. Another would be to ask the portfolio assessment team to give a pass/fail grade to the portfolio and leave the letter grade for the course to the teacher.

If the composition staff decides to use a team approach to assessment, a series of decisions will have to be made about ways to foster communication between the team and the teachers, as well as about procedures for scoring. The communication issue I leave to those who know the local situation, but five of the most prominent procedural issues are

- content of the portfolio,
- leaving or removing original grades and comments,
- scoring procedures,
- criteria for scoring reliably, and
- appeals procedures.

Content of the Portfolio.   I mentioned earlier some possible components of class portfolios. When an assessment team is evaluating portfolios, the staff needs to attend even more closely to portfolio content than the individual instructor does; the class situation usually makes clear what is important and what the grading expectations are, but as soon as we move out of the class context these matters must be made explicit and put in writing. The number of items in the portfolios must be limited so that they can be graded in a reasonable amount of time, but the papers must represent what matters for the course, as defined by the staff. What is to be included, and why? Before those questions can be answered, some decisions must be made about the purpose of the evaluation.

One such purpose might be to determine or strongly influence the student's grade in the course; the teacher might not be permitted to vary more than, say, one grade from the assessment team's portfolio grade. For the assessment team to be able to proceed, it must reflect the staff consensus about what determines a student's grade for the course. This consensus will shape the decision about the required content of the portfolio.

- Perhaps the portfolio should contain the first paper in several drafts, the last paper in several drafts, two examples of in-class writing, and a reflective letter to readers relating the contents to the course goals.
- Perhaps the class teacher and the student could agree on the three best papers the student has written, along with a reflective letter.
- Perhaps all that is needed is the research paper, including all notes and drafts.
- Or the team may want to see specific kinds of writing and to apply particular standards to that writing, so specific papers may be needed.

Whatever the grading and selection criteria, they must be written out well in advance and distributed to all students and faculty. A few sample or composite portfolios, exemplifying a variety of grades, should be available in the library to anyone interested (with suitable care for privacy issues).

Another purpose might be to evaluate the first-year course, or an entire curriculum — not individual students. How much writing is in fact being required, how is it being responded to, and what are the standards? For this purpose, the portfolios may have to be as complete as possible, but only a sample of them needs to be evaluated. Every student will file a full portfolio of all work done in the course, an administrative assistant will randomly select a few from each class (concealing the instructors' names unless everyone agrees otherwise), and the assessment team will read without preconceptions to find out what these portfolios indicate is going on in the course as a whole. This is close to the Outcomes Assessment described in the following section of this chapter.

Still other purposes will require different definitions of what the portfolio must contain. The essential principles to keep in mind are the need to match the purposes of the assessment to the curriculum — what is actually being taught — and then to the portfolios, being clear about just what is being measured. Remember, a portfolio is not a test; it is only a collection of materials. Those materials must be specified, and an evaluation procedure must then follow, if the operation is to make sense.

Leaving or Removing Original Grades and Comments.   If the portfolio is to be used for the generation of some sort of new grade, it seems fair to remove all the comments and grades of the teacher or to include a copy of the original before the teacher responded to it. Otherwise, the new grade will surely be influenced by the original grade and by the comments written on the paper. However, two major problems must be confronted if the staff decides to do this. First, the clerical work is enormous, either in collecting unmarked originals or in erasing or obliterating what the original teacher wrote. Second, the assessment team will lose the expertness of the original comments, with their reflection of the class context and the details of the assignment. (The actual assignment as handed out is, of course, a necessary attachment to each paper, but it is often only a skeleton of the task in context.) For essays based on reading material, this expertness may be crucial, unless the assessment team members complete all the assigned reading themselves. If the course allows a wide range of reading materials, it may be impossible for the assessment team to know every piece of reading, and instructor comments may then be necessary.

A further issue arises if the teacher comments are left on the student papers: assessment of those comments themselves. Some assessment is inevitable, even if we try to avoid it; the quality of teacher comments is an important aspect of teaching, and readers will notice their colleagues' high-quality work or the reverse. But perhaps we should not avoid it, as so much time and work is represented by those comments. This added component of teacher evaluation strikes terror in the hearts of some teachers and makes them apprehensive about portfolios; conversely, the opportunity to be evaluated (and presumably rewarded) for a major teacher activity that has rarely been noticed seems to other teachers yet another positive aspect of this complex assessment. For these reasons, as well as for practical economy, I am in favor of retaining all teacher commentary on work in the portfolio, particularly if Phase 2 scoring is to be used.

Scoring Procedures. Experience with essay tests has shown that reliable readings can take place only in controlled sessions — with all readers reading at the same time and place, under the direction of a chief reader. The need for a controlled reading for portfolios is even more important, as the scoring of portfolios seems in every way even more difficult than the scoring of essays. The portfolio programs that report the most consistent scores are the ones that conduct controlled scoring sessions with scoring guides and sample portfolios. Hence, if the evaluation is to be consistent and therefore meaningful, careful planning of a scoring session will be necessary.

Such planning involves many details, including facilities, time management, funding, and personnel. Sample portfolios, illustrating different levels of performance, and scoring guides will have to be prepared in advance, for consistency training. Each portfolio should be read twice, independently, with discrepant scores (more than 1 point on a 6-point scale) given a resolution reading. The size of the portfolios and the complexity of the scoring will determine how fast the reading can go; leaders of the reading should be sure to score a small sample in advance to make a reasonable estimate of the pace. For example, if readers can score five portfolios an hour, forty readers will require (after training) two hours to score two hundred portfolios twice. One particular advantage of the Phase 2 scoring procedures outlined below is that the reading, focused on the reflective letter, can proceed much more quickly — two to three times as quickly — than readings in which each item in the portfolio must be read and rated.

Resist using informal procedures, such as parceling out the portfolios to faculty to take home and treat as they wish. Though that may seem less burdensome, it merely disguises the nature of the work and makes it unreliable. Sometimes it seems too much trouble to work for consistency in scoring, particularly when the results may be as crude as a pass/fail score. But unreliable results are unfair and unprofessional. Instead, we should seek funding to make a controlled reading as pleasant and as rewarding as possible. Evaluation worth doing is worth doing well, which means in a fair way that gives dependable results.

Criteria for Scoring Reliably.   This is the weakest aspect of traditional portfolio assessment. If the faculty attempts to use holistic scoring procedures, it will likely take considerable effort to get all readers to use the same scoring criteria. In addition to developing a scoring guide that is responsive both to the goals of the assessment and to the students and to compiling sample portfolios to illustrate the points on the scoring guide, one more step is needed: deciding on the weighting of the various components of the portfolio. Are the same criteria to be applied to first-draft, in-class writing as to a research paper that has gone through multiple drafts? If not — and good sense suggests not — how are the criteria to be applied? A much better solution is to work from the start to use the procedures of Phase 2 scoring, based on clear goals statements and the students' reflective letters.

Though these are difficult problems, they are manageable as long as they are dealt with in advance. Composition staff working together to decide the purpose, then the content, and then the scoring criteria for portfolios are really deciding on the meaning and standards for the composition course, a most worthwhile activity. The crucial first step is to come up with a goals statement that is appropriate for the institution, the students, and the curriculum. The second step is to provide the students with sufficient materials and help so that they can be the initial assessors of the work they have done in terms of those goals.

Appeals Procedures.   If the portfolio evaluators will be making grade or advancement decisions, some appeals procedure will be necessary. As with any other kind of assessment, portfolio assessment is not perfect, and some mistakes will be made. If the assessment team hands down a grade that a student (perhaps backed by the instructor) feels to be wrong, the case should be heard. However, because portfolio assessment tends to be so time-consuming, it is a good idea to think through in advance just how appeals can be minimized and handled expeditiously.

The most effective way to minimize appeals is to develop a demonstrably careful and reliable method of scoring. A simple description of the complex and expensive scoring mechanism will sometimes make the student realize that the scoring decision was made with care. A requirement for a written statement of appeal will discourage frivolous requests, and a requirement for evidence of procedural or other error for an appeal to be heard will reduce requests to the truly serious ones. When the appeals board reviews the portfolio, it needs to reestablish the context of the original scoring, using the same scoring guide and sample portfolios at the various score levels. Too many appeals will choke the system; more than an occasional one is a sign that insufficient care and groundwork have gone into the program.

Even if the focus for your portfolio assessment is individual student scores, try to find ways to use the portfolios for program outcomes assessment as well. Perhaps after the scoring session is completed, a half hour reflecting on what the students are learning, or might be learning, would be more productive than any series of staff meetings dealing with the subject in the abstract.

Outcomes Assessments

There are two important differences between traditional fine arts portfolios and the writing portfolios that we have been discussing: fine arts portfolios are selected to represent the *best* work produced by the student, while writing portfolios tend to require *representative* work — including early drafts and less successful products; in addition, fine arts portfolios normally do not require a reflective letter, whereas writing portfolios often do. This difference reflects the emphasis on process in writing instruction, allowing the reader of the portfolio to note and value the learning as well as the best products of the student. The second difference incorporates metacognitive theories of learning, which ask the student to think about the learning that the portfolios demonstrate. It is surprising that those working with and writing about portfolio assessment, including me, have until recently failed to appreciate fully the major importance of these differences, even though these are the theoretical underpinnings of writing portfolio assessment itself.

Both of these matters — the selection of portfolio content and the criteria for the reflective letter — are key to the second phase of portfolio assessment, and both depend on careful consideration of the goals of the assessment. I will not say much here about the first, since it is obvious that the content of the portfolio should reflect its purpose: for instance, a course portfolio should probably contain the most important papers written for the course, including drafts and outlines, while an outcomes assessment for an English major should contain enough term papers in final draft for the readers to assess whatever the goals of the major happen to be. But it may not be as obvious that both decisions — what content to include and whether to require a student reflective letter — depend on a clear understanding of the goals of the assessment, and that is a decision calling for careful consultation among the faculty and careful writing of a document for the students.

A portfolio presented for assessment is essentially a set of evidence for an argument, in the rhetorical sense. What does the evidence demonstrate? In most cases at present, that crucial matter is left unstated — somehow to be worked out by the readers of the portfolios during the scoring session, with the unsteady assistance of a holistic scoring guide. But Phase 2 portfolio scoring requires that the goals for the portfolio assessment be well understood from the start by the students as well as the readers. In that case, the portfolio content constitutes evidence that the student will use to argue that the goals of the assessment, and hence the goals of the course or program, have been met (in whole or in part). Thus the student needs to have a document explaining these goals in hand from the very beginning of the portfolio process. The reflective letter the student prepares after the portfolio has been compiled becomes the overt argument, using the portfolio content as evidence that the goals have been met. If the evidence does not demonstrate that the goals have been met, the reflective letter can discuss why, and if the discussion demonstrates powerful thinking about that issue, the portfolio might still receive a high grade. For these reasons, a goals statement — developed by the faculty who will score the portfolios, and well understood by the students preparing the portfolios — is essential for Phase 2 portfolio grading. Indeed, some will argue that a clear understanding of one's goals is crucial for responsible teaching itself, a matter that goes beyond our discussion here.

The Appendix at the end of this chapter gives four examples of goals statements for portfolio outcomes assessments. The first is from the English department of California State University at San Bernardino (CSUSB), the second is a very brief one from the first-year writing program at Northern Arizona University (NAU), the third is a very extensive one from the first-year writing program at Arizona State University (ASU) (based in large part on the Outcomes Statement developed by the National Council of Writing Program Administrators), and the fourth is from the department of Electrical and Computer Engineering at the University of Arizona (ECE). While the four statements are widely different in many respects, each of them was developed in a similar way. In the first place, the faculty of the departments involved agreed to put together a goals statement; they spent a substantial amount of time, well over a year, debating the important issues involved and putting together a satisfactory statement; and they tested the goals statement, refining it as they went, over the first few years of implementation. Their interest was multidirectional. The assessment sought to determine whether students were completing the program with acceptable course grades without meeting the goals of the program — and if so, what changes could be made to the program in order to help students meet those goals. In each case, after completing the portfolio assessment, the faculty readers spent considerable amounts of time considering what the experience had taught them about the program itself.

The goals statement for the English major at CSUSB reflects the typical "big tent" English department, including linguistics, creative writing, composition, and literature. Students have considerable latitude in choosing courses that fit within the structure of the various tracks. Before the portfolio assessment, the department had no way of knowing — aside from course grades and anecdotes — whether students completing the major had met the goals for the major. The assessment seeks to provide that information. The students are informed that no one student is likely to have met all the goals of the department, but that they should demonstrate that they have met most of the goals. The department was encouraged to find that most students had indeed met most of the goals. But programmatic problems emerged as readers reflected on their portfolio reading experience. One of the stated goals reflects current concern about literary theory. Students completing the CSUSB English major should be able to demonstrate an awareness that there is no single "correct" way to read a piece of literature, but rather that there are a variety of ways to read depending on the literary theory one adopts. The goals statement put it simply: students are expected "to know that literature can be studied in a variety of ways, and to be familiar with some of these critical approaches." After the first few portfolio readings, the faculty recognized that this goal was not in fact being met by most graduating seniors. Few students understood the role or the importance of theory, and most of them continued to believe that there was one "best" way to read a literary work — usually the teacher's. This realization led to a series of faculty meetings about more effective ways to help students meet this goal, and then to a revision of requirements for the major.

A second aspect of the curriculum came under review after the portfolio readers observed that the portfolios contained almost no papers over six pages in length. There were many reasons for this, including a heavy faculty workload, students who needed to work to support themselves in college and had limited time for schoolwork, and the compression of a ten-week quarter system. Nonetheless, the department decided to take steps to ensure that graduating senior English majors would have some experience writing longer papers. Yet another recent discovery, that many graduates had been assigned *The Great Gatsby* in three different courses, led to additional curricula discussions and revisions.

The CSUSB example demonstrates the value of shaping a departmental outcomes portfolio assessment around a carefully developed goals statement. Such a statement as a key part of the assessment makes clear that an English major is not merely a collection of distinct courses but also a coherent program designed to impart certain abilities and ways of thinking. It also turns an outcomes assessment into a program assessment as well as an evaluation of individual student performance.

The last item in the appendix is a goals statement for writing from an unlikely source, a department of Electrical and Computer Engineering, but it demonstrates the flexibility and power of Phase 2 portfolio assessment. The ECE department at the University of Arizona, keenly aware of the need for its graduates to be able to write competently, adopted these goals after much internal debate. The goals are made clear to students early on in their studies, and an increasing number of faculty are designing assignments that will help students meet the goals. The preparation of the portfolio with its reflective letter is part of a senior-level required course, and the scoring of the portfolios follows a scoring guide that focuses on that letter. ECE faculty do the scoring, with a few additional raters from a major local engineering firm and with professional leadership. Each portfolio receives two independent scores, with about 10 percent requiring a resolution reading, and the entire reading is accomplished in a morning.

An additional bonus for this kind of portfolio assessment is the positive response to it from faculty and students. With the focus of the assessment on the degree to which the student's reflective letter demonstrates awareness of and accomplishment of the goals, portfolio reading can proceed relatively quickly and with high levels of agreement. The assessment makes sense to the readers and also to the students, who find the entire operation a useful — even creative — way to envision the studies they have completed. "I never realized how much I have learned, since I was just interested in passing courses," students will say. "Now I see that every course was part of an overall program." The most effective part of the portfolio in helping students to come to that realization is the reflective letter.

The Importance of the Student Reflective Letter. Phase 2 portfolio scoring depends heavily on the student reflective letter — a document that many students find difficult to prepare, since few of them are accustomed either to thinking of their own written work as evidence of learning or to taking responsibility for their own learning. The four programs whose goals are listed in the appendix have found it necessary to provide instructional support for students writing this letter. CSUSB requires a one-unit course for seniors preparing their portfolios, while NAU, ASU, and ECE include the preparation of the portfolio as an important part of the required course curriculum. If this support is not provided to students, they will not take the portfolio or the reflective letter as seriously as they need to, often hastily putting it together at the last moment and attaching a quickly written and superficial letter. Indeed, the increasing use of portfolios in many different contexts has led to a destructive pattern of writing, since most programs and teachers do not attend much to the reflective letter. Without instruction, students are likely to give a hasty overview of the portfolio contents, including much personal experience about the difficulty of writing and revising — along with some fulsome praise of the teacher — without attending to the goals of the program at all. But when sufficient faculty attention is given to the demands of the portfolio, and to genuine reflection in the letter, the effort is rewarding to students as well as portfolio readers. In fact, in over three decades of experience with assessments of writing, these portfolios are the only assessments I have known that students genuinely find interesting, useful, and worth doing. Students rarely care enough about tests to retrieve them after they receive grades. But these portfolios are valuable to students, who normally not only retrieve them after they are graded, but carry them to job interviews and preserve them as a record of their college years.

The reflective letters are of unusual importance when the portfolio assessment is at the program level, as in the ECE, ASU, and CSUSB examples. While faculty tend to envision programs and program-level goals, students are more focused on particular courses and professors. When the reflective letter requires them to consider what they have learned and accomplished in terms of the program rather than individual courses, they gain a new sense of responsibility for the choices they have made. While they may have chosen to take Modern Fiction instead of Advanced Composition for several reasons, including time of day and friendships in class, now they need to consider that course as part of their major and the outcomes of that course as part of the program outcomes. How, the reflective letter asks, have they spent their time, and what have they gotten for that expenditure? If the program failed to meet their needs, they are quite ready to say so and to apportion (perhaps even avoid) responsibility. But they can no longer see their college careers as a random set of courses; they must somehow put them together and seek coherence. If the program gave them many, perhaps too many, choices (as perhaps CSUSB did), they make recommendations for the future. If the program is highly structured, as ECE is, they are ready to evaluate that structure in terms of the program goals. But however the students proceed, they must think about and assess what they have done or not done in terms of the goals statement that has been before them for some years. In most cases, they much appreciate this opportunity to do mature reflection — even if they wind up condemning themselves, or the institution, for failing to measure up.

Similarly, when the portfolio reflects a single course, the reflective letter allows the students to evaluate the course in terms of their own experience of it. With their writing in front of them, they are less likely to praise or blame the teacher for what they did; more often than one would think they ask themselves what they got out of the course and why they didn't work harder to learn more.

Scoring Portfolios Based on the Reflective Letter

Phase 2 scoring does not intend or need to regrade papers that have already been read and commented on; its concern is the portfolio as a whole. It focuses on the reflective letter and the references in that letter to work in the portfolio as evidence for the argument in the letter. If one goal of the program is to show that the student has learned how to cite sources and then to use those sources as evidence (rather than as a substitute) for ideas, then the portfolio reader need only refer to the cited page of the portfolio to check on the student's argument that the page demonstrates that accomplishment; at most, a quick skimming of the full contents should suffice. The reader essentially grades the reflective letter, and the portfolio as evidence in that letter, as the portfolio grade.

Since in Phase 2 scoring the reader is relieved of the necessity of giving new grades to each item in the portfolio, it is now possible to give a reliable and reasonably quick reading to the portfolios in hand. This may sound shocking to faculty used to spending, say, half an hour or more rereading and regrading student work in portfolios. But this has been the fallacy behind portfolio scoring from the start: rereading and putting grades on everything at hand. If the purpose of the portfolio is to demonstrate that the student has achieved certain stated goals, the portfolio contents are important not as individual graded papers but as part of the student's entire learning experience. Does the portfolio support the argument in a well-considered reflective letter? Has the student taken responsibility for evaluating their own work? Have course or program outcomes been achieved? In contrast to the multiplicity of portfolios, the reflective letter is a single document that needs to meet certain quite specific criteria, and therefore it is appropriate to score it using our standard assessment tools, including scoring guides. We are back to a single document, the basic material for which holistic scoring was designed, and we can usually agree on the quality of that document. With some labor, we can come up with a scoring guide and sample portfolios representing various scores, just as we do with single essays. The variation in the portfolio from item to item and from genre to genre is of no real importance now (we can expect such variation over an extended period of time, with a great variety of kinds of writing to many different assignments); we are not trying to average grades on the items but rather scoring the portfolio as a whole, from the perspective of the reflective letter.

And as we do so, we find that instead of scoring two portfolios an hour we are scoring from six to ten an hour, or more, and achieving substantial agreement on the grades. Phase 2 scoring reinforces the entire point of portfolios by making the assessor of first resort the student submitting the portfolio, who in the reflective letter performs the self-assessment that is the true goal of all academic assessment. The faculty assessment then focuses on that student assessment, which must be done in the light of clearly stated faculty goals, and evaluates the student's overall awareness and achievement of those goals. The faculty assessment can be done relatively quickly and responsibly, yielding reliable grades at reasonable cost in time and effort. Furthermore, the entire experience is valuable in its own right. It supports student learning by requiring self-assessment and responsibility, provides direct information to faculty on the outcomes of their programs, and uses existing documents in a new way that is demonstrably direct and valid.

I do not mean to suggest that Phase 2 scoring is problem-free, nor the answer to all portfolio issues. As I have said, there will be some portfolio assessments that are not interested in evaluating reflection. The reflective letter is a genre itself, and a difficult one to do well; thus it adds a new burden to both the preparation and scoring of portfolios even as it simplifies measurement. There may well be important qualitative differences between the reflective letter and the content of the portfolio, and the scoring team will need to decide how to handle such differences consistently. There seem always to be students who will ignore course or program goals in their reflective letters, sometimes writing engaging personal narratives or flattering course evaluations that are hard to dismiss despite their avoidance of the task assigned. In writing assessment, every solution seems to bring forth new (if more interesting) problems, and Phase 2 scoring will no doubt need to be adapted to local conditions wherever it is adopted.

APPENDIX: SAMPLE GOALS STATEMENTS

A. California State University at San Bernardino, Department of English

GOALS for English Majors

1. To be familiar with the major writers, periods, and genres of English and American literature, and to be able to place important works and genres in their historical context.

2. To be able to analyze, interpret, and compare literary works, and to write about literature in a clear, coherent, literate way that demonstrates a high level of understanding both of a text's technical merits and of its emotional impact.

3. To know that literature can be studied in a variety of ways, and to be familiar with some of these critical approaches.

4. To have read several important works in non-western, ethnic, and women's literatures that illustrate the diversity of literary studies and the interconnectedness of literary traditions.

5. To understand writing as process and, in their own writing, to demonstrate an awareness of audience, purpose, and various rhetorical forms as well as a high level of control of the conventions of standard written English.

6. To have some basic understanding of the phonological, morphological, and syntactic structures of English and their development, as well as to be familiar with theories of sociolinguistics and language acquisition.

7. In addition, students who are planning to teach English should be more specifically acquainted with pedagogical approaches to literature, language, and writing, and with the theories that underlie those approaches.

8. Students taking the creative writing track are expected to be able to demonstrate a high level of competence in some genre of imaginative writing and the forms and techniques of that genre.

B. Northern Arizona University Goals for English 105

1. To develop critical reading skills through close attention to text content and to the skills needed to interpret texts effectively

2. To develop expository writing skills through attention to the writing process

3. To apply critical reading and writing skills to formal writing tasks, including an extended writing project

4. To develop technological literacy skills to rhetorically analyze online resources based on the audience addressed, the purpose explored, and the language used

C. Arizona State University Writing Programs Course Goals, Objectives, and Outcomes

The composition program at ASU supports the Conference on College Composition and Communication (CCCC) and Writing Program Administrators (WPA) outcomes for first-year composition students. The goals and objectives we have developed from these outcomes are provided here to help teachers better understand what materials and knowledge students will be expected to acquire in ASU Writing Programs courses. Since learning to write effectively is a complex task that requires lifelong practice, any composition class should never be seen as "the" course that will make the student an effective writer. Rather, any writing class, including our first-year courses, should be seen as a step toward gaining the strategies necessary to engage in that practice.

Rhetorical Knowledge

Our writing courses will focus on helping students develop and use a rhetorical framework to analyze writing situations in a number of ways. Students will learn how to

- use heuristics to analyze places, histories, and cultures
- be aware of the components of argument and create their own arguments in conversation with other members of their discourse communities

- synthesize and analyze multiple points of view
- use a variety of argumentative strategies to write for a variety of audiences
- express a working knowledge of key rhetorical features, such as audience, situation, and the use of appropriate argument strategies
- adopt appropriate voice, tone, and level of formality
- use conventions of format, structure, and language appropriate to the purpose of the written texts
- be able to focus on a specific rhetorical purpose

Critical Thinking, Reading, and Writing

One of the key goals of our writing courses is to provide students with strategies to gather, analyze, and write about issues that are important to specific audiences in specific contexts. Students will learn to

- work with demanding, nonfiction readings and learn to interpret, incorporate, and evaluate these readings
- develop and support an argument that is convincing to a particular audience
- explore the multiple facets (ideological, social, cultural, political, economic, historical) of issues and to use writing to construct informed, critical positions about these topics
- engage in a variety of research methods to study and explore the topics, including fieldwork as well as library and Internet research
- write empirical, historical, and cultural analyses of issues of social relevance
- conduct inquiry-based research and writing which is driven by the desire to study a cultural phenomenon and asks "what kind of research needs to be done in order to understand this issue?"
- analyze differing cultural and historical perspectives on issues so as to encourage students to understand that multiple perspectives of an issue are in operation at the same time. This analysis will help students to broaden and enhance their own perspectives on these issues
- ascertain the significance of situation in adopting rhetorical strategies in their writings and readings
- identify the kind of ideological work a text undertakes and how it serves to persuade readers to accept a particular account of an issue as accurate and effective
- pursue an issue across projects in order to understand the complexity of the issue and to make connections between empirical, historical, and cultural aspects of an issue
- use writing as a way of thinking through topics and ideas

Processes

Our writing courses will focus on the writing process and will ask students to engage in a variety of practices to research, develop, and write their projects. During the course of the semester, students will learn to

- propose, plan, and undertake research projects that involve a number of writing activities that build toward a final project that meets the audiences' needs
- interact with texts as they read and re-read, by underlining, taking notes, and commenting in the margins, in order to arrive at a strong reading that supplies a starting point for writing
- write and revise drafts and integrate feedback into their writing
- engage in collaborative work at a variety of levels (research, invention, writing, etc.)
- better respond to audiences by revising work based upon feedback (peer response, teacher conferences) from others
- discuss readings, writings, and other kinds of research with others and use those discussions as brainstorming, invention, or revision exercises
- respond to their classmates' work and learn how to supply effective peer editing feedback. Peer response techniques include group workshops, class discussion and examination of content, organization, syntax, and mechanics
- actively participate in class discussions about readings and writings
- engage with instructor, peers, and other members of the writer's audience in order to better understand and meet their needs and goals as readers

Conventions

We strive to teach students to analyze the writing conventions of different discourse communities and to begin to write effectively within these communities. Throughout the semester, students will learn to

- understand the ways that different discourse communities have different strategies for conveying information, for researching information, and for evaluating and analyzing information
- employ a variety of organizational tactics
- learn how to deploy supporting evidence
- analyze what audiences' expectations about conventions are and to address them in critical ways
- understand the ways that information technologies aid and change writing conventions

- examine the conventions of empirical, historical, and cultural writing conventions and to analyze and question those conventions
- effectively integrate a variety of sources into their writings
- use grammatical and mechanical conventions of a variety of discourses in appropriate ways
- learn and use at least one system of documentation responsibly

D. University of Arizona, Electrical and Computer Engineering Writing Outcomes

Graduates of the ECE Department should be able to:

1. Document a procedure, how something works, how to perform an operation, or how to solve a problem.

2. Write a clear and succinct definition of an open-ended problem including a summary of known attempts to solve the problem.

3. Write a proposal to perform a project, undertake research, develop a program, solicit funding, or some combination of the above.

4. Write an abstract or summary of a technical document.

5. Write a letter or memorandum taking a clear position defending or selling an idea to an audience.

6. Document a project in a professionally written design report.

7. Explain technical information to a non-technical audience.

SELECTED REFERENCES

Belanoff, Patricia, and Marcia Dickson, eds. *Portfolios: Process and Product.* Portsmouth: Boynton-Cook, 1991.

Belanoff, Pat, and Peter Elbow. "Using Portfolios to Increase Collaboration and Community in a Writing Program." *WPA: Writing Program Administration* 9.3 (1986): 27–40.

———. "Using Portfolios to Increase Collaboration and Community in a Writing Program." *Portfolios: Process and Product.* Eds. Pat Belanoff and Marcia Dickson. Portsmouth: Boynton-Cook, 1991.

Black, Laurel, et al., eds. *New Directions in Portfolio Assessment: Reflective Practice, Critical Theory, and Large-Scale Scoring.* Portsmouth: Boynton-Heinemann, 1994.

Diederich, Paul. *The Measurement of Growth in English.* Urbana: NCTE, 1974.

Hamp-Lyons, Liz, and William Condon. *Assessing the Portfolio: Principles for Practice, Theory, and Research.* Cresskill: Hampton, 2000.

Haswell, Richard H., ed. *Beyond Outcomes: Assessment and Instruction within a University Writing Program.* Westport: Ablex, 2001.

Larson, Richard L. "Portfolios in the Assessment of Writing: A Political Perspective." *Writing Assessment: Politics, Policies, Practices.* Eds. Edward M. White, William Lutz, and Sandra Kamusikiri. New York: MLA, 1996. 271–83.

White, Edward M. "An Apologia for the Timed, Impromptu Essay Test." *College Composition and Communication* 46.1 (1995): 28–43.

———. "The Scoring of Writing Portfolios: Phase 2." *College Composition and Communication* 56.4 (2005): 581–600.

———. *Teaching and Assessing Writing: Recent Advances in Understanding, Evaluating, and Improving Student Performance.* 2nd ed. San Francisco: Jossey-Bass, 1994.

White, Edward M., William Lutz, and Sandra Kamusikiri, eds. *Writing Assessment: Politics, Policies, Practices.* New York: MLA, 1996.

Williamson, Michael, and Brian Huot, eds. *Validating Holistic Scoring for Writing Assessment.* Cresskill: Hampton, 1993.

Yancey, Kathleen Blake, ed. *Portfolios in the Writing Classroom: An Introduction.* Urbana: NCTE, 1992.

———. *Reflection in the Writing Classroom.* Logan: Utah State UP, 1998.

Yancey, Kathleen Blake, and Brian Huot. *Assessing Writing across the Curriculum: Diverse Approaches and Practices.* Greenwich: Ablex, 1997.

Yancey, Kathleen Blake, and Irwin Weiser, eds. *Situating Portfolios: Four Perspectives.* Logan: Utah State UP, 1997.

CONCLUDING NOTES ON ASSESSMENT AND THE TEACHING OF WRITING

This book provides many writing assignments along with much practical advice on teaching, responding to, and assessing writing. The last three chapters also deal with one major assessment problem many writing faculty find themselves confronting: program assessment. In Chapters 6 and 7, I suggest ways to achieve moderately reliable and economic pretesting and posttesting of students, to allow a statistically significant demonstration that they have improved in writing skill over the course of study. But we should note that the sample writing assignments in Chapter 1 and the portfolio mdel in Chapter 8 more accurately represent the complexity of the world of writing instruction than the pretesting/posttesting models do. If you need to conduct a program assessment, I suggest you consult my "The Rhetorical Problem of Program Evaluation and the WPA" in *Resituating Writing: Constructing and Administering Writing Programs,* Joseph Janangelo and Kristine Hansen (Eds.), Portsmouth, NH: Heinemann Boynton/Cook, 1995.

The first edition of this book included parallel forms of a multiple-choice test, which examined only one aspect of the writing process (editing) and assumed that editing skills will improve as writing improves. The evidence for such an assumption is skimpy (see George Hillocks, *Research on Written Composition,* Urbana, IL: National Council of Teachers of English, 1986) and uncertain, particularly for racial and ethnic minorities. Subsequent editions dropped those tests, and most writing teachers (familiar with earlier editions or not) will sigh with relief that they are gone. The essay tests examine much more of the construct "writing ability" but still omit much that is taught in the writing course: drafting, revision, development of complex ideas, and use of sources, for example. In addition, the composition course ought also to teach some matters that almost never appear on writing tests: use of the dictionary and the complex meanings of words, ability to cope with ambiguity of ideas, understanding of complicated reading—even a love of reading, thinking, and writing for their own sake. This edition, fully revised, now gives a prominent place to portfolio assessment, the assessment methodology of choice in the twenty-first century. The four editions of this book thus reflect the enormous strides that have been made in writing assessment over the last two decades.

In short, ironic as it may seem, this book (which began as a rather simple testing manual) has developed into an argument against simple uses of evaluation to trivialize the composition course. Wherever I have included an assessment device or a scoring guide, I have tried to hedge it with cautions, warn of its limitations, and guard against its misuse. The assignments in Chapter 1 show the broad range of advanced skills that college composition courses teach, and they demonstrate the great complexity of evaluation involved in responding usefully to student writing. No one should imagine that the writing assessments included here (or those used anywhere) measure more than they do; nor should the concern for measurable outcomes reduce the composition course to a mere matter of editing just because editing is relatively easy to test. Assessment is immensely useful for teaching and is certainly worth much more attention than it has usually gotten from composition teachers. A good composition course always involves regular evaluation of student work. But as I have suggested throughout this book, the misuse of assessment is a serious problem in American education. The student who has moved from some ability to handle the first personal-experience essay in Chapter 6 to competency at handling the research paper assignment given at the end of Chapter 1 has made immense progress in a vast range of thinking, reading, and writing skills. Most composition courses in fact do bring students some distance along these largely uncharted paths. Assessment in composition should support this complex and difficult job: assessment should help students and teachers see how far they have come and how far they need to go without diminishing the adventure of the journey.

INDEX